LANDSCAPE
GARDENS
on the HUDSON *a history*

ROBERT M. TOOLE

The Romantic Age, the Great Estates &
the Birth of American Landscape Architecture

BLACK · DOME

www.blackdomepress.com

Published by Black Dome Press Corp.
1011 Route 296, Hensonville, New York 12439
www.blackdomepress.com
Tel: (518) 734-6357

First Edition Paperback 2010

Library of Congress Cataloging-in-Publication Data

Toole, Robert M.
 Landscape gardens on the Hudson, a history: the romantic age, the great estates, and the birth of American landscape architecture: Hyde Park, Sunnyside, Olana, Clermont, Lyndhurst, Montgomery Place, Locust Grove, Wilderstein, Springside, and others / Robert M. Toole. — 1st ed.
  p. cm.
 Includes bibliographical references and index.
 ISBN 978-1-883789-68-8 (trade pbk.)
 1. Landscape gardening—Hudson River Valley (N.Y. and N.J.)—History—19th century. 2. Landscape gardening—New York (State)—History—19th century. 3. Landscape architecture—Hudson River Valley (N.Y. and N.J.)—History—19th century. 4. Landscape architecture—New York (State)—History—19th century. 5. Gardens—New York (State)—History. 6. Dwelling—New York (State)—History. 7. Historic sites—New York (State) 8. Historic buildings—New York (State) 9. Hudson River Valley (N.Y. and N.J.)—History, Local. I. Title.
 SB470.54.H83T66 2010
 712.09747'309034—dc22
        2010016352

This book was made possible in part through a grant from Furthermore:
 a program of the J.M. Kaplan Fund.

Front cover: Montgomery Place, photograph by Bryan Haeffele,
 courtesy of Historic Hudson Valley.

Design: Toelke Associates

10 9 8 7 6 5 4 3 2 1

Contents

for
Margaret and James Fehily

"A Taste for rural improvements of every description is advancing silently, but with great rapidity in this country. While yet, in the far west the pioneer constructs his rude hut of logs for a dwelling, and sweeps away with his axe the lofty forest trees that encumber the ground, in the older portions of the Union bordering the Atlantic, we are surrounded by all the luxuries and refinements that belong to an old and long cultivated country."

Andrew Jackson Downing, Preface, *A Treatise on the Theory and Practice of Landscape Gardening, Adapted to North America*, 1841

FOREWORD

Every unspoiled landscape has its unique personality, a distinctive character that is perceived through the senses. It is an ineffable quality, something vaguely mythic. Alexander Pope advised consulting "the genius of the place"—the preexisting spirit of nature—before attempting to make a garden. For Pope and other English progenitors of Romanticism, genius of place was linked to a landscape's potential for scenic enhancement as an alternative to *de novo* design. In terms of both landscape painting and landscape design, this alliance with nature was fundamental to the development of Romanticism during the eighteenth and nineteenth centuries.

In America no place has fulfilled this aspect of the Romantic ethos more completely than the Hudson River Valley. The estuarine river's broad, commanding presence with striking views both north and south ensured this distinction. It was, however, the river's role as a major artery of commerce that provided the original motive for the settlement of its adjacent banks and exploitation of their wilderness hinterlands.

When the country between New York Harbor and Albany was under the authority of the Dutch West India Company, a few scattered forts were established as outposts. At the same time, large tracts were offered to patroons—grantees charged with colonizing their lands and operating them as business enterprises. The same profit motive extended into British colonial times when English petitioners were awarded land by the crown. Thus, manor houses such as Philipse Hall and Van Cortlandt Manor were the centers of farming operations as well as the location of sawmills and other commercial activities. As a result, their grounds were cluttered with utilitarian structures, and the notion of ornamental landscaping did not exist.

But this did not remain the case for long. Large landholdings were subsequently divided among heirs such as Robert Livingston, Jr., who took possession of 13,000 acres of his father's vast estate south of Albany in the first half of the eighteenth century. Livingston was the most prominent among the heads of families who aggrandized their properties' old manor houses. The trend continued as their children ennobled the further-subdivided estates they inherited with new mansions and adjacent gardens. Their handsome manors, which now functioned exclusively as homes rather than as part-residence and part-business headquarters, were for the most part sited so as to take advantage of their river views. This may be seen as an indication of the burgeoning appreciation of the area as a romantic setting. In addition, they were located so as to overlook the river landings from which estate owners still shipped the products of their yet extensive landholdings. Since these properties were accessible principally by water, the nearby landings also provided a dimension of convenience for the owners and their guests.

By the middle of the nineteenth century, new transportation technologies had opened the region to a different kind of settlement pattern. The construction of the Erie Canal between 1817 and 1835 prompted a great increase in commercial barge traffic, and steamboats also plied the Hudson, carrying passengers to various stops between New York and Albany, causing the populations of towns such as Newburgh to grow. The construction of the Hudson River Railroad between 1849 and 1851 further promoted the purchase of estates on the eastern bank. These properties usually consisted of a single farm and were therefore much smaller in size than the hereditary properties of the Livingstons and other descendents of the seventeenth- and eighteenth-century land grantees.

Educated and reasonably affluent, the owners of these farm estates often engaged in such activities as the growing of fruit trees, but the ease of routine travel to New York and other cities opened up a much wider range of possibilities as far as gaining a livelihood. Writers such as Washington Irving and painters such as Thomas Cole were attracted to the region's incomparable scenery, thereby initiating an important trend that made the Hudson River Valley a subject for literature and art as well as a romantic retreat from urban life.

These later denizens of the region distinguished themselves from their agrarian neighbors by the construction of what became known as rural villas, and no one was a more influential guide in terms of the style in which they landscaped their grounds than Andrew Jackson Downing. A nurseryman by trade and a prolific writer on horticultural and landscape subjects, this charismatic figure and his frequent architectural collaborator, Alexander Jackson Davis, advised clients and undertook commissions to design villas and prepare landscape plans for their grounds. In books by Downing, with illustrations by Davis, they further assisted the general public in acquiring what was commonly referred to as "taste" in such matters.

Robert Toole has done what few if any authors have done before by describing the Hudson River Valley's historic properties in terms of the layout of their grounds as well the architectural character of their manors, mansions, and villas. He prepares the reader for an understanding of the distinctions once made in their different kinds of landscape design by first summarizing the development of the Romantic style in England during the eighteenth and nineteenth centuries. Being the parent country for most Americans at the time, it was natural that ideas and fashions would come from this source, although there was a general lag in their provincial adoption. Thus, we find some of the early Livingston gardens laid out in the manner of the Anglo-Dutch gardens of the period of William and Mary, rather than in the contemporary style prevalent in England during the reign of George II when Whig lords were consulting the geniuses of their places and ushering in the naturalistic idiom that would become the language of Romantic landscape design.

To the English philosopher Edmund Burke's distinctions between the aesthetic categories known as Beautiful and Sublime, the eighteenth-century clergyman and early travel writer William Gilpin added a further category of aesthetic discrimination—the Picturesque. In his *Observations on the River Wye* (1782) Gilpin urged an appreciation of the wild scenery found in Wales and the western regions of England. Such scenery was considered picturesque in that it could be viewed according to the same compositional principles found in painting.

At the same time that Gilpin was promoting a new way of viewing natural landscapes, Richard Payne Knight and Sir Uvedale Price initiated a fierce debate with the professional landscape gardener Humphry Repton over the manner of laying out designed landscapes. With considerable invective directed toward Repton's predecessor, the well-known landscape improver "Capability" Brown, they advised estate owners to abandon the smoothly undulating topographical grading and gently curving paths and shorelines associated with the Beautiful in favor of the rugged irregularity of the Picturesque, as exemplified in the dramatic wildness of the Italian artist Salvatore Rosa and the humble rusticity of the Dutch painters Jacob van Ruisdael and Meindert Hobbema.

Being the quintessence of Romanticism, the Sublime—with its penchant for untenanted wilderness, mountain peaks, craggy precipices, and rushing cascades—was not really an option within the sphere of domestic landscape design, so it is the distinction between the Beautiful and the Picturesque that Toole attempts to parse in his tour of the great estates that are the subject of this book. Landscape painting was unfettered by the limitations of a piece of domestic property, and therefore the representation of the kind of scenery categorized as Sublime was well within the grasp of Cole, Asher Durand, Jasper Cropsey, and other painters of the Hudson River School, and it is this that marks their works as quintessentially romantic. In a sense, however, the landed gentry along the river were able to incorporate sublimity into their grounds because of the fortunate fact that their views of the scenic Catskills, as well as the Hudson's towering highlands, sheer bluffs, and tributary falls, constituted a form of "borrowed" scenery. It is this advantage of site selection more than anything else that places them within the realm of Romanticism.

With Toole's explanation of the distinctions between the aesthetic categories of Beautiful, Picturesque, and Gardenesque (John Claudius Loudon's name for design intended to display the numerous exotic horticultural species that botanical exploration had recently brought into cultivation), we are prepared to follow his Hudson River Valley itinerary. Our stops include: Robert Livingston's Clermont; Dr. Bard's and his son Samuel's Hyde Park estate (today's Vanderbilt National Historic Site), subsequently turned into a virtual botanical garden by Dr. David Hosack; Janet Livingston Montgomery's Montgomery Place; Edgar Allan Poe's fictional Landor's Cottage; Washington Irving's Sunnyside; Robert Donaldson's Blithewood; General William Paulding's and his son Philip Rhinelander Paulding's Knoll (renamed Lyndhurst after the construction of a magnificent Gothic Revival mansion, A. J. Davis's masterpiece); Henry Sheldon's Millbrook, with a Davis-designed cottage extolled by Downing; Joel Rathbone's Kenwood, a Downing-Davis collaboration; Samuel F. B. Morse's Locust Grove farm where Davis made over the existing Federal-style house as an Italianate villa; Downing's own Highland Gardens estate; Matthew Vassar's Springside, Downing's only surviving landscape design; Idlewild, the Cornwall-on-Hudson property of writer Nathaniel Parker Willis; The Point, Geraldine Livingston Hoyt's and Lydig Hoyt's 100-acre property near Rhinebeck with a Picturesque-style house designed by Calvert Vaux; Thomas and Catherine Suckley's nearby Wilderstein with its Italianate house, later remodeled in the Queen-Anne style at the same time that Calvert Vaux's son, Downing Vaux, combined picturesque and gardenesque elements in his reconfiguring of its landscape; and—what most people, including Toole, consider to be the queen of them all—Olana, Frederic Church's striking Moresque-style house with its unrivalled river views and surrounding landscape, believed by the eminent painter to be his greatest work of art.

Today parts of this tapestry of Romantic landscape design adorning one of America's most naturally romantic landscapes have been obliterated by subsequent development. Fortunately, some properties have been protected as historic sites under the aegis of such organizations as New York State Office of Parks, Recreation and Historic Preservation and the National Trust for Historic Preservation, while Scenic Hudson works to protect the natural beauty of the entire valley. Unfortunately, many of the sites Toole discusses are in such serious disrepair, lacking in grounds maintenance and imperiled by lack of funding, that their future is in jeopardy. Even where they are protected and preserved, it is mostly the manors' and mansions' historic associations with personages and events that are the focus. At best, the stories of their owners' original use of these estates as farms and business operations or as scenic retreats are told in educational programs offered by their custodians, but to date there has been very little attention paid to the aesthetic intentions underlying their landscape designs. Robert Toole's important contribution in this book, therefore, is to perform what amounts to a feat of garden archaeology, bringing to light the many-layered landscape palimpsests of these historic Hudson River places. This kind of knowledge is indispensable if their grounds are (as is happily underway at Olana) to be restored to a semblance of their former romantic glory.

Elizabeth Barlow Rogers
New York City
May 2010

Elizabeth Barlow Rogers is a leading landscape preservationist and president of the Foundation for Landscape Studies. She was the first Central Park Administrator and the founding president of the Central Park Conservancy. Her several books include Landscape Design: A Cultural and Architectural History *and* The Forests and Wetlands of New York City, *which was nominated for a National Book Award.*

PREFACE

Landscape Gardens on the Hudson is the result of my thirty years of professional involvement with historic landscape gardening in the Hudson River Valley. While individual historic sites have distinctive, idiosyncratic histories, it was apparent to me from the start—when completing the landscape "Inventory and Evaluation" for properties in the Sixteen Mile and Clermont Estates Historic Districts (Dutchess and Columbia counties) in 1980—that historic landscape gardening in the Hudson River Valley was more than the sum of its parts. Rather it was a holistic story, where the valley was the crucial venue for landscape gardening in America and represented the genesis of my own profession of landscape architecture.

I followed the career of one of the giants of American landscape design, Hudson Valley native Andrew Jackson Downing (1815–1852). While Downing's only surviving design work, at Springside in Poughkeepsie, brought him within the scope of this book, Downing's writings contribute immensely to our understanding of many other landscape garden compositions created during the fleeting but significant Romantic period.

Compiled herein are discussions of all the gardens open to the public at historic sites, together with descriptions of several others now lost or in private hands. Enough detail and illustrative material has been discovered to re-imagine these landscapes, their layouts, their purpose and aesthetic intent within the context of New York's cultural history. The presentation here is often a historical reinterpretation of these established historic sites. For those visiting these landscapes, it is hoped that the information adds interest and appreciation to their enjoyment.

Background studies related to landscape gardening on the Hudson are well-advanced. Historic landscape reports, as well as published monographs and other investigations, have accumulated over time. Today, these efforts stand as valuable research into the nineteenth-century life of some of the valley's most important historic properties and their residents. It is time to bring the story together. Heightened knowledge and appreciation of these exceptional historic landscapes would lead to better efforts at interpretation, preservation and restoration.

Over many years it has been an honor to work with the sponsoring agencies and private not-for-profits that provide stewardship over this landscape patrimony. Dozens of past and present curators, site managers, librarians, research interns and others, too numerous to name individually, have aided this effort. I especially recognize the New York State Office of Parks, Recreation and Historic Preservation, the National Park Service, and the National Trust for Historic Preservation. At Historic Hudson Valley, Waddell Stillman, Director, graciously provided the cover photo of Montgomery Place by Bryan Haeffele. At Wilderstein, Duane A. Watson, Curator, provided valuable follow-up on several issues. At Springside, thanks for special help from Virginia Hancock. At Locust Grove, the generous support of Kenneth F. Snodgrass, Director, is gratefully acknowledged.

In bringing this compilation to fruition, special thanks to editor Steve Hoare, who first read the manuscript, and publisher Deborah Allen. Proofreader Matina Billias provided valuable input. The color reproduction of this work was subsidized by a generous grant from Furthermore. I salute Joan K. Davidson, President of Furthermore, who has championed the Hudson Valley's designed landscapes for many decades, always ahead of her time. Sara Johns Griffen, President of The Olana Partnership, sponsored the grant request. Her leadership in encouraging historic landscape studies, including this publication, has been most appreciated. I am also indebted to J. Winthrop "Wint" Aldrich, Deputy Commissioner for Historic Preservation, New York State Office of Parks, Recreation and Historic Preservation, who read the manuscript at an early date and offered many helpful and substantive suggestions, as always. In turn, I thank Linda McLean, Site Manager at Olana, John H. Braunlein, Director at Lyndhurst, Kathleen Eagen Johnson, Curator at Historic Hudson Valley, and Wint Aldrich for their supportive letters.

It has been an honor and privilege to have this work reviewed and the foreword written by Elizabeth Barlow Rogers, whose leadership in historic landscape preservation and success in revitalizing Central Park I greatly admire.

For the book's creative design, appreciation is extended to Ron Toelke and Barbara Kempler-Toelke. I thank Steve Benson for his photographs and Dahl Taylor for his illustrations. Additional and most grateful appreciation goes to Wint Aldrich, John Braunlein, Sara Griffen, Elizabeth Barlow Rogers and Waddell Stillman for gracing the back cover of this book with their generous commentary.

Robert M. Toole
Saratoga Springs, New York
May 2010

CHAPTER 1

HISTORICAL BACKGROUND

ENGLISH LANDSCAPE GARDENING
A standard dictionary defines "landscape gardening" as "the art of designing or arranging large gardens or estates." Landscape gardening is often associated with England, where it originated and where numerous and splendid eighteenth-century examples of landscape gardening can be visited. In America landscape gardening was practiced sparingly, without the wealth of an English aristocracy or the large estates that prompted the finest English examples. Still, there are many historic properties in New York State's Hudson River Valley where excellent examples of landscape gardening have been preserved. Along the Hudson River, landscape gardening is a hidden but unequaled historic resource.

This volume highlights a dozen or so historic sites that are open to the public. Today, most of these museum properties focus interpretations on their historic houses, while the historic landscapes are not fully restored or appreciated. Yet these are some of the most significant designed historic landscapes in America.

Landscape garden design was an important facet of cultural expression in nineteenth-century New York. In all ages, gardens and landscape design have reflected broad interests, involved numerous disciplines, and attested to widely held social values and ideals. In the historic garden, unlike other artistic endeavors, our ancestors interacted with their physical environment. Professional designers were involved, but in the vast majority of the examples the property owners played decisive roles. Landscape gardening on the Hudson was by and large an amateur's pursuit, but then, that had always been the case.

Appreciation for the fine examples of landscape gardening evidenced in the Hudson River Valley requires an understanding of their historical roots. It is necessary first to summarize the history of landscape gardening that came before these examples, for indeed landscape gardening in America had a long-established background.

In the western world, from the Roman Empire through the Middle Ages and the Renaissance—for over a thousand years—garden design relied on rational, formal, geometric layouts. Trees, shrubs and flowers were arranged architecturally into rows, *parterres* (geometric garden beds) and topiary (shrubs sheared into geometric and animal shapes). Garden designers dreamed of organizing

Figure 1. Drawing Showing Holkham Hall, Norfolk, by William Kent, early 1740s. The illustration shows the placement of landscape features in an irregular arrangement determined by the site's topography and vegetation—the *genius loci*. William Kent was an early prominent landscape gardener. Note the open clumps of trees and the deer grazing in the left background. Courtesy of Viscount Coke and Trustees of the Holkham Estate, Norfolk, England.

nature into elaborate geometric concoctions, the products of the genius of man over nature. Then, in the early decades of the eighteenth century, a naturalistic and thus irregular approach to garden design became fashionable in England—known today as the English landscape garden. Its earliest development occurred in the decades between 1710 and 1740 and was the product of English Enlightenment, the so-called "Augustan Age." Gardens were often emblematic—that is, full of allusions to classical and literary themes, reflected in statuary and evocative features. But these classical elements were arranged in the landscape in a new way, irregularly, based on the natural characteristics of each garden site. The designer's "genius" was to stand aside, discarding preconceived notions of "taste" or "style." The guidance for landscape gardeners was to "consult the genius of the place" (called the *genius loci*) in directing the design work, and the designer was typically one with the wherewithal and land to pursue the avocation of an informed and cultured amateur.

This concern for the natural world and the distinctive "spirit" of a given place was a new idea in garden design, in many ways revolutionary, and it would be a fundamental principle of landscape gardening in England and in the Hudson River Valley. Old-fashioned rigid geometry imposed on nature as a garden was suddenly passé. William Kent (1685–1748), a painter and stage-set designer, was the earliest notable landscape gardener. After his death, English garden historian Horace Walpole said William Kent had "leaped the fence, and saw that all nature was a garden" (Figure 1).

The Augustan intellectuals—most notably Joseph Addison (1672–1719) and Alexander Pope (1688–1744)—had a special

interest in landscape design. They discussed the topic routinely, and it was considered a high-minded amateur pursuit. Joseph Addison prefigured the later popularity of landscape gardening when he concluded, in 1711, "But why may not the whole estate be thrown into a kind of garden ... [so that] a man might make a pretty landscape of his own possessions." It was Alexander Pope, a friend of William Kent, who sounded the mantra of landscape gardening—"Consult the Genius of the Place." Landscape gardening was from that moment an important expression of artistic thought in eighteenth-century England, melding man's works to nature and ultimately to God.

By the mid-1700s numerous English theorists were publishing treatises on landscape gardening, attempting to describe design principles and interpret worthy examples. One such author was Henry Home (Lord Kames) (1696–1782), whose home was outside Edinburgh, Scotland. Lord Kames's book, *Elements of Criticism*, published in 1762, included a discourse on landscape gardening. In that same year a medical student in Edinburgh, Hudson Valley native Samuel Bard (1742–1821), came to know Kames's book and may have visited his home. In 1763, Samuel wrote to his father, John Bard, who was just beginning to develop the family's farm estate, Hyde Park, on the banks of the Hudson River in Dutchess County. Samuel sensed the possibilities of landscape gardening, and the twenty-one-year-old enthusiast encouraged his father to study Lord Kames's precepts "before you go to improving your place on the North River."

Samuel Bard's advice, reciting Kames, ranged from generalities—"I find those [landscape gardens] the most beautiful where nature is suffered to be our guide"—to specific ideas—"I would have in my garden alcoves and temples dedicated to the memory of my best friends." Samuel Bard's reading of Lord Kames and his consideration of landscape gardening led Samuel to advocate a natural appearance and to reject design geometry and symmetrical arrangements, except perhaps in areas close to the house. There, Kames favored regularity as a complement to what in that period was always classical architecture. Kames's design approach amounted to a transition from the geometric past to the naturalized future, and it was accepted practice in Great Britain by the 1750s and '60s. The whole idea of design in the outdoors was in flux at that time. For the avant-garde connoisseurs of landscape gardening, any hint of geometric regularity might be thought outdated.

Around the time of America's Revolutionary War, England's greatest landscape gardener was Lancelot "Capability" Brown (1716–1783). He and others continued the innovations of the earliest landscape gardens by making natural effects the dominant design goal. Built elements, such as the "alcoves and temples" mentioned by Samuel Bard to his father, were no longer the chief concerns. Brown saw rural landscapes with "capabilities" for aesthetic improvement. His projects typically were expansive, domesticated parks, some of the largest ancestral properties in England. With limited man-made features, Brown and his many followers relied instead on the enjoyment of composed, idealized, pastoral scenery, often with an artificial lake as its feature (Figure 2). In England, sophisticated gentleman farmers adapted this approach in their farm operations to realize the *ferme orneé*, an ornamental farm, an English concept (despite the French words) that was perfected in the decades from 1730 to the 1760s, following Addison's advise on making "a pretty landscape of his own possessions" (Figure 3).

Capability Brown's gentrified appreciation of nature and the ascent of the *ferme ornée* coincided with the rise of the Romantic Movement in England. International romanticism was inspired by a heartfelt rejection of the rigid formality and perceived decadence of French absolutism. This cultural reaction was seen most ardently in garden design. For romantics, the sumptuous, rigidly arranged gardens at

Figure 2. Engraving Showing Blenheim, Oxfordshire, c. 1800. A vast estate property, Blenheim is Capability Brown's most famous designed landscape. This image shows his transformation of what had been a straight canal into the naturalized lake, with a garden-scaled sailboat and hand-cranked ferry, surrounded by rolling parkland. Courtesy of Bodleian Library, University of Oxford.

Versailles, outside Paris, epitomized landscape design in stifling excess. The naturalized landscape garden was the English response.

All of the arts became infatuated with the English Romantic Movement. A broad cultural spectrum was affected, from political thought and philosophy to the arts of literature, painting, poetry, and architecture, in addition to our interest here, garden design. Romantics came to believe that "Nature" (often capitalized in this era) and man's reverential response to it offered the potential for a highly charged aesthetic experience in the design of landscapes and gardens. The English romantic felt a heightened appreciation for local scenery and, with nature as the guide, it followed that gardens and residential landscapes should be given sympathetic design treatment. Proponents of landscape gardening in the Romantic era—which included many of England's leading connoisseurs—considered the French formal landscapes, as at Versailles, and the fussy geometry of then old-fashioned English gardens to be unnatural and therefore contrary to logic and reason. Across the English countryside, design was soon freed from formality and geometry, over time swept away and replaced by the tenets of naturalistic landscape gardening.

English landscape gardening allowed romantic sentiments to be expressed within the spirit of local settings. It was the landscape garden's expression—its effect on those experiencing it—and explicitly not the garden's overt design form that distinguished these artistic works. Where the ancient focus had been on the impressive exactitude and sculptural embellishments of a formal geometric garden, the interest now was on the emotional reaction to man-made but natural-appearing scenery modeled on nature and local distinctions. This was a profound change in design intent, and the legacy of landscape gardening was eventually adapted across

Figure 3. Engraving Showing Woburn Farm, Surrey. At Woburn, a modest property outside London, a farm became a garden—and the quintessential example of the *ferme ornée*—with agricultural improvements and landscape gardening by Philip Southcote in the mid-1730s. Courtesy of Bodleian Library, University of Oxford.

the western world. In 1969 historian Kenneth Clark called the Brown-era landscape garden "the most pervasive influence that England has ever had on the look of things."[1]

Despite his paramount importance, Capability Brown did not write down his design principles. Fortunately, however, several of his contemporaries did put pen to paper on the topic of landscape gardening. One such effort, *Observations on Modern Gardening*, by the influential English garden design theorist Thomas Whately, served as a popular style manual. Whately, writing in 1765–70, closely followed Brown's ideas.

Whately's book went through several editions. In about 1811 it was eagerly read by a young American artist studying painting in London, Samuel F. B. Morse (1791–1872). Today, Morse is best remembered as the inventor of the telegraph, but he was also a pioneering American artist. His home on the Hudson River, Locust Grove at Poughkeepsie, is one of the valley's finest and best-preserved landscape gardens.

Morse's early reading of Whately led him to include landscape gardening in a comprehensive discourse on the arts, *Lectures on the Affinity of Painting with the Other Fine Arts*, which Morse laboriously prepared and presented to the public, initially in 1826 at the New York City Athenaeum.[2] Whately's documented influence on Morse (Morse called Whately "an accomplished writer as well as gardener," even fifty years after his death) illustrates the persistence of the long-evolving tradition of English landscape gardening as established in the age of Capability Brown. Morse's lectures on landscape gardening, as with Samuel Bard's earlier discussion of Lord Kames's ideas, show that garden design theories were transmitted directly to America even while local conditions clearly limited the actual practice of landscape gardening throughout the colonial period.

Even after the colonial period ended, and on until the 1820s when Morse presented Thomas Whately to the New York City intelligentsia, very little landscape gardening had been practiced in America, while English landscape gardening had continued to evolve. At the height of the Romantic period, in the 1790s, there was in England an inevitable interest in ever more varied, intricate and wilder, more truly "natural," designs in landscape gardening. In a word, the model became the "picturesque" as experienced in Nature.

Initially, a search for picturesque beauty (literally meaning "a scene a painter would select for a picture") was available to anyone out on a countryside tour. Picturesque touring was guided most notably by William Gilpin (1724–1804), a very popular English writer whose books, including the "Observation" Series

(1782–1800), visited the English Lake District, the Wye River Valley along the Welsh border, and the Scottish Highlands, analyzing the visual world in painterly terms and seeking out real scenes that were reflective of landscape paintings (Figure 4). Gilpin discussed landscape gardening, but held out little hope that man could equal "the superior effects of nature."

At first the public's interest in a picturesque aesthetic had little impact on garden design. There was little motivation to insert picturesque situations into the Brownian landscape garden, where a tidy, idealized landscape was the objective. Besides, as Gilpin suggested, the grounds of a country house would almost always be inferior as dramatic scenery to the waterfalls, crags and wild prospects that attracted picturesque touring. In turn, garden design in this period was increasingly focused on smaller properties, and garden art in England was moving towards a showier and more ornamental focus during what would be the Regency period, roughly 1800 to 1830. In these years it seemed that only a few valued wilderness as a garden theme. Instead, professional landscape designers and theorists, such as Humphry Repton (1752–1818), Capability Brown's most prominent successor, brought back the geometry and artificial forms banished in Brown's idealized naturalism. These changes were notable, especially in garden elements close to the house, and were made out of concern for elegance and status, in the name of good sense: "In whatever relates to man," wrote Humphry Repton in 1795, "propriety and convenience are not less objects of good taste than picturesque effects."

But the purists who favored picturesque beauty challenged that accommodation and demonstrated that natural effects could in fact be made the central theme of landscape garden design. The different approaches prompted the so-called "picturesque controversy." English writers and amateur garden makers such as Richard Payne Knight (1750–1824), Uvedale Price (1747–1829), and others active in the 1790s argued for a truly natural and localized spirit in landscape gardening. They were referred to as the "picturesque improvers."

What would a picturesque landscape garden look like? Richard Payne Knight's influential, self-described "didactic poem" *The Landscape* (1794) included two contrasting engravings, each showing a country house set beside a stream in two very different designed settings (Figure 5). Plate I represented the natural, picturesque setting, while Plate II is the same scene "dressed in the modern style" of landscape gardening, i.e., the style of Capability Brown. Of course, both examples looked "natural" as compared to Versailles or the older geometric garden designs, but there were real differences between them. In Plate II, the Capability Brown-inspired scene was of a classical-style house, refined and austere. It stood, as Richard Payne Knight described it, "but a lump" in an open, tidy landscape that Knight criticized as "dressed by the improver" (i.e., by Brown and his followers). In its foreground, a "dressed" stream was shown, cleared of wild vegetation and grass-edged, "shaved," as Knight contemptuously concluded, by the arrogant designers who, like Brown, "advance triumphant, and alike lay waste the forms of nature." Plate I exhibited Knight's preference. It showed the stream's "deep-embower'd shade" preserved. There, amid a facsimile of nature, the house is a picturesque edifice, in this case a venerable Elizabethan pile, richly framed in mature foliage in what Knight called an "undressed" landscape, the picturesque landscape garden.

For Richard Payne Knight, the principles of landscape gardening were best exemplified in nature and designed landscapes that blurred into nature. Knight practiced what he preached at his 10,000-acre property, Downton in Herefordshire. The Gothic-style house, designed in 1772 just prior to the American

Revolution, was one of the earliest "picturesque" (i.e., not classical) designs in the English countryside. Downton's landscape, centered on the wild gorge of the River Teme, has been restored and interpreted in recent years. It remains one of England's earliest and finest examples of picturesque landscape gardening.

Close by, at a property called Foxley, also in Herefordshire (it is no accident that the picturesque aesthetic found favor in the hilly and wooded Welsh border districts), Uvedale Price, in his *Essays on the Picturesque* (1794), rejected Humphry Repton and what he called "the cold monotony of Mr. Brown," and championed the vision of romantic landscape artists, who would appreciate the "neglect and accidents" of nature. Price's manifesto described how the simple forms of nature and the ordinary circumstances of rural England could be made into evocative garden features. Price practiced his landscape gardening at the 4,000-plus-acre Foxley estate, which remains a private residential property to this day.

Four decades after the "picturesque controversy" raged in England, during the 1830s, a young, inquisitive nurseryman

Figure 4. Drawing Showing Mountainous Landscape with Lake, by William Gilpin, c. 1780s. In the late eighteenth century, nature became a more direct model for residential landscapes, reacting to the "genius of the place." One influential proponent was William Gilpin, who analyzed the components of "picturesque" scenery, identifying, as in this example, a foreground, middle distance (with castle ruin), and background, artistic principles that could be applied to landscape gardening. Courtesy of Gainsborough's House, Sudbury, Suffolk.

from the Hudson River Valley, Andrew Jackson Downing (1815–1852), began to read the works of Richard Payne Knight, Uvedale Price and William Gilpin. His understandings were a bit fragmented, but enthusiastic. In 1840 he wrote to a friend:

[William] Gilpin's works occupy an important place in the theory of the art. His "Observations on Forest Scenery" 2 vols. I have in my collection and have found them of much value in preparing a

Figure 5. Plate I, *Undressed*, and Plate II, *Dressed in the Modern Style*, engravings from *The Landscape*, by Richard Payne Knight, 1794. In these contrasting images, poet Richard Payne Knight found the landscape gardening of Capability Brown with its groomed, "dressed" parkland (at bottom) inferior to a picturesque house embowered in a naturalized landscape, which Knight called "undressed" (at top). This distinction would influence Picturesque-style landscape gardens along the Hudson.

description of the peculiar effects of trees in Composition: indeed this is considered the standard work on this branch of the subject. His [Gilpin's] "Tours in search of the Picturesque" to which you allude are exceedingly scarce and I have never been able to get them having only seen extracts. How is it that the edition to which you refer as being in N.Y. is in 12 vols. The "Tour to the Lakes" 1772 & "Tour to the Highlands" 1782 were each published in London in 2 volumes & the "Forest Scenery" in 2 making in all only 6 vols.? …

The most important work on this department is undoubtedly Price's "Essay on the Picturesque" London, 3 vols. 1794 with which I am thoroughly familiar. Sir Uvedale Price is said to have contributed more than any other English author to raise the scale for the art from the mere copying of a few simple forms in nature to the initiation of her more characteristic and expressive features. In his own residence (Foxley) also as I have been informed by those who visited it, he illustrated practically in a most complete manner what he enforced in his essays: viz the superiority of Picturesque over merely elegant or beautiful nature; and the practicability of introducing it in the grounds of a country residence. Brown & Repton, as you are well aware, were his opponents at the time, contending for the smooth and polished alone, and his portion of the argument between them is one of the keenest pieces of controversial writing on such a subject in the language. [3]

While unaware of many of Gilpin's works, A. J. Downing instinctively understood "the superiority of Picturesque over merely elegant or beautiful nature" and appreciated the appropriateness of this design approach in the near wilderness and otherwise pastoral settings of his New World home. Many New York connoisseurs felt the "genius" of the Hudson Valley. Downing's special role will be discussed shortly, but it is clear that the design approach of the picturesque improvers, notably those practicing in the 1790s in the rugged west counties of England and in Wales, eventually influenced landscape gardening in the Hudson River Valley.

In England's Regency period a strong counter-fashion to picturesque landscape gardening put renewed focus on formality in a "fancy" garden. This meant that actual use of a Picturesque design approach in England was limited. Today,

a dozen or so picturesque creations remain and several are accessible. These are usually evaluated as late variants within the grand sweeping traditions of English landscape gardening, which reached a crescendo earlier with Capability Brown at about the time of the American Revolution. Only later did the picturesque design approach to landscape gardening find a worthy setting and achieve its intrinsic distinction in the Hudson River Valley.

The evocative picturesque aesthetic, melded as it was to romanticism, would have an important role to play in the cultural underpinnings of the young United States. The evolution of design changes in English landscape gardening—from ancient formal geometry to the tentative asymmetry of William Kent, to the idealized sweeping parkland of Capability Brown and the heightened romance and naturalism of the picturesque improvers—occurred while the Hudson River Valley languished in cultural doldrums. In America's colonial period, to be discussed in the next chapter, the last remnant of geometric gardening was the so-called Anglo-Dutch style, common in England during the late 1600s reign of William and Mary (Figure 6). Colonial Williamsburg in Virginia reflects this style well, but it was also prevalent in New York State. The formal, symmetrical and insular Anglo-Dutch designs predated the English landscape garden and were decidedly conservative and old-fashioned when applied to American residential estates after the Revolutionary War, fifty years into the landscape gardening era. Still, even in the early nineteenth century, as Samuel F. B. Morse asserted in his art lectures, "[landscape gardening] is little known or practiced in our country." This neglect was noted by several English travelers, as in this observation as late as 1830: "Gardening, laying out grounds, etc., with the idea of embellishment, 'tis out of the question. 'Here,' say the Americans, 'the English miss it when they come to this country—these things don't pay.'"[4]

In the Hudson River Valley the earliest design work that can be described as being in the English landscape garden tradition came in the 1790s, when the house (at this date always a classical design) began to be located away from the farmstead in a naturalized park-like setting, isolated from outbuildings, kitchen gardens and stable areas that had earlier been closely attached to the house. This was the Brownian tradition finally arrived in the New World, and some of these properties bore a strong resemblance to the "dressed landscape, bare and bald" criticized by Richard Payne Knight in his poem "The Landscape" (1794). The early American approach to landscape garden design typically emphasized this "dressed" (i.e., embellished) appearance, made common practice on the strength of the wide acceptance of Capability Brown's work in England. Wealthy and sophisticated Americans, living in otherwise rural circumstances, appreciated a certain polish in their house grounds. Carriage drives were carefully raked and the grass was kept short and smooth, formed into idealized parkland. New plantings included regularly spaced avenue trees and ornamental shrubberies. One motivation was to offer a contrast to wilderness conditions. As one commentator explained it in 1815:

> In embellishing on country seats in the United States, where the features of nature have as yet undergone but little change, an appearance of human labor and skills, and even of formality, produces the agreeable effect of variety, and awakens the pleasing ideas of progressive civilization and improvement.[5]

Local conditions in the Hudson River Valley and along the eastern seaboard retarded the advance of landscape gardening even into the late 1790s and early 1800s, a full half-century after its genesis in Augustan-era England, and only just in time to be contemporary with the picturesque controversy, described above as the final chapter of English landscape gardening. Of necessity landscape gardening matured rapidly in the New World, in essence shifting through sixty years of English evolution in a single generation.

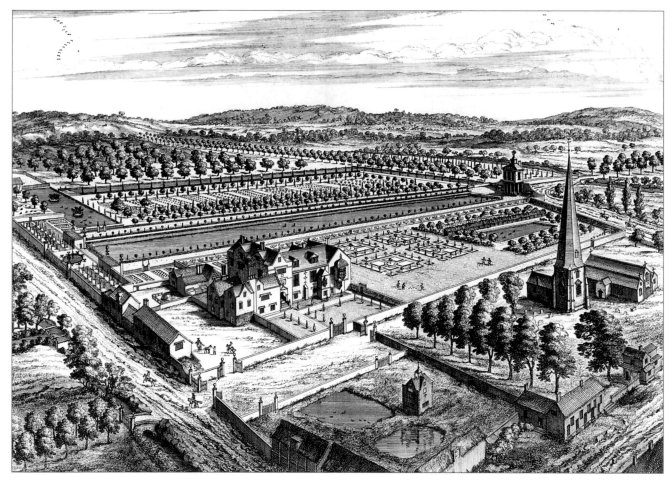

Figure 6. Engraving Showing Westbury Court, Gloucestershire, by Kip, c. 1707. The age-old regimentation of European gardening is apparent in this bird's-eye view of Westbury Court. The house is in the center foreground surrounded by considerable acreage of geometric gardens, bowling greens and water channels. Westbury is one of the best surviving Anglo-Dutch gardens in England. Courtesy of the National Trust Picture Library.

❧ The Romantic Hudson

By 1825 the Hudson River Valley awakened from the aftermath of the Revolutionary War with great vigor. New York City grew from a post-war population of about 25,000 to a metropolis of 125,000 people. Americans migrated from New England, and new immigrants arrived from Europe; commerce and farming flourished. At the end of the era, the Erie Canal opened the West to settlement, and New York State prospered. After 200 years of lackluster colonialism, New York City and its river valley to the north settled into the domestic life of a nascent republic.

Fashionable Americans still recognized the excellence of European models, but they began to look to their own country for local inspirations. Writing led the way, with the imported works of Englishmen such as Sir Walter Scott (1771–1832), quickly augmented by locals such as James Fenimore Cooper (1789–1851) and Washington Irving (1783–1859), who recounted revolutionary heroics and glorified the sublimity of the American wilderness.

Notably, Americans of romantic persuasion began to appreciate the greatness of their vast and varied land. In 1825, Thomas Cole (1801–1848), was the first of what came to be known as the Hudson River School of landscape painters. He was "discovered" after exhibiting three modest oil paintings of identifiable Hudson Valley scenes. An indigenous focus developed in all the arts, championing the "genius of the place," and a Romantic period blossomed. In the Hudson River Valley, the Romantic period was a golden age. This was a distinct regional phenomenon of place and people where, for a time, popular culture celebrated human emotions and feelings over purely intellectual and practical judgments. The romantics valued above all else the affections of the heart. While persons of romantic persuasion have lived in many periods, and romantic thought remains important today, its historic expression in America was noteworthy because it coincided with the earliest manifestation of cultural ambition in the United States. American romanticism provided a context that influenced landscape gardening on the Hudson.[6]

American romanticism had its particular themes. The idea that "all men are created equal" was its political manifesto; for the arts, freedom of imagination and freedom of expression were the message. Individual freedoms were essential to romantic stimulation. Romanticism in the arts represented not the choice of subject or objective fact, but individual sensibilities. By asserting that the emotions of each individual mattered, it was assumed that an individual had natural rights that made

them so. Now, in America, a new nation was to be governed on these values. It took time for these lofty revolutionary thoughts to filter down, but when they did, in the first decades of the nineteenth century, the depth of idealism provided heady substance for would-be romantics and the arts.

In turn, American religious life in the Romantic period supported romantic sensibilities. Modesty, restraint and chasteness, born of Puritanism and mercantile thrift, were common values. Simple and spontaneous reflections, pleasurable sensations of awe, delight, contentment, and even melancholy, were deeply felt. In this period, experiencing a beautiful garden provided an insight to the divine. This pleasure was spiritual, transient and elusive, yet sustained not only by the formal churches, but by a national philosophy of individualism epitomized by the Transcendentalism of Ralph Waldo Emerson and Henry David Thoreau.

The sense of America as "Nature's Nation" was a central theme for romanticism in the early republic. Europeans knew the natural world was important, but in America wild nature was an essential component of the "genius of the place." America was seen as special, distinguished by its wilderness condition. "In the beginning," wrote the English philosopher John Locke, "all the world was America."

In the alliance of the arts, the role of landscape painting was crucial. In the earliest English landscape gardens, the painterly works of seventeenth-century artists such as Claude Lorrain, Nicolas and Gaspard Poussin, and Salvator Rosa guided garden designers in incorporating classical temples, stone ruins, and other landscape features into idyllic garden settings. Later, for the picturesque improvers, the landscape paintings of such artists as Thomas Gainsborough (1727–1788) suggested appropriate visual images—a modest cottage embowered in dense foliage, cows roaming along tranquil streams, a happy rural lifestyle. The Hudson River School constituted New York's regional approach, with dozens of artists led by Thomas Cole epitomizing the search for picturesque scenery on canvases that often celebrated local settings (Figure 8).

❧ The Gardens

Added to the expressions of romantic thought in the Hudson River Valley in the region's golden age are its historic designed landscapes. During the pre–Civil War decades, the Hudson Valley saw extensive developments in landscape gardening as nowhere else in America. These were the works of informed amateurs, as was typical of the era. Today, many of the largely unaltered grounds of numerous riverfront properties are pre-served as historic sites open to the public. Some of the region's premier historic attractions are, in fact, landscape garden compositions where architecture is but a part of the holistic historic artifact (Figure 9).

From the south, these museum properties include **Knoll** (today called **Lyndhurst**) and **Sunnyside**, close to one another on the Tappan Zee in Tarrytown. Moving north to Pough-keepsie, **Locust Grove** and **Springside** are nationally significant examples. **Hyde Park** (the so-called **Vanderbilt Mansion National Historic Site**) is farther north towards Rhinebeck, as is **The Point**, often called the **Hoyt House** property, now part of the Mills-Norrie State Park in Staatsburg, and **Wilderstein**. Beyond Rhinebeck dozens of residential landscapes

glorify a continuous string of eighteenth- and nineteenth-century estates. These expansive designed landscapes constitute today's **Hudson River National Historic Landmark District**, at thirty-two square miles the largest such district in the United States. This is "Livingston Country," named for its most prominent family. On nearly all these sites land-scape gardening influenced the historic arrangements. **Clermont** and **Montgomery Place** were significant Livingston family homes, not so much for their links to any one historic person, but as indicative of the valley's long residential and landscape garden heritage. Other properties in the landmark district, with lesser pedigrees, remain in private ownership, such as **Rokeby**, **Steen Valetje**, and **The Locusts**. A few sites have largely disappeared—most regrettably **Blithewood**.

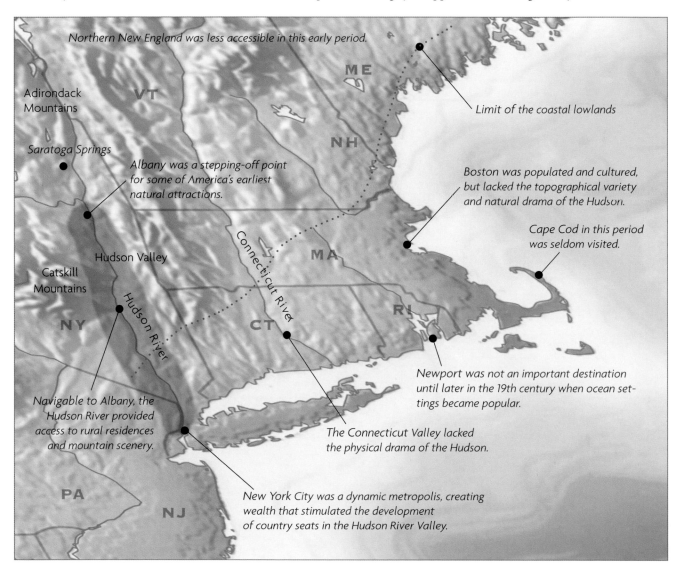

Figure 7. Bird's-Eye View Showing Northeast U.S.A., by Ron Toelke. In the early nineteenth century, the Hudson River Valley was unique on the Atlantic seaboard as a route to the mountainous and picturesque interior. First were the Catskills and Saratoga Springs. Beyond were the Adirondacks and Niagara Falls. Here, America had some of its earliest romantic encounters and artistic attachments to the land.

Millbrook at Tarrytown, **Idlewild** at Cornwall, **Highland Gardens** at Newburgh, and **Kenwood** at Albany have also succumbed to changing circumstances. While these last cannot now be visited, their importance dictates that they be included. Several others will be mentioned here in passing. Finally, one of the most popular museum properties in the Hudson Valley, and very well preserved, lies just south of the city of Hudson in Columbia County. This is **Olana**, the aesthetic crescendo of American landscape gardening, unique and famed for its creation by a renowned landscape painter, Frederic Edwin Church. Olana has been rightly called by a recent commentator "one of the most perfectly realized Romantic landscape gardens in the world."[7]

❧ THE LANDSCAPE GARDEN DECONSTRUCTED

The general characteristics of the Romantic-period landscape garden can be concisely described (Figure 10). All of these landscapes were associated with gentleman farming and, with a few exceptions, amateur designers—the property owners themselves. Unlike a building or formal garden where the design is semi-permanent, a naturalistic landscape garden requires season-to-season adjustments with the growth and decline of vegetation in a largely organic composition. Owners lived with their landscapes. Then, too, the expertise of the landscape gardener was gained primarily from broad-based academics and exposure to artistic principles, an education seldom found in the lower status of a gardener. The few professionals available did impact local examples, and their writings (and imported written advice from England) offered comprehensive coverage of landscape gardening as the art form it was then considered to be, at least for the inquisitive and literary-minded. In this context landscape gardening became a genteel and erudite pursuit. Alexander Pope had referred to it as the "pursuit of innocent pleasures."

Sometimes the designed landscape, or "pleasure grounds" as it was called, were separate from the farmland, but often the two landscapes melded. Turning a profit was not the point of a gentleman's farm, but farming was part of an idealized rural lifestyle. In the nineteenth century, farming remained integral to residential life and to the heightened landscape design aesthetics required of romantic taste. The emphasis was on a purely ornamental purpose.

The acreage of the era's gentleman farms varied widely, from less than twenty acres to hundreds. The house was always the central focus, but in the landscape the house was certainly

not the only important component. Some of the house sites discussed here predated the practice of nineteenth-century landscape gardening; these sites were modified in response to the new aesthetic. Other residences were constructed when the Romantic-period landscapes were designed, so that the results were a set piece that can be attributed to one owner at one moment in time. The earlier houses were classical designs, but after the mid-1830s a variety of eclectic styles emerged. These "picturesque" house designs complemented the landscape gardening, so that an Italianate house might have a more formal and grand landscape, while a Gothic cottage would be associated with more casual and intricate grounds.

In general there were no large-scale restructurings of the landscapes in the Romantic-period designs, because the idea was to work harmoniously with the natural "lay of the land"— the *genius loci*—with its opportunities and constraints, rather than imposing an intrusive overlay. This has meant that some designed landscapes have been dismissed as indistinguishable from nature, with only the use of native or long-introduced plantings, and in layouts that can appear to be unconscious and haphazard. For some Hudson Valley house museums, the landscape is now reduced, in thought, to trees and mowed lawns, a consequence of naturalistic design, changing use and a loss of subtleties inherent in modern maintenance practices. Originally all these properties were farms, an activity no longer practiced at modern museum properties. One consequence is that many of these landscapes are severely overgrown, with detrimental aesthetic impact.

Typically, Hudson Valley landscape gardens were created from farmland or by clearing existing woodlands to create open spaces. Occasionally, previously cleared land was selectively replanted to form the intended spatial design. The distribution of the site's vegetation was critical. Any landscape garden was a mix of parkland—wooded and open acreage—and the drama of this juxtaposition often determined the garden's visual interest. Where new plantings were carried out or where there has been removal of existing vegetation to affect the appearance of the landscape, that activity was landscape gardening.

Carriage drives and their pedestrian cousins, footpaths, played the single most important role in determining how the designed landscape was experienced. Drives were especially critical in defining the arrival experience, i.e., how one was brought from the property's gateway to the house. This was always a carefully contrived route, and the resulting visual sequence fixed the landscape's personality and largely defined the visual experience and the property's sense of place. Footpaths were almost always present so that visitors and owners could stroll the grounds at leisure and take in the landscape's features and scenery. Drives and footpaths varied in their upkeep, from meticulously raked and edged gravel to scruffy dirt paths ("dug out and walked hard," as one owner described it). The level of care depended on the design intent and on the context within the landscape garden.

Water was always a prime component of these designs. This began with the unequaled splendor of the Hudson River, the era's grandest and most scenic river. Views to the Hudson were available from all the properties discussed here. Some were from perched overlooks, while others were set low and close to the shoreline. After 1820 the animation of sailing ships was enhanced by increasing numbers of river steamers. As the vast majority of the residential properties lay on the east bank of the Hudson (because of historic land grants and the evolving transportation infrastructure), the relatively undeveloped western shoreline, punctuated by the Palisades, Highlands, and Catskills, offered highly scenic and distinctive backdrops. In addition the numerous small streams that joined the Hudson offered very different watery pleasures. These tributaries often descended to the river over waterfalls and rapids, and elsewhere were formed into decorative pools set into small valleys and glens, all enhanced by the practice of landscape gardening.

Water almost always incorporated planted edges and, because they were typically intended to appear natural (even dammed impoundments were to look like natural water bodies), the plantings were mostly indigenous, melding with the woodsy surroundings. Trees formed the fabric of the landscape garden, and these were almost always indigenous varieties or long-established imports. In the early post-Revolutionary War period, columnar Lombardy poplars (*Populus nigra italica*) were popular, seen often in old illustrations planted in rows, forming lines on the land. Their use in the Hudson Valley was modeled on the tall Italian

Figure 8. *View on the Catskill, Early Autumn*, by Thomas Cole, 1836–37. Thomas Cole, the founder of the Hudson River School of painters, celebrated America in its distinct landscapes where nature embraced a new republic. Cole created the imagery of America's *genius loci* and inspired a love for nature and place. Courtesy of The Metropolitan Museum of Art.

cypress (*Cupressus sempervirens*), an evergreen evoking classical scenes from the Mediterranean world. Lombardy poplars were also associated with republican values (initially a French idea), but they were cloned exotics—introduced trees—and thus unnatural to the genius of the place in the Hudson River Valley. It is indicative of the changing taste in landscape design that Lombardy poplars were seldom planted after 1830.

In the Romantic period such native stalwarts as red, white and chestnut oaks (*Quercus rubra, Q. alba and Q. prinus*), sugar, red and silver maples (*Acer saccharum, A. rubrum, and A. saccharinum*), and beloved natives such as the American elm (*Ulmus americana*) and basswood (*Tilia americana*) were valued landscape trees. Some of the smaller native trees also gained favor beginning in this era, including the white birch (*Betula papyrifera*), redbud (*Cercis canadensis*), honey locust (*Gleditsia triacanthos*) and black locust (*Robinia pseudoacacia*). Evergreens were represented by white pines (*Pinus strobus*) and hemlocks (*Tsuga canadensis*), both common on the Hudson, as well as balsam fir and spruce. Shrubs were used sparingly, given the scale of the average landscape, but there were a few designed botanic collections that earned the title "shrubbery." Flowers, per se, were not an integral part of the landscape garden. Flowers were often included in the kitchen garden, isolated from what was otherwise expansive, park-like scenes. Still, at least some bedding-out annuals and longer-lived perennial flowers were incorporated as features, typically arranged in separate, well-defined enclosures or in "lawn beds," where seasonal bedding-out flowers enlivened areas close to the house. The informal, mingled flower garden, precursor to our modern perennial borders, was also popular.

Finally, the landscape garden was embellished with built features. Buildings in the landscape garden played a supportive role at most properties. Essential outbuildings, such as farmers' cottages, gatehouses, barns and stable buildings, were set up as major landscape features. In addition, greenhouses, icehouses, mausoleums, water towers and dovecotes (pigeon houses) were given ornamental roles beyond their practical usefulness. Purely decorative buildings varied widely, from sizable pavilions

Figure 9. Map of Hudson River Valley Showing Sites, by R. M. Toole. "There is no part of the Union where the taste in Landscape Gardening is so far advanced, as on the middle portion of the Hudson," was the claim in 1844. In the Hudson River Valley there remains a string of nineteenth-century landscape gardens representing a unique heritage and historic resource. Many of these designed landscapes are preserved at today's historic sites. This map also illustrates the concentration of estate properties in the Hudson River National Historic Landmark District. Many of these properties preserve documented, nineteenth-century designed landscapes, notably Clermont near the northern end and Hyde Park on the extreme south. In between are Blithewood, Montgomery Place, and dozens of others, all fronting on the river.

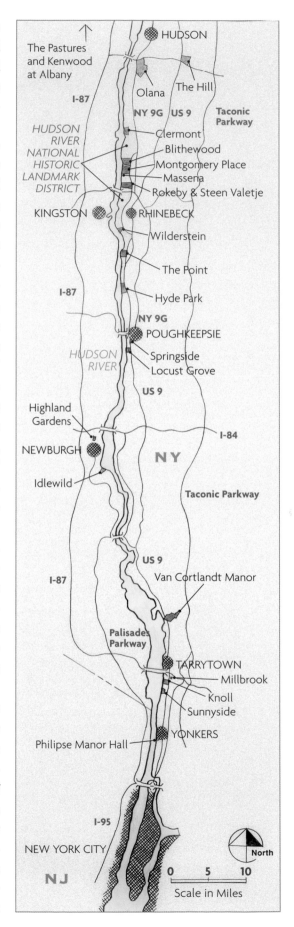

Figure 10. Bird's-Eye Sketch Showing Typical Residential Property, by Dahl Taylor. Illustrated here are some of the components often included in Romantic-period landscape gardens along the Hudson River. The gateway was usually modest, with a low wall along the public road and possibly set off by a diminutive gatehouse (A). A densely wooded buffer was maintained for privacy (B). The meandering entrance drive provided a dramatic approach to the house, introducing a variety of open spaces and views (C). Water, in streams, ponds and waterfalls, was employed to enliven the scene (D). The house was set in a dramatic position, typically fitted with a loop driveway and terraced earthworks towards the river (E). Flower gardens were informal, sited along footpaths that led to shelters and seats that exploited the views (F). The kitchen garden and agricultural elements were isolated, but designed as an ornamental gentleman's farm (G). Together, landscape elements formed a distinctive sense of place.

and summerhouses to small individual seats. They provided shelter and rest for those touring the grounds and were also landmarks and artistic highlights in the garden. Urns and sundials, planters and commemorative constructions were also inserted as features. One owner excavated and propped up an old tree stump and presented it on his front lawn for all to see. Pride in a sculptural tree stump was a design conceit peculiar to the Romantic period.

But then, the Romantic period was a proud time in America. There was enthusiasm and optimism, if innocent and naïve. Romantic sensibilities were upbeat. There was an ease in New York's social, economic and political life that was seldom bitter but, rather, prideful, optimistic, and irrepressibly vital.

"Can there be a country in the world better calculated than ours to exercise and to exalt the imagination?" asked New York's Governor Dewitt Clinton in 1816, going on to find his muse in the American landscape, "this wild, romantic and awful [awe-inspiring] scenery ... calculated to produce a correspondent impression in the imagination—to elevate all the faculties of the mind, and to exalt all the feelings of the heart."

Fueled by sympathetic political, religious and nationalistic principles, after a period of assimilation America's cultural aspirations joined with the nation's physical assets, the landscape, to achieve a distinctive artistic expression. This garden design work stands at the center of historic events that decisively shaped the concept of scenic beauty in America. It was undeniably indigenous, because it reflected America's "genius of the place"—the *genius loci* of the Hudson River Valley.

⧫ ANDREW JACKSON DOWNING

> "In Landscape Gardening the country gentleman
> of leisure finds a resource of the most agreeable
> nature."

A. J. Downing, Preface: *A Treatise on the Theory
and Practice of Landscape Gardening, Adapted
to North America*, 1841

The role of Andrew Jackson Downing (1815–1852) in Hudson Valley landscape gardening is so important as to require preliminary discussion to introduce the personality ahead of extensively quoting him throughout the text that follows.

A. J. Downing (as he was often called) was a native of Newburgh-on-Hudson. As noted earlier, he was a nurseryman and horticulturist by training, and had a knack for writing and a curiosity for sophisticated culture (and a handsome and suave personality, according to those who knew him). Downing became America's most prominent landscape gardener in the mid-nineteenth century, known widely for his early important books, *Treatise on the Theory and Practice of Landscape Gardening Adapted to North America*, with three editions in Downing's lifetime (1841, '44 and '49) and *Cottage Residences*, with four editions (1842, '44, '47 and '52), and as editor of the popular periodical, *The Horticulturist*, from July 1846. Over the years Downing added material to new editions and revised some of the text, so that the later editions represented his mature understandings. (In quoting from *Landscape Gardening* and *Cottage Residence*, all these editions will be used interchangeably or as indicated in the text.)[8]

For social historians, Downing is most important for his influence on domestic architecture as a prominent proponent of America's earliest picturesque house designs. In this he partnered with another A. J. D.—Alexander Jackson Davis (1803–1892)—an architect by training who provided the younger Downing with many of the architectural sketches that illustrated Downing's books. As with Downing, Davis saw architecture in the context of landscape settings. A. J. Davis was a New York City native and knew the Hudson Valley well. He provided architectural designs for several of the historic sites examined in this book. When his friend and kindred spirit, A. J. Downing, died at age thirty-six in a tragic steamboat accident on the Hudson, Davis lived on to see the picturesque aesthetic play out for several more decades. Still, Davis did not have a horticultural or landscape design background and never wrote extensively on landscape gardening, despite its known importance to him.

While a singular voice, A. J. Downing's thoughts on the topic of landscape gardening are not easily read today. Except for professionals, his topic is obscure, even incomprehensible, because few practice landscape gardening in Downing's terms. Today we have little cultural context to appreciate its purposes or design tenets. Landscape gardening in America is an historic phenomenon, the concern of curators. Its study is most critical for the historic sites that preserve worthy examples and are valued historic resources. Most of these landscape resources are today poorly maintained and poorly—and sometime wrongly—interpreted.

In revisiting historic landscape gardening on the Hudson, no one is a better guide than Andrew Jackson Downing. In the first and subsequent editions of his *Treatise on the Theory and Practice of Landscape Gardening*, Downing reported on "a taste for rural improvements," as he described it in the first words of his preface. Later in the book's introductory remarks Downing claimed that "nothing is more instructive than a personal inspection of country seats, where the grounds are laid out in a tasteful manner." It is his role as a guide to the Romantic-period properties that most interests us as we tour historic sites today. Downing knew the Hudson Valley region intimately and with great pride. Touring properties amid the modest hills outside Boston, he wrote to a Hudson Valley friend whose residential landscape fronted the river, "I wished quietly when the Bostonians were laboring to show me the 'fine views' from their country places that [I] could have transplanted them to the grand coup d'oeil of the Catskills from your veranda."9 In his *Treatise*, Downing proclaimed, "There is no part of the Union where the taste in Landscape Gardening is so far advanced, as on the middle portion of the Hudson."10

Downing was no fan of older colonial designs, such as the Hudson's old-fashioned Anglo-Dutch gardens, which he chided as "the Ancient or Geometric Style" for their "regularity, symmetry and the display of labored art" and "a fertility of odd conceits" (Figure 13). Instead, Downing made himself a champion and student of landscape gardening as it had evolved in England over the previous century, where Downing felt "Landscape Gardening was first raised to the rank of a fine art."

Downing sought out and read the standard works on the topic, from Alexander Pope, Joseph Addison, Horace Walpole and Thomas Whately to Uvedale Price, William Gilpin, Richard Payne Knight, and Humphry Repton, so that he understood the century-long evolution of English landscape gardening. He

had the intellectual inquisitiveness, and connections, to visit the Hudson Valley's premier estate properties, and he had the design background to evaluate the situation in mid-century America vis-à-vis what had gone before. As such, Downing was the most important chronicler of antebellum landscape gardening in America, and his focus on the Hudson River Valley is of great benefit to a regional study.

In addition to Downing's studied background in landscape gardening, he was also influenced by more contemporary ideas, notably the prolific writings of John Claudius (J. C.) Loudon (1783–1843). Loudon was England's most prominent garden authority during Downing's lifetime. Downing appreciated Loudon's professional success and modeled his own career accordingly. As befit his English audience, Loudon covered all varieties of garden and landscape design in his works, providing a shopping list of eclectic ideas in contrast to the more consistent, dogmatic tenets of eighteenth-century landscape gardening in the age of Capability Brown. A modern, Loudon ushered in the plethora of stylistic approaches that characterizes international landscape design to this day.11

In 1832, J. C. Loudon coined the term "Gardenesque," a design philosophy that emphasized individual plants placed in the landscape to show their particular attributes. The garden was a collection of plants. Loudon promoted the Gardenesque as elevating what he called "the botany of trees and shrubs" above wild nature. For Loudon, domestic grounds modeled on picturesque themes weren't much of a garden. He proclaimed:

Mere picturesque improvement is not enough in these enlightened times: it is necessary to understand that there is such a character of art, as the gardenesque, as well as the picturesque. ... Any creation to be recog-

Figure 11. Photograph Portrait of A. J. Downing, c. 1851. Youthful, articulate and well-grounded in horticultural expertise, Andrew Jackson (A. J.) Downing was the premier spokesperson for landscape design in pre–Civil War America. A resident of the Hudson River Valley, Downing also reported on regional landscape gardening, providing knowledgeable commentary on many of the important properties that remain historic sites today. Courtesy of George Tatum.

Figure 12. Portrait of A. J. Davis, by George Freeman, no date. An architect with romantic sensibilities attuned with A. J. Downing's, Alexander Jackson Davis expanded on Downing's interest in picturesque architecture. Davis's designs, presented in Downing's popular writings, evolved into indigenous Hudson Valley styles. Courtesy of Avery Library, Columbia University.

The "Beautiful design mode" (sometimes he used the term "Graceful") took inspiration from nature, but sought a refined polish that resulted in a man-made appearance. A "Beautiful" landscape garden would be clearly artificial, with a tidy and unnatural look, often using exotic plants and formal placements. Beautiful landscape gardens, wrote Downing, were "characterized by curving and flowing lines" and "an idea of beauty calmly and harmoniously expressed." Maintenance was increased by the need for "grass mown into a softness like velvet, gravel walks scrupulously firm, dry and clean; and the most perfect order and neatness should reign throughout."

Downing did not dismiss the Beautiful approach, which he knew well from recent English fashion. The Beautiful was J. C. Loudon's taste, and Downing, in *Landscape Gardening*, called the Gardenesque "but another word for what we term the Graceful [i.e., Beautiful] school." The Beautiful style also incorporated French influences popular in America in Downing's time. For Downing, the Beautiful was an amalgam going back to English precedents, both old and new, from Capability Brown to J. C. Loudon. In a sense, the Beautiful was everything in landscape gardening, except the Picturesque.

Downing's "Picturesque design mode" was the legacy of the picturesque improvers, notably Uvedale Price. A Picturesque design, said Downing in imitation of Price, produced "outlines of a certain spirited irregularity, surfaces comparatively abrupt and broken, and growth of a somewhat wild and bold character." The Picturesque is:

> An idea of beauty ... strongly and irregularly expressed, [where] every object should group with another; trees and shrubs are often planted closely together; and intricacy and variety—thickets—glades—and underwood—as in wild nature, are indispensable. Walks and roads are more abrupt in their windings, turning off frequently at sudden angles. ... In water, all the wildness of romantic spots in nature ... The keeping [i.e., maintenance] of such a landscape will of course be less careful than in the

nized as a work of art, must be such as can never be mistaken for a work of nature.[12]

While admitting Loudon's influence, Downing was understandably concerned that the American situation was an awkward fit with pretentious Gardenesque goals. In later editions of *Landscape Gardening*, Downing called Loudon too scientific, labeling him "somewhat deficient as an artist in imagination," preferring "mere artistical beauty to that of expression," and the Gardenesque style suited to "artificial planting only." In a review of *Landscape Gardening* that appeared in the periodical *The Cultivator*, J. C. Loudon was cited as "extensively read in America with a corresponding influence on this art [i.e., landscape gardening]," but the reviewer added that Loudon presented "far less appreciation of the picturesque than is contained in the work before us [i.e., Downing's *Landscape Gardening*]."[13]

Related closely to this comparison of the Gardenesque to the earlier picturesque, the most important design discussion provided in A. J. Downing's writings was the distinction he made between "Beautiful" and "Picturesque" design. Downing grounded this description in the history of English landscape gardening, and he explained the difference simply, but in great detail and without bias (Figures 14 and 15).

graceful [i.e., Beautiful] school. ... The lawn may be less frequently mown, the edge of the walks less carefully trimmed, where the Picturesque prevails.

In short, a Picturesque landscape garden would be modeled on natural occurrences and be of a natural appearance. While the Picturesque design was not wilderness, man's presence was benign. The term "vernacular" (local circumstances) had design implications, modeled on the ideal of yeomen farmers working agrarian pursuits in settled but primitive landscapes—a wilderness landscape garden that embraced connections to common and pioneer life. Downing suggested that the appeal of the Picturesque design was not for everyone:

Artists, we imagine, find somewhat of the same pleasure in studying wild landscape, where the very rocks and trees seem to struggle with the elements for foothold, that they do in contemplating the phases of the passion and instincts of human and animal life. The manifestation of [nature's] power is to many minds far more captivating than that of beauty.

While the Beautiful mode was often employed in the pre–Civil War era and increasingly thereafter in the stampede to Victorian excess, it is the Picturesque design mode that distinguished landscape gardening in the Hudson River Valley's Romantic period. Initially, A. J. Downing felt only one in a thousand would

Figure 13. *The Geometric style, from an old print,* engraving from *Landscape Gardening* by A. J. Downing (1844). Downing's illustration shows a late seventeenth-century residential landscape reminiscent of Westbury Court (Figure 6). He derisively called it the "ancient style," because of its fussy geometry and heavily sheared shrubbery (topiary). The Old World scene furthered Downing's argument for the superiority of naturalized landscape gardening based on America's distinctive *genius loci.*

Figure 14. Engraving Showing Contrasting Residences, from *Landscape Gardening* by A. J. Downing (1841). Downing used this vignette to contrast two separate styles. On the left a classical house is shown fitted with a straight avenue and set off with a regular spacing of identical trees. In the left foreground is a formal-appearing columnar evergreen. These design elements were indicative of the Beautiful design approach. In contrast, on the right is a crenellated Gothic-style house with an approach drive that curved through a naturalized park. A gnarly tree forms an appropriate foreground to the Picturesque design.

prefer the Picturesque, but by 1844 he claimed it was "beginning to be preferred." Even if public acceptance of the Beautiful was widespread, Downing called the Picturesque "appropriate" in the setting of the Hudson Valley and, as it was more practical to maintain, he thought the Picturesque should grow in appeal to Americans.

Today the Romantic-period appeal of the picturesque aesthetic and Picturesque landscape gardening are recognized as precursors of other cultural achievements. Notably, the development of America's urban parks, beginning with Central Park in New York City (1858), was directly related to the earlier practice of landscape gardening in the Hudson River Valley. As an urban park, Central Park had its appropriate Beautiful components, but the inspiration behind its plan was Nature and the appeal of the picturesque aesthetic. Central Park, it was said, brought the Catskill Mountains to New York City. Picturesque design sensibilities were also factors in the early history of the American national and state park systems of the late nineteenth and early twentieth centuries. In turn, America's suburban home, with its reliance on mown lawns and shade trees overhanging a swing chair or a sundial or bird bath, owes its aesthetic foundation to designs that fit Downing's definition of the Picturesque.

Downing's synthesis of the Picturesque and Beautiful was effectively illustrated in *Landscape Gardening* by using contrasting engravings (Figure 15). The images bore a resemblance to those presented as part of Richard Payne Knight's poem "The Landscape." However, unlike Knight, Downing did not include these illustrations to argue in favor of one design approach

over another so much as to make clear the distinction between them. In Downing's illustration of the Picturesque, a Gothic-style house, a rustic summerhouse, and woodland surroundings dominated the scene. Low mountains resembling the Catskills loom in the distance. A man with a gun, accompanied by a dog, introduces a decidedly rustic domesticity. It is clear that the Picturesque emphasized design in harmony with mid-eighteenth-century conditions along the Hudson. In contrast, in the Beautiful landscape, a woman and child stand before a classical (Federal-style) house, flanked by elegant urns and a fountain, emblematic of the more refined, "dressed" approach of Beautiful landscape gardening.

Today, scholars have an easier time evaluating many of the Hudson Valley's historic landscape compositions because of Downing's period descriptions. Touring the valley ahead of the 2nd edition of *Landscape Gardening*, published in 1844, Downing provided expert analysis and made the point again that it was "important and instructive ... to examine, personally, country seats of a highly tasteful character." He visited numerous sites "newly laid out, or greatly improved within a few years." Downing was often accompanied by the property owners, thus seeing the landscapes as they were intended. This was key to understanding the historical character of so ephemeral an art as landscape gardening. Downing understood the unity of residential life and the Hudson Valley's *genius loci*, describing it in intimate terms:

> The natural scenery is of the finest character, and
> places but a mile or two apart often possess, from the

Figure 15. Engravings Illustrating the Picturesque and Beautiful Design Modes, from *Landscape Gardening* by A. J. Downing (1844). The Picturesque (at top) emphasized an appearance in harmony with mid-nineteenth-century conditions along the Hudson. A Gothic-style cottage, a rustic garden shelter (far right), and indigenous woodland surroundings dominate the scene. A man with a gun, accompanied by a dog, introduced a decidedly New World domesticity. The Beautiful design mode (at bottom) contrasted a woman and child standing before a classical (Federal-style) house flanked by urns and a fountain, creating a refined and formal appearance.

constantly varying forms of the water, shores, and distant hills, widely different kinds of home landscape and distant view. Standing in the grounds of some of the finest of these seats, the eye beholds only the soft foreground of smooth lawn, the rich groups of trees shutting out all neighboring tracts, the lake-like expanse of water, and, closing the distance, a fine range of wooded mountain. A residence here of but a hundred acres, so fortunately are these disposed by nature, seems to appropriate the whole scenery round, and to be a thousand in extent.

Downing's role in the study of Hudson Valley landscape gardening was as a reporter and a critic and, to a lesser extent, as a designer. He designed a number of landscapes, but in an age of limited media coverage his actual works were little known to the public. Owing to the loss of Downing's office files and records, attribution of his work has been difficult. The facts of his professional life—his clients' names and billings for example—are fragmentary. In this volume a virtual tour of his own "Highland Gardens" home at Newburgh will lend insight on his design preferences, but the site is now an inner-city neighborhood without a trace of its past use or appearance. Fortunately, one of Downing's best landscape garden designs is preserved at Springside in Poughkeepsie and is a strikingly well-crafted design responsive to the owner's needs and the genius of the place. It is the Hudson Valley's most significant garden.

Andrew Jackson Downing's reporting and his few discernable design efforts enrich the study of landscape gardening on the Hudson. His writings outlined his interpretation of the basic elements and design tenets. These presentations were often broadly sketched, presenting universal design principles of form and expression, of unity, harmony and variety. On the specifics of how to lay out grounds and select plantings, Downing recited a varied agenda, often influenced by his distant mentor, J. C. Loudon. In these recitations the particularities of a site and the varied needs of owners were identified as critical factors. Myriad circumstances led to idiosyncratic results. This eclectic approach did not generate rigid design guidelines likely to inspire a set "fashion" or amount to a "Downingesque style," as is sometimes claimed. Downing did not promote an American version of the British picturesque style, as one recent author asserted, nor did Downing invent landscape gardening or define it as a new art form, as is sometimes claimed. Instead, Downing called his landscape gardening advice "my hints," representing a humble approach much less than dogma or innovation. Typically in the nineteenth century, professional landscape gardeners worked as part of a long organic process where the owner's decisions decisively influenced the design scheme. In this way landscape gardening was an art reflective of varied owners and aspirations and influenced by the dynamics of broadly felt fashion, where professionals took on bit parts in the drama of man's interface with nature and design in the outdoors. ✦

CHAPTER 2

PRELUDE:
THE COLONIAL PERIOD

In 1609, Henry Hudson, employed by the Dutch East India Company, explored the river that would bear his name. A few years later, settlers from what is today Belgium sailed up the river and established an outpost at what would become Albany. So began the Hudson River Valley's 166-year colonial history, culminating in the Revolutionary War. During this century and a half, landscape design in the Hudson River Valley was uniquely influenced by the Netherlands, but the most notable links would be with England. In either case, the reliance on geometric layouts and regimented plantings was common to all European landscape design in this period.

The Hudson River was initially operated by the Dutch West India Company as a trading post. The impact of early settlement was meager, and the area's growth was lethargic. Only one Dutch estate (patroonship) was established before the English took over administration of the Hudson Valley after 1664. For several generations residential life was restricted to a few fortified centers. There was the small port of New Amsterdam (New York after 1664), and another upriver at Albany (the earlier

Dutch outpost of Fort Orange and Beverwyck), and one mid-valley enclave, Kingston (called Esopus, and later Wiltwyck, by the Dutch). Scattered tenant farmers worked modest farmsteads, isolated across an otherwise wilderness landscape. On the banks of the Hudson River, a few manor houses were seats of administration for large landowners. Manor house sites were milling, shipping and market centers, as well as points of refuge.

With the rare exception, landscape development in these circumstances focused on agricultural efficiency. Ornamental gardening was limited to modest pursuits. An owner might lay out a straight driveway with trees planted at regular intervals and maintain a well-ordered and productive kitchen garden. Landscape planning was otherwise haphazard, indifferent to aesthetics and answering to practicality. The benefits of previously cleared land, reliable fresh water, soil characteristics, and optimum solar orientation determined the layout of agricultural and residential landscapes. There was an emphasis, and considerable satisfaction, in utility and good keeping. Gardens in colonial times were derived

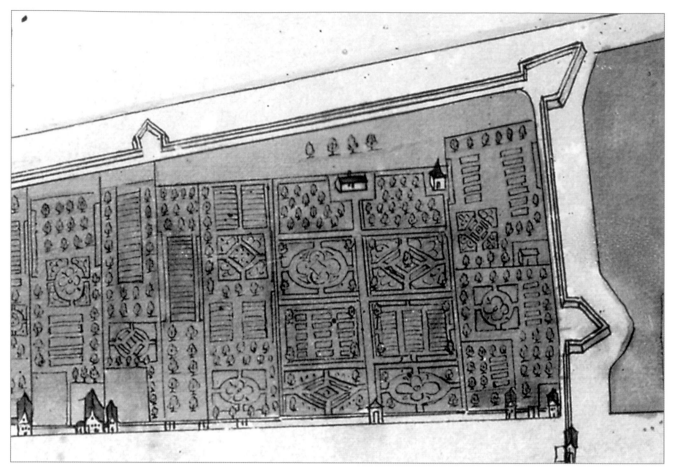

Figure 16. Detail from the Costello Plan of New Amsterdam (New York City), 1660. A portion of this old map of New Amsterdam (north is to the right) reveals residential landscapes that are exclusively formal geometric designs with symmetrical garden beds. The Hudson River is at the top; the future Wall Street is the fortification line shown on the right. Courtesy of the New York Public Library.

from the Middle Ages, when horticulture was practiced along functional lines and adhered to orderly arrangements. In the New World, garden layouts with their geometric designs (*parterres*) attest to long-standing European taste (Figure 16).

Decades passed. Because of the sluggish economic circumstances, a society of landed owners emerged very slowly in the Hudson River Valley. By 1700 less than 20,000 colonists inhabited the region, the majority close to Manhattan. The rest of the valley was a true frontier. Few settlers, let alone wealthy settlers likely to undertake ornamental landscaping, lived in the valley. The only Dutch patroon, Kiliaen Van Rensselaer, was a successful Amsterdam jeweler, but he never set foot in the New World. Instead he sent agents to extract a profit, and certainly not to engage in elaborate garden making.

It was not until the end of the seventeenth century that several aspiring immigrants took up residence and began to assert themselves as wealthy entrepreneurs, loyal to English rule. A look at several of these elite colonial residences, today

museum properties, illustrates the typical situation. In the lower valley, Frederick Philipse (1626–1702) arrived in New Amsterdam from the Netherlands before 1653. As a builder with skill, ambition, and English loyalties, he worked his way to the top. By the late 1690s he was established on Philipse Manor, a huge tract extending for miles along the eastern bank of the Hudson River from New York City to Croton in today's Westchester County. His estate would last a hundred years and is today represented by the surviving manor house, Philipse Manor Hall State Historic Site, at Yonkers (Figure 17).[14]

Acquired initially as a business enterprise, the manor soon became the Philipse family's chief residence. While a family home, the surroundings were workmanlike. The manor hall site was selected for its proximity to the river and to several mills along Neperhan Creek (today the Saw Mill River). The mills were of crucial economic importance, developed even before the manor was established. The adjacent manor hall allowed easy scrutiny of these operations and convenient access to the river landing, a lifeline to commerce and social interaction in the early colonial period. The manor house yards and gardens were built on raised, open ground above the river, positioned to exploit a southern orientation and a healthful breeze, even while the house site was cramped by the proximity of roads and the milling complex. Only north of the house was land available for storage, work yards and kitchen gardens. All in all, this was a utilitarian scene with discordant elements clustered together. Its landscape had little aesthetic purpose (Figure 18).

Another colonial estate, close to Albany, was that of the Livingston family. The "patriarch," Robert Livingston (1654–1728), was an audacious Albany businessman born in Scotland, who struck it rich after being granted Livingston Manor, south of Albany, in 1686. This extensive holding spawned the many later properties developed by the Livingston family. The original manor house, built in 1699, was a no-nonsense workhouse built close to a saw- and gristmill enterprise, and later a boat yard, located where the Roeliff Jansen Kill empties into the Hudson River in southern Columbia County. This pioneer house and its workyard surroundings was soon hopelessly outdated as a residence. The complex was dismantled and the house demolished before 1800. Today, the original manor house site is unrecognizable, although the old manor hamlet of Stadtje, today sleepy Linlithgo, does survive a short distance inland.

Farther south, development of Van Cortlandt Manor at Croton-on-Hudson (now operated as a museum by Historic Hudson Valley) mirrored the typical colonial approach to landscape design. The landscape layout was established at a very early date, even earlier than the property's purchase by Stephanus Van Cortlandt (1643–1700) in 1688.[15] The main structure was a fortified, stone workhouse (Figure 19). The distinctive wraparound veranda was added before 1700. While the view is today screened by highways,

Figure 17. *Philipse Manor Hall,* unknown artist, 1784. Philipse Manor illustrates typical conditions along the Hudson River, which is seen here on the left with the Palisades as a backdrop. Manor house sites were integrated with commercial activities. A large mill is shown fronting the house, and other utilitarian barns, sheds and work yards are clustered nearby. The view can be compared with Figure 18. Courtesy of Historic Hudson Valley.

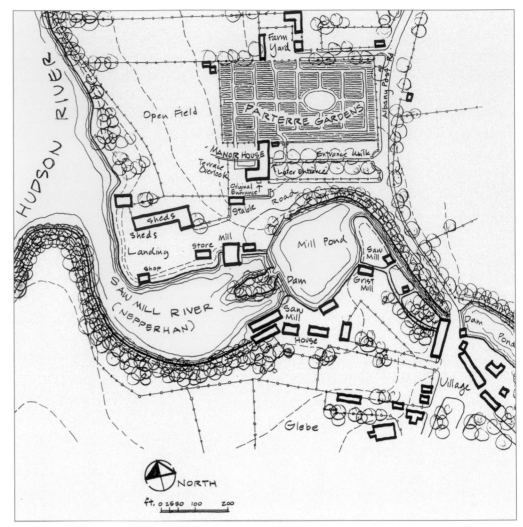

Figure 18. Plan of Philipse Manor Hall Site in the Late Colonial Period, by R. M. Toole. The manor house is shown adjacent to the extensive two-acre "Parterre Gardens" to the north. The manor house was hemmed in by sheds, mill buildings and yards, limiting its potential for landscape gardening.

bridges and vegetation, the manor house originally was exposed at a point where the Croton River entered the Hudson. From the house, there was an expansive panorama over the Tappan Zee, a wide portion of the lower Hudson River. While early settlers were not oblivious to a fine view, the Van Cortlandt house site otherwise conformed to the colonists' preoccupation with practicality and good order and a geometrical layout that was the hallmark of landscape and garden development in this early period.

In the 1950s the Van Cortlandt house site was researched and restored. These investigations showed that the siting and layout of the house grounds had much in common with the Philipse manor hall and the early Livingston development upriver. Here, at Van Cortlandt, a steep hillside buffered winter winds from the north, enhancing the preferred southern orientation of the house and gardens. The sheltered anchorage on the Croton River became a vital economic installation and later turned a profit as the site of a toll ferry linking the

earliest public highway, the Albany Post Road, today's U.S. Rt. 9 (Figure 20).

The Van Cortlandts exploited the soils and drainage of the site, which were studied to maximize cultivation on the narrow land between the Croton River and the hillside. The Anglo-Dutch approach to design was employed to incorporate kitchen gardens with self-contained fenced yards and work spaces for the active household and its minions. Barns, storage sheds and other outbuildings were clustered nearby. In order to accommodate these needs in so confined a space, the landscape layout could not be structured formally on the center line of the house, which under ideal circumstances would have been used to organize the immediate landscape. Here, there was very limited level land, and what was available curved around to the east, following the shoreline of the Croton River. Given the constraints, the gardens were set off to the side of the house, where a so-called Long Walk was established, angled away from the house but serving as the central axis for the garden's geometric arrangement. The Long Walk also linked the house with other landscape components stretched out along the cramped river bank (Figure 21).

Once established, colonial-period estate properties on the Hudson were improved by family descendents—at Philipse Manor by Frederick Philipse II (d. 1751) and Frederick Philipse III (d. 1786), and at Van Cortlandt Manor by Philip Van Cortlandt (d. 1748) and Pierre Van Cortlandt (d. 1814). Still, in these second and third generations, the landscape arrangements often remained unchanged, showing a persistence of the original design.

The colonial-period rules of primogeniture, whereby the oldest son alone inherited the entire estate, were occasionally broken. For example, in 1728, Philip Livingston (1686–1749) succeeded his father on Livingston Manor while his younger brother, Robert Livingston, Jr. (1688–1775), took possession of a 13,000-acre property subdivided from the main estate. This mini-estate, called Claremont, was given to Robert Livingston, Jr. by his appreciative father who, by bending the rules of primogeniture, set seeds for the active subdivision of the Hudson River shoreline that would occur after the Revolutionary War.[16]

In 1730, Robert Livingston, Jr. developed a manor house and farm on his Claremont property following ideas similar to his father's. Today this is the Clermont State Historic Site, operated by New York State, on the Hudson River in southern Columbia County.[17] The basic landscape layout of this new, second-generation manor site was not much different from the earlier residences. The house was set on a narrow terrace

Figure 19 . Van Cortlandt Manor. Originally a stone hunting lodge and trading post, the house was expanded to its present appearance in the mid-eighteenth century. Courtesy of Historic Hudson Valley .

Figure 20. Map of the Van Cortlandt Manor Farm (detail), by George W. Cartwright, 1837. This map (north is up the page) shows the manor house on the north side of the Croton River, fronted by a "Lawn" and the "Garden" off to the east side along the narrow river bank. This was a cramped spot, but important for its situation in a sheltered harbor off the Hudson River at a critical ferry crossing along the river road. Courtesy of Historic Hudson Valley.

close to the river. Concurrent with house construction, a close-by river landing was set up where the access road would pass close to the manor house under the watchful eye of the landlord. Accessory buildings and fenced yards, slave quarters and outbuildings, soon clustered around in a chaotic, workaday scene typical of the period. It appears that modest garden beds, laid out in geometric, *parterre* arrangements, were located east of the house on artificially leveled terraces.

As seen in all the colonial-period examples, the residential landscape typically amounted to a composition of roughly arranged, loosely rectilinear forms, beginning with a straight approach drive—sometimes called the avenue—and extending out from the house in large and small enclosures, a few purely ornamental (a flower garden perhaps), but most functional work yards, laundry yards, firewood yards, and stable areas. The kitchen garden mixed ornamental flowers with vegetables, fruits and herbs. The house grounds formed a somewhat haphazard division on the land, regular and symmetrical when possible, but adaptable when the particulars of the natural situation, and practicality, made an irregular arrangement preferable. Refined garden effects were appreciated. This was the Anglo-Dutch garden design style common in England since the late 1600s, recreated in colonial New York.

Even as garden and landscape design traditions began to change radically in England during the 1740s and '50s, with age-old, geometric formality giving way to irregular naturalism, earlier ways persisted in provincial New York. With an old-fashioned, traditional outlook, the estate owners brought the Anglo-Dutch style to a zenith of elegance before the Revolution. At the Philipse manor hall the last landlord, Frederick Philipse III, and his family lived a

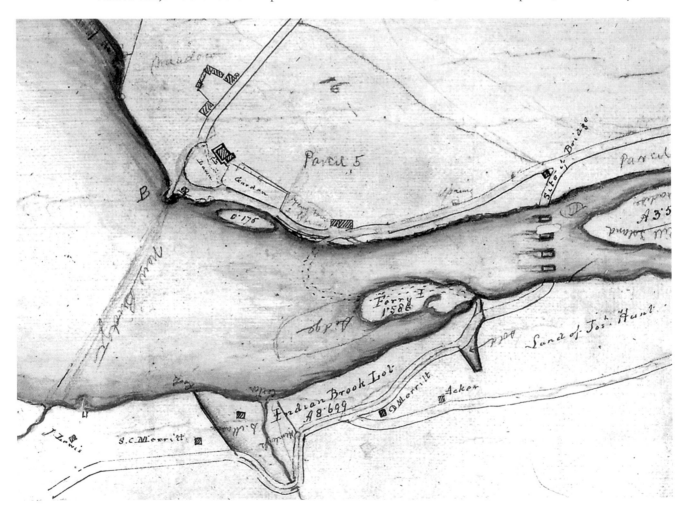

Figure 21. Photograph Showing Gardens at Van Cortlandt Manor, c. 1890. This overview gives a good indication of the garden's cramped layout along the narrow banks of the Croton River against the hillside on the left. The "Long Walk" is visible, together with geometric garden beds (right) reflective of the Anglo-Dutch style. The circle beds in the foreground are late-nineteenth-century modifications in an area of the garden reserved for ornamentals. In the 1950s extensive archaeological investigations revealed the early layout, which has been restored. Courtesy of Historic Hudson Valley.

genteel and cultured existence as aristocratic, anglicized gentry. In these years the manor hall was enlarged and given its surviving Georgian form. A large formal garden occupied a raised terrace, about 400 feet by 200 feet (nearly two acres), expanded and remodeled from the original, more workaday, kitchen garden. As was the taste of his generation, Frederick Philipse III showed an interest in exotic plants, which were increasingly available. There is evidence, in the poetry of a traveler, that the Philipse manor hall was an idyllic rural situation, perceived in the then-popular classical idiom:

> The eastern banks [of the Hudson] are crown'd
> with rural seats,
> And Nature's work, the hand of Art completes.
> Here Philips's villa, where Pomona joins
> At once the product of a hundred climes;
> Here, ting'd by Flora, Asian flow'rs unfold
> Their burnish'd leaves of vegetable gold.
> When snows descend, and clouds tumultuous fly
> Thro' the blue medium of the crystal sky,
> Beneath his painted mimic heav'n he roves
> Amidst the glass-encircled citron groves;
> The grape and luscious fig his taste invite,
> Hesperian apples glow upon his sight;
> The sweet auriculas their bells display,
> And Philips finds in January, May.[18]

Despite the refinements, the landscape at Philipse manor hall was cramped and outdated, with incompatible neighbors

crowding in (Figure 18). The residential landscape was compromised by its pioneer layout and close proximity to discordant mills, barns, stables, and work yards. These antiquated conditions were difficult or impractical to alter. Although lovely for its wealthy owners, and although the landscape had become more ornamental in purpose and more elaborate in scope late in the colonial period, Philipse Manor illustrated the artistic limitations of outdated needs and the traditional design emphasis on geometric arrangements and practicality.

This compromised approach was typical, affecting even new developments. Consider, for example, The Pastures, the late-colonial construction in Albany by Philip Schuyler (1733–1804). Schuyler was a prominent New Yorker, the descendent of an early Dutch family. He was a local leader and statesman, thoroughly provincial, infused with the memory of three pioneering generations before him. He was also fully anglicized and a cultured member of the colonial elite. His Georgian house and handsome property, created after its purchase in 1761, was visited by important dignitaries and distinguished travelers. Today, the house and a tiny portion of its original landscape are preserved in an urban setting at the Schuyler Mansion State Historic Site (Figure 22).[19]

Despite Schuyler's sophisticated background, and possibly owing to his provincial perspective, documentation shows that the layout of The Pastures was, by and large, a continuation of the regimentation seen earlier. The house site sloped to the east, looking out over the Hudson River about a quarter mile away. A level lawn terrace extended across the east façade of the house, planted with a formal, double row of trees and a symmetrical, curving picket fence. Between the house and the public road was a five-acre field, set apart, planted with an arrangement of regularly spaced trees. The area may have been scythed, rather than grazed, so that it was set off from the common agricultural fields. Around it the natural and pastoral valley scenery would have been a contrast.

Directly attached to the west (back) side of the house was an enclosed "yard," as Philip Schuyler himself called it, that included a wide variety of dependencies including slave quarters, the kitchen, offices, outhouses and sheds, grouped around a utility open space. Close by and south of the house was a formal garden that seems to have included kitchen gardens arranged in geometric rows. In 1790 this area was described as "laid out in all the elaborate art of French landscape gardening, with here and there parterres, some of which are nicely lawned."[20] This may represent a refinement of the original garden. North of the house, a straight approach drive angled downhill towards the center of Albany. A coach house/stable was inelegantly sited along this drive. Given contemporary practices in England, The Pastures illustrates the persistence of the colonial tradition, although the layout was less haphazard, a bit grander, and the aesthetic effect more overtly ornamental.

In the years just before the Revolutionary War, several river estates were laid out by Livingston descendents, and one by an outsider, John Bard, at his Hyde Park estate, that provide further insights into the slowly evolving practice of landscape and garden design late in the colonial period.

The children and grandchildren of Robert Livingston, Jr. of Claremont developed numerous residential farm properties, although most did so only after the Revolutionary War, an era that will be discussed shortly. Before the war, at the 1730 house, Robert's oldest son, Robert R. Livingston (1718–1775), sometimes called "The Judge," married Margaret Beekman (1724–1800) in 1742 and by so doing added a stupendous 240,000 acres to Claremont's original 13,000-acre property. Margaret Beekman Livingston is known to have been an avid gardener,

Figure 22. The Pastures, from a Map of Albany (detail), 1794. This is a detail from the so-called "Simeon De Witt Map" of Albany (north is to the right). It shows the Schuyler house with garden beds (south) and a large barn (west). The approach drive is awkwardly set to one side, reaching a stable building before arriving at the classical-style house. The lawn area to the east is planted with an alignment of evenly spaced trees. Courtesy of the New York State Library, Manuscripts and Special Collections.

and documentation shows that there was a fountain in her formal Claremont garden.

In 1775, Robert R. Livingston died and his eldest son, twenty-nine-year-old namesake Robert R. Livingston (1746–1813), became the third master of Claremont (Figure 23). This Robert was the most important of all the Livingstons. He was a son of the Enlightenment who, despite aristocratic trappings and his role as country squire, understood that at a time of revolution the future was with a new order. He helped secure the Declaration of Independence, participated actively in the war, and later served as the United States Minister to France. He partnered with Robert Fulton in pioneering steamboat travel on the Hudson a few years later. Robert R. Livingston was the first Chancellor of New York State, and he was called "The Chancellor" to distinguish him from his father and grandfather.

When Chancellor Robert inherited the Claremont property, his mother, the dowager Margaret Beekman Livingston, stayed on at the forty-five-year-old manor house. Robert occupied a separate house built nearby, which he called "Belvedere." Little is known of Belvedere's residential grounds, but its proximity to the Claremont house and the clutter of the river landing suggests a compromised position. In any event

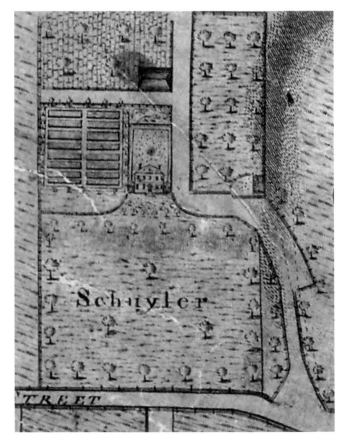

Figure 23. *Portrait of Chancellor Robert R. Livingston,* by Gilbert Stuart, c. 1795. Robert R. Livingston was the most famous of the Livingstons. His landscape gardening at old Claremont would be a notable contribution in the immediate post–Revolutionary War period. Courtesy of New York State Office of Parks, Recreation and Historic Preservation, Clermont State Historic Site, Taconic Region.

Figure 24. Clermont (Claremont). Photograph by Kjirsten Gustavson. The present house had it beginnings with the reconstruction after 1777. Many alterations followed in the nineteenth century. Courtesy of New York State Office of Parks, Recreation and Historic Preservation, Clermont State Historic Site, Taconic Region.

Belvedere did not survive for long, as all this development was swept away by the turmoil of the Revolutionary War. In October 1777 the British military on a foray up the Hudson River burned both the Claremont and Belvedere houses and their outbuildings. The owners escaped and, immediately after the British retreated, Margaret Beekman Livingston had the Claremont house rebuilt on its old foundations. This house, much altered, survives (Figure 24).

The wartime events at Claremont denote a certain benchmark in the evolution of the region's landscape design heritage. When the house was rebuilt on its original site, it had a strikingly new landscape. Most significantly, the colonial-era

Figure 25. Drawing Showing Claremont from the East, by Alexander Robertson, 1796. This drawing shows the grounds fifteen years after the house was reconstructed. As part of that remodeling, the formerly cluttered landscape was rearranged as a park, with a simple fence line separating animals from the pleasure grounds east of the house. Courtesy of the Albany Institute of History and Art.

complex of outbuildings and work yards, slave quarters, and Anglo-Dutch garden forms was not rebuilt in its old proximity to the house, freeing up the immediate landscape for a more gracious treatment. The immediate house grounds were formed into a park of lawn and trees, wherein the rebuilt house was presented as a sculptural object in an idyllic landscape setting. In 1782 a reception, attended by George Washington, was held at the manor house, and the house grounds had no doubt been reassembled to some extent by that date. It is fitting, perhaps, that this event can be cited as introducing English landscape gardening to the Hudson River Valley (Figure 25).

While his mother reigned at the new house, Chancellor Robert R. Livingston, depressed over the wartime destruction of Claremont and Belvedere, initially thought of moving on. But soon his role in public life proved a distraction that lasted well into the postwar years, after which he returned to the

area and created a new residence and landscape. This era saw the rules of primogeniture dismantled, and so the Claremont holdings were subdivided by Robert's many brothers and sisters who, in time, developed residential estates and designed landscapes of their own.

The Revolutionary War marked a break between continents and empires, between old and new ways, and also between the old and the new in garden and landscape design on the Hudson. By the 1780s landscape gardening, as established in the age of Capability Brown, was readily transmitted to the newly independent colonies. The disruption and eventual renewal brought on by the Revolution provided a new start. After a long, unsettled period, landscape design in the young American republic focused somewhat belatedly on English landscape gardening.

CHAPTER 3

CLERMONT, "IN COMPLETE FAIRY LAND," AND LANDOR'S COTTAGE

The Hudson Valley emerged slowly from the Revolutionary War and its aftermath during what we now call the Federal period. Many of the old manors and farm estates, with their workaday landscapes and old garden beds, remained intact. Few new residential properties had been developed during the years of war and disruption. In this context, renewed building late in the eighteenth century provides an opportunity to study the shifting trends in garden design and the emergence of English landscape gardening from its first appearance at war-torn Claremont.[21]

An interesting example is Hyde Park, today confusingly and arbitrarily called the Vanderbilt Mansion National Historic Site in Dutchess County, operated by the National Park Service. The Hyde Park estate was consistently developed over a period of seventy years from the early 1760s until 1835. As

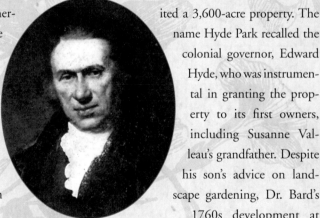

Figure 26. Detail of *Portrait of Samuel Bard*, unknown artist, not dated. John Bard's son, Samuel, developed a new residential landscape at Hyde Park in the late 1790s. Courtesy of the New York Public Library.

such, Hyde Park provides a casebook study of the evolution of landscape design in the Hudson River Valley.

The initial development was by Dr. John Bard (1716–1799), who was described as receiving advice from his son, Samuel Bard (1742–1821), when the latter was studying in Edinburgh, Scotland, in the 1760s (see page 2). The elder Bard was a physician from the Philadelphia area who married Susanne Valleau in 1737 and thereafter inherited a 3,600-acre property. The name Hyde Park recalled the colonial governor, Edward Hyde, who was instrumental in granting the property to its first owners, including Susanne Valleau's grandfather. Despite his son's advice on landscape gardening, Dr. Bard's 1760s development at Hyde Park fell into line with long-established colonial practices and there was little art to the landscape. Instead, quite appropriately, Dr. Bard concentrated his efforts on establishing a viable farm and milling operation. He built a modest house in a Dutch-influenced style that was frankly old-fashioned and inelegant, although it answered to practical concerns. Red House, as it was called, was built close to older barns and work yards, fronting the public road and notably (and incredibly) just out of sight of the Hyde Park terrace, which overlooked a fine Hudson River panorama (see Figure 43).

After the Revolutionary War, Dr. Bard's early landscape was radically improved with the grand residential layout developed by his son Samuel, who practiced medicine in New York City. In the late 1790s, in order to be closer to his aged father, Samuel built a new house a few hundred feet from Red House, at the edge of the Hyde Park terrace (see Figure 41). Samuel's documented understanding of landscape gardening from his studies in Edinburgh in the period 1763–66 was transitional in a period when landscape design was not yet driven by romanticism. Certainly Samuel Bard recognized the splendor of the terrace, but he also fitted his new house with a straight approach drive. His house was a classical, brilliant white, Federal-style structure set intrusively as a prominent object, both from the river and from the public road (Albany Post Road). The house was approached on a driveway aligned with the symmetry of the architecture. Trees were planted in a regular way along the straight driveway, and there were open fence lines set out to control animals and extending out from the house and fronting the approach drive. Close to the house, the fencing may have been decorative; elaborate, white-painted fencing was typical in this period. Samuel was not ready to give up his preferences for an orderly, even geometric landscape layout, despite nature's dominance over the property's *genius loci*.

The dichotomy of Samuel Bard's Hyde Park landscape improvements is that, while conservative, it did incorporate some new ideas. Critically, the new Hyde Park house was sited in open, park-like surroundings (Figure 27). The necessary stable complex, and associated smells, were isolated in a grove of trees 500 feet north of the house, and the kitchen/flower garden complex was located about 1,000 feet to the south. This was a response to the Brownian era's separation of divergent estate functions, so that the house was alone in an uncluttered sweep of parkland. The practice of enveloping the house in parkland was a basic theme of English landscape gardening, but in America it was atypical before 1800. At Hyde Park this effect was enhanced by the spectacular character of the terrace, perched high above the river. Also, the relatively level house site was

stately and studded with many mature trees, including old oaks that predated John Bard's ownership, trees described as a "celebrated belt of forest trees" in 1829. These venerable trees provided a sense of long-established maturity to the landscape.

While Samuel Bard built his new Hyde Park, the Livingston family's residential development in the post–Revolutionary War years also confirmed the ascendancy of landscape gardening as a fashionable concern. While exhaustive research has not been carried out on all the Livingston properties, even a superficial look at a few of their layouts confirms that landscape gardening was being actively pursued.

John Livingston (1750–1822), a great-grandson of "patriarch" Robert Livingston, built "Oak Hill" on the Hudson River in about 1794. The house and landscape survive about a mile north of the original manor house at the confluence of the Roeliff Jansen Kill. As at Hyde Park, a Federal-style house at Oak Hill was erected on a high bluff, 500 feet back from the river's edge. The dramatic perch-like location afforded extensive views, and it was the views, not practical concerns, that seem to have been decisive in the selection of this spot. John Livingston is said to have climbed a tall oak tree to decide the matter based on the views. His family worried about the exposed site, understandable given the previous emphasis on finding a sheltered southern orientation with higher ground to the north to buffer the prevailing winter winds. But, as at Samuel Bard's Hyde Park, these considerations seem to have mattered less to John Livingston than concerns for aesthetics and spectacular scenery. The landscape layouts at Hyde Park and Oak Hill reveal artistic sensitivity to the residential landscape that a previous focus on practicality and domestic good order had ignored. No longer a work place, the house grounds were now dedicated to genteel domestic life.

The most famous residential building spree in Hudson Valley history was tied to the exploits of the ten children of Judge Robert R. Livingston and Margaret Beekman, who with their spouses developed a score of estate properties from the 1790s into the early decades of the nineteenth century. Today, many of these properties are well-preserved and several are important historic sites open to the public, all within the recognized Hudson River National Historic Landmark District (see Figure 9).

As discussed earlier, the oldest son, Chancellor Robert R. Livingston, spent the war and postwar years engaged in affairs of state. He lived in New York City, and his sporadic visits upriver were spent with his mother at the rebuilt Claremont house. Then, in 1793, married with two young children, Robert built a new house several hundred feet south of the destroyed Belvedere.

He called this "Clermont," using the French spelling of the original "Claremont," which is notable as a reflection of French cultural influences along the Hudson River following the Revolution. It is the French spelling of Clermont that has been used from that point forward, and today for the name of the historic site administered by New York State. On the other hand, the site of Chancellor Livingston's 1793 house was later called "Idele." For clarity, that name is used here to describe its landscape development after 1790 and to differentiate it from the earlier 1730 house and grounds. The Idele house burned in 1909 and only ruined remnants remain today, while the landscape retains faint clues of what was an expansive landscape design at the end of the eighteenth century (Figure 28).

As an important public figure, Chancellor Livingston was visited by many notables, and there is considerable documentation to aid an accurate recreation of his landscape. Still, despite its importance, Clermont's historic, designed landscape has not been systematically studied by the New York State Bureau of Historic Sites, which has focused much of its time on concerns for architectural preservation.

Idele house was an unusually elegant and unique Federal-period design with four pavilions forming a distinctive H-shaped structure (Figures 29 and 30). The river façade of the house was set along a graded, level lawn terrace, which served as an architectural platform for the house. A carriage drive crossed just below the house, hidden in the river views. The drive was called Locust Avenue and it seems to have been an older roadway referred to as an "alley" [i.e., *allée*] by a visitor in the 1790s.[22] It was lined with mature

Figure 27. Aerial Photograph Showing Hyde Park, by Marcia A. Toole. Samuel Bard's landscape gardening placed the house in parkland, with the cultivated kitchen gardens set off to the south, shown here on the left, and the stable areas out of view to the right (north). The present house is the fourth classical-style building to occupy this spot.

black locust trees (*Robinia pseudoacacia*) and traced the edge of the immediate river bluff linking the old and new Clermont houses. When Chancellor Livingston built his house, he removed some of these locust trees that fronted the house and planted an alignment of tall, columnar Lombardy poplars in their place. As discussed earlier, the use of Lombardy poplars had French origins and reflected republican values. East of Locust Avenue and north of the house was a large, level lawn, possibly an earlier kitchen garden, terminated by a garden feature, a little "stone building with a steeple," that may have been an older well house mentioned by a local historian who described an informal scene, "backed by ground rising precipitately to a rocky ridge covered with shrubs, trees, and evergreens, affording a fine rich background."[23]

The backdrop of woodland was notable. Later referred to as the Clermont woods, it was a rocky forested area that separated the riverfront from the nearest public road. The driveway twisted through this distinctive landscape, which Chancellor Livingston called his "park." Close to the house, the driveway entered what was termed "the pleasure grounds," where the river views were seen before finally approaching the house along Locust Avenue from the south. All this is nearly indecipherable today.

In 1797 a visitor described an "English garden with only flowers and rare bushes" as located along a path leading southwest from the new house. This would have been a loosely defined, open lawn area, set off with ornamental shrubbery and fencing, amounting to a protected glade featuring flowering plants. It was meant for strolling and no doubt was traversed by a path system. The visitor explained that "this little garden adjoins and loses itself in the wild promenade which descends to the river"[24] (Figure 30).

Figure 28. Photograph Showing the Lawn at Clermont State Historic Site, 2009, by Steve Benson. The great lawn at Clermont is enjoyed by today's picnickers even while few visitors know of the historic landscape design or its significance as an early example of landscape gardening. Today, Clermont's landscape is more state park than historic artifact.

In this context, the term "wild" is quite important, referring to an area near the house where a natural appearance was retained and where plantings and visual effects were augmented to give an ornamental, but still "wild," effect. As such, this is one of the earliest recorded references in the Hudson River Valley to what was later termed Picturesque landscape gardening by A. J. Downing. It came only a few years after the design style was first articulated in England by the picturesque improvers. The fragmentary quotations that remain suggest that the taste of Chancellor Livingston was strikingly in line with current English fashion, which might be expected given the pre-1783 makeover of the old grounds and the Chancellor's exposure to the latest practices. Livingston was familiar with European fashion from his service as American Minister to France until 1805. When he returned from France, a greenhouse was quickly added to the south façade of the house. In 1824 it was reported that this greenhouse "overlooks the pleasure grounds and a fine grassy vale in the highest cultivation, skirted with flowering shrubbery, with a rich and extensive background of various fruit trees."[25] This "fine grassy vale" may be the "English garden" described thirty years earlier. Only the land forms remain today.

After Chancellor Livingston's death in 1813, Idele's designed landscape was initially maintained consistently by direct descendents. Thirty years later, Andrew Jackson Down-ing, in the 2nd edition of *Landscape Gardening* (1844), spoke of the relatively recent practice of landscape gardening in America, but noted that examples of the art form could be found as early as the mid-1790s and specifically cited as an example the "celebrated seat of Chancellor Livingston." This, Downing said, was "highly remarkable for extent, elegance of arrangements, and the highest order and keeping" (i.e., maintenance). He called the overall Clermont property "the show place of the last age ... still interesting [and] a noble place [for its] undulating lawn ... rich native woods ... added to its fine water views." Also noted were the "long vistas of planted avenues ... a pleasure-grounds, [and] gardens contain[ing] many specimens of fruit trees, the first of their sort introduced into the Union." Finally, Downing provided this comment: "The mansion, the green-houses, and the gardens, show something of the French taste in design, which Mr. [Chancellor Robert] Livingston's residence abroad, at the time when that mode was popular, no doubt, led him to adopt."

Chancellor Livingston's experiences in France in the period 1801 to 1805, and the continued direct involvement of the Livingston family with France until the 1830s, profoundly influenced the family's artistic preferences. Their landscape gardening may have been atypical of the more fully English-inspired examples. The popularity of "the French taste in

Figure 29. Watercolor Showing Idele from the North, by P. Lodet, 1807. Chancellor Robert R. Livingston built the stylish H-shaped house in 1793. Here it is shown with the Hudson River to the west and a promenade, called Locust Avenue, paralleling the river. Note the distinctive Lombardy poplars fronting the house. Courtesy of the Franklin D. Roosevelt Library.

design" referred to broadly felt French cultural influences in post–Revolutionary War America, but for the Livingstons there were also close personal links. The results can be seen throughout the Livingston family. Already mentioned was the changed spelling of the estate's name to "Clermont."[26]

Despite the French connection, however, French impact on Clermont's landscape design is uncertain. After all, this was a period when garden and landscape design in France was being heavily influenced by the English landscape garden. The cosmopolitan elite likely to have interacted with the Livingstons in France may have shown their interest in landscape design by attempting to reconcile English naturalism with the French traditions of elegance, geometry and symmetry. This was a complex and esoteric situation, and its impact on individual Livingstons and on New York's Hudson River Valley awaits further study. Downing's comments hint at some level of elaborate formality and refined elegance, a landscape character not otherwise recorded or documented at Idele (except, perhaps, for the row of Lombardy poplars fronting the house). Possibly Downing's comments were focused more on the older house grounds. There is no reference in Downing's account to the "wild" effects at Idele that were described in 1797.

As a counterpoint to the ambitious, complex landscape gardening represented at the old Claremont house, and Idele after the Revolution, consider the building career of Alida Livingston (1761–1822), another of the ten children of Robert and Margaret Beekman Livingston. In 1791, Alida married a hardworking Pennsylvania war veteran, John Armstrong (1758–1843).

Figure 30. Drawing Showing Idele from the South, by Alexander Robertson, 1796. This view shows the house, with a fence line extending along the Locust Avenue promenade to restrict grazing in the garden areas. Landscape gardening south of the house resulted in extensive pleasure grounds. A greenhouse was constructed on the south façade of the house after 1805. Courtesy of the Albany Institute of History and Art.

Fortified with an ample dowry, the Armstrongs set about developing a farm property that they called "The Meadows." (Today, this is the site of the Fisher Center for performing arts on the Bard College campus in Annandale-on-Hudson.) From the start, it seems that the Armstrongs were intent on being no-frills farmers. Their house at The Meadows was not sited on the river, although it does seem to have been positioned in an open, park-like setting that provided expansive views towards the Catskills. Still, the residence retained a close proximity to the farm operations, river landing, orchards and fields that testifies to the functional concerns of Hudson Valley farmers since colonial times.

In addition to this farmstead, the Armstrongs developed mill operations on the Sawkill, a substantial stream that emptied into the Hudson a mile south of The Meadows. In 1796 they left The Meadows and built a new house close to these mills, calling their new home, appropriately, "Mill Hill." (Today, Mill Hill is the Blithewood site on the Bard College campus.) The Armstrongs enjoyed the river and mountain views, but they wasted little time or effort on ornamental landscaping or even on their accommodations. A Federal-style brick house was quickly constructed. The farmyard environs appear to have been developed close by.

The Armstrongs were a practical couple, seemingly unaffected by the art of landscape design. In 1797, The Meadows was sold to Colonel Andrew DeVeaux (1758–1812), a southerner who married a local girl. DeVeaux undertook landscape improvements and renamed the property DeVeaux Parc. Although not much is known of these improvements, a local historian writing in 1931 asserted:

> Out of this property, Colonel DeVeaux created an estate after the manner of the great parks of the gentry of England. The ground was gently undulating and he cleared it in such a way as to surround the house with open sweeps of lawn, studded here and there with veteran trees, singly or in groups. ... When it was in its prime this place was probably unsurpassed on the Hudson for natural beauty and for the age-old standards of cultivation in accordance with which it was laid out.[27]

The Armstrongs' initial reaction to all this was summarized in a 1798 letter, when a somewhat disapproving John Armstrong hinted that the eye of his neighbor, Col. DeVeaux,

was attuned to landscape design aesthetics. Speaking of his old property, Armstrong remarked, "The wood has suffered somewhat by DeVeaux's rage for distant prospects and a wide horizon," implying that he would have been a bit more conservative in altering the practicality of the landscape—in this case removing valued woodland—for a purely ornamental purpose. All this confirmed Armstrong's family reputation as "more of an agriculturist rather than a landscape gardener."[28]

In 1801, Alida and John Armstrong left Mill Hill to pursue public life; first, John served in the U.S. Senate, and later as Minister to France, until 1810. In 1811 the Armstrongs, in their fifties, returned to Dutchess County with six children and developed a third farm estate, two miles south of Mill Hill. This they called La Bergerie ("the Sheep Farm"), in testimony to a gift of Merino sheep given by Napolean and, no doubt, in deference to the continued cultural influence of France felt especially by the Livingstons in this period. La Bergerie was soon to be renamed Rokeby (Figure 31).

While the documentation is not definitive, it seems that the landscape layout at La Bergerie was decisively influenced by the presence of several former tenant farms that the Armstrongs incorporated into their unified scheme. Also, there was apparently an older, straight, tree-lined driveway in existence prior to the Armstrongs' development, and this was used as an access to the new house, which was a French-inspired Federal-style structure that looked out to the south and west over a wide panorama. But the house was built more than a half mile from the Hudson River, with intervening high ground, and its siting ignored the impressive northwestern views towards the Catskill Mountains. Alas, the Armstrongs' workaday concerns were again on display as a counterpoint to landscape gardening. The house at La Bergerie was located close to the farm infrastructure, a layout not radically different from that of The Meadows, developed fifteen years earlier. The Armstrongs seemed incapable of grand landscape design gestures, remaining farmers. John Armstrong wrote a treatise on agriculture and he seems to have considered all his properties as agrarian operations, a testimony to American no-nonsense practicality.

By the end of the 1790s, another example of Livingston development came from Janet Livingston Montgomery (1743–1828), Chancellor Robert's oldest sister, who initiated one of the Hudson's most celebrated residences, Montgomery Place, in Annandale-on-Hudson (Figure 32). Today this is a 400-acre museum property administered by Historic Hudson Valley.[29]

Figure 31. Aerial Photograph Showing Rokeby, by Marcia A. Toole. This bird's-eye view (north is to the right) shows the house site set back from the Hudson River scenery, yet adjacent to service areas, barns and farmyards north of the house. The area to the east (foreground here) was landscaped in the mid-nineteenth century.

In 1773, Janet Livingston married Richard Montgomery, a recent immigrant from an Anglo-Irish landowning family. In a peaceful prelude before the Revolutionary War, the Montgomerys spent two years building a house at "Grasmere," a farm that survives just south of Rhinebeck. Then, General Richard Montgomery became one of America's earliest war heroes when he died a revolutionary, storming British-held Quebec on December 31, 1775.

After the Revolutionary War, Widow Montgomery grew committed to honoring a request in her husband's will that their estate benefit one of Richard's relatives. In 1797 a potential heir arrived from abroad in the person of William Jones (1780–1815), a Montgomery nephew who immigrated to America hoping for Janet Montgomery's benevolence. By 1802, persuaded by Jones's interests and ambitions and tending to dote over his wishes, Janet

Figure 32. Sketch Portrait of Janet L. Montgomery, by Coralie Livingston Barton, early nineteenth century. Janet Livingston Montgomery developed Montgomery Place as "Chateau de Montgomery" beginning in the early 1800s. Courtesy of Historic Hudson Valley.

decided to build a new residential property that Jones would help to develop and, presumably, inherit.

For Janet, aspirations for a Hudson River frontage and proximity to other Livingston family members made Grasmere unsuitable for the new project. She left her melancholy former life and relocated to a strategically positioned property beside the Sawkill between Mill Hill and Massena, the home of her brother, John R. Livingston (1755–1851). The 242-acre tract was earlier part of the John Van Benthuysen farm, but it was the property's residential attributes that made it of special interest to Janet Montgomery and William Jones.

As planned, young Jones was actively involved, supervising house construction and landscape development. Janet Montgomery, by then in her sixties, was an active businesswoman. She no doubt remained in control of the expenditures and, ultimately, of design decisions as the property took shape. She called her new home Chateau de Montgomery, yet another direct reflection of the enthusiasm for France felt by this generation of Livingstons. Indeed, French themes seem directly

reflected in the landscape design developed here in the Montgomery/Jones period.

The house siting was of first concern. Janet Montgomery found the river front unsurpassed, boasting in a letter to her brother, Chancellor Robert R. Livingston, "My situation is most charming and one beyond John's [i.e., Massena] and commands the south and north views."[30] Her appreciation for the site's aesthetic potential was matched by William Jones's ambition, with Janet reporting that he was determined that it would "go far beyond any on the River"(Figure 33).[31]

The relation of the new house and landscape to the older farm arrangements is not fully understood. The new house was built on the foundation of the old Van Benthuysen farmhouse, and the old black locust trees (*Robinia pseudoacacia*) that fronted the house remained from the colonial-era structure. If there had been close-by barnyards and outbuildings, these seem to have been removed. The project did not represent a complete site revision, but rather incorporated older elements. From the evidence and from what can be surmised,

Figure 33. Aerial Photograph showing Montgomery Place, by Marcia A. Toole. This view (north is to the left) shows the house and terraces facing the river. Behind the house, running east, is the long, straight approach drive that swung around a former garden area close to the house. The riverfront was traversed by a formal promenade, called the "morning walk," that led into the wooded Sawkill Valley, seen as the wooded area on the left in this view.

Figure 34. Engraving Showing the Catskills from Montgomery Place, from *The Hudson: from the Wilderness to the Sea* by Benson J. Lossing (1860). This view evoked the close link between river scenery and agricultural operations in the Hudson Valley's Romantic period.

the initial landscape was dominated by encompassing, park-like grounds that opened onto the grandeur of the magnificent Hudson River Valley setting. Close to the house, the parkland was formed from native woodland, with the existing conditions enhanced by new plantings. Some open fields remained in agriculture. The Sawkill ravine was reserved for milling operations, although the scenery of waterfalls and old woods was appreciated at an early date.

The "Chateau" was itself a rather austere Federal-style building, but it faced east-west, responding to the views rather than to the practicality of a sheltered southern orientation. On the west side, toward the river, there were dramatic lawn terraces that may have existed in some form in the Van Benthuysen period. If so, they were retained and probably expanded. The terraces served as a platform for the house and as an overlook to the majestic prospect to the west. The sloping foreground park and the wide, island-studded river and mountain backdrop produced a remarkably well-proportioned and varied

panorama that is certainly one of the finest in the Hudson River Valley (Figure 34).

The long approach drive into Chateau de Montgomery was laid out as a straight avenue, in keeping with prevailing taste, but manifest in an unusually grand way with a heightened aesthetic effect. Planted with a variety of avenue trees (black locusts, horse chestnuts, beech and lindens) spaced in rows about fifty feet apart, the striking formality of the avenue was further enhanced when the road bed was raised on a high causeway that carried the drive across a ravine. Some of this work is documented as occurring in 1815.[32] Filling over the ravine, rather than having the road drop down onto a lower crossing, created an approach drive with an elegant and impressive appearance, a fitting approach for the Chateau de Montgomery. Years later, A. J. Downing described it as "a long and stately avenue of trees, like the approach to an old French chateau."

The house came into view as one climbed the moderate grade up from the causeway. A tree-studded rolling meadow, backed by woodland, bordered the driveway as it approached the house. While it was a majestic arrival, the driveway was not aligned with the house. Today the approach drive bends to the southwest and curves around to approach the house obliquely. The final driveway segment was edged with black locust trees, resembling those on the lawn terrace west of the house. This evidence indicates that there was originally a courtyard fronting the house. It may be that today's looping arrival drive was an earlier service access, as the south side of the house was the service wing.

By her own admission Janet Montgomery's "favorite subject" was "Shrubs, Plants, Flowers & Seeds." Putting her business acumen to work on this interest, Janet developed a commercial nursery at Chateau de Montgomery. This operation continued for more than fifteen years. During this period Janet elicited plants from her brother, Chancellor Robert, in France, and from her younger brother, Edward Livingston (1764–1836), who lived at the time in Louisiana. She established business dealings that included supplying native American plants to English collectors.

Documentation shows that four to ten acres of land were fenced for the nursery, but the location of this production area is not known with certainty. It seems possible that the well-drained and properly oriented piece of ground located south of the house was used for this purpose, as well as serving as the kitchen garden. This siting, somewhat isolating a utilitarian landscape element away from the house, was in keeping with design practices observed elsewhere. Today this garden has been partially restored to its twentieth-century appearance, when it took on a more ornamental character.

In addition to this historic nursery/kitchen garden, miscellaneous and extensive farm production, including orchards, contributed to the property's income during Janet Montgomery's ownership, but Chateau de Montgomery was only secondarily a commercial farm. It was first and foremost an elegant residence and a superlative landscape in an increasingly fashionable stretch of the Hudson River Valley.

In 1808, William Jones married and Janet Montgomery formalized her will, leaving Chateau de Montgomery and other inheritance to the Montgomery heir. Two children were born, and the Chateau briefly took on the trappings of a family place, with Janet serving as matriarch. Then, in 1815, William Jones suddenly died. For a time, Janet Montgomery shifted her inheritance to Lewis Livingston, Edward Livingston's oldest son, who had been raised at neighboring Mas-

sena and who was especially close to his Aunt Janet. But in 1821, at the youthful age of twenty-three, Lewis Livingston also died. Janet Montgomery, nearly eighty, quickly reorganized her papers yet again, leaving the property to her brother, Edward Livingston, youngest of the ten Livingston siblings. Janet Livingston died in 1828, age eighty-five. Edward was then sixty-four years old.

After his inheritance, one of Edward's first decisions was to rename the property Montgomery Place. He further deemphasized agriculture, determining that this would be primarily a residential landscape. Despite his plans to make changes, and some footpath construction in 1829, the landscape was not immediately altered. Edward's career in public life kept him from the property for long intervals, and the family used the estate sparingly in the early 1830s. Only in the last year of his life, after he had retired, did Edward get actively involved in making landscape improvements that would be continued by his family well after his death. This story belongs squarely in the Romantic period to be discussed in Chapter 5.

Andrew Jackson Downing, in the first edition of his book *Landscape Gardening* (1841), wrote, somewhat obscurely, of "one or two old and celebrated country residences on the Hudson, in the possession of the Livingston family, in the neighborhood of Barrytown." While Downing does not name these places, the reference was to Montgomery Place and nearby Massena. Downing noted:

> The magnificent single trees, groups, masses, and rolling woods, which seem as if tastefully disposed in the modern style over an extensive undulating park, covered with the finest turf, give these seats very much the air of an old European residence; which perhaps they resemble, more than any mansion residences that we have in the United States.

One other Livingston Manor property merits comment here, as its landscape was certainly one of the most expansive, ambitious, and finest ornamental schemes undertaken by a Livingston family member in the post–Revolutionary War period. This property was called "The Hill," and its 270-acre house grounds were developed from the late 1790s by Henry Walter Livingston (1768–1810), a nephew of Oak Hill's John Livingston. While Henry Livingston died only a decade after house construction began, the property remained the home of his wife, Mary Allen Livingston (d. 1855), who lived to see it

Figure 35. *Manor of Livingston* [The Hill], engraving from *Landscape Gardening* by A. J. Downing (1844). The Hill was developed beginning in the late 1790s. When A. J. Downing visited fifty years later, it was a showplace of landscape gardening. Downing perceived "an air of great dignity and grace."

evolve into a notable landscape garden composition. The house built by Henry Walter Livingston was an impressive, classical, French-influenced pile that tragically burned in the mid-1970s (Figure 35). A smaller modern house replaced it at the same location. With this exception, The Hill is well preserved as a private residence at the intersection of Rt. 9H and Rt. 82, a few miles south of Claverack in Columbia County.

From the house site, the landscape at The Hill oriented toward the west, with the same Catskill panorama as along the eastern shoreline of the Hudson, except that here the location is about five miles inland and at a raised elevation 350 feet above the river. The property fronted the Albany Post Road and was surrounded by active farmland. While The Hill was an agricultural operation, Henry Livingston separated his house and grounds away from the farm infrastructure, choosing a dramatic position atop an isolated hillock dominated by mature forest trees. Skirting the hill on the east was the Taghkanic Creek. The house took several years to construct, and an elaborate landscape scheme complemented the house development. A gatehouse and an approach drive were laid out, and other carriage drives traversed a park-like landscape of lawns and old trees. Before 1810 a large lake (now known as Bell's Pond) was constructed below the house to the west. At the shore of this lake, a mausoleum was built for Henry Livingston, set into the scene as a landscape garden feature.

In 1841, A. J. Downing, actively investigating examples of landscape gardening, visited The Hill, which by then was a fully mature property with Mary Livingston still in residency. He wrote to a friend, praising it, astonished at the quality of the designed landscape:

You have no conception of the Landscape beauty of some of our finest North [Hudson] river places! ... What do you think of a residence when the eye from the terrace sweeps over half a million dollars worth of the proprietor's domain & the <u>park</u> filled with noble trees, some 6 ft. in diameter, is kept in such perfect order by 10 men that even the carriage tracks are <u>rolled out</u> everyday [emphases Downing]. ... Such is Mrs. Mary Livingston's residence, the 'Upper Manor,' certainly the grandest place in America.[33]

In the revised 2nd edition of *Landscape Gardening* (1844), the author called the house "one of the chastest specimens of the Grecian style," and added:

The mansion stands in the midst of a fine park, rising gradually from the level of a rich inland country, and commanding prospects for sixty miles around. The park is, perhaps, the most remarkable in America, for the noble simplicity of its character and the perfect order in which it is kept. The turf is, every-where, short and velvet-like, the gravel roads scrupulously firm and smooth, and near the house are the largest and most superb evergreens.

Given the expansive scale and quality of its development, and its consistent management over a half century, The Hill, along with Samuel Bard's Hyde Park, Chancellor Livingston's Idele, and Montgomery Place, is a good example of the sort of designed landscape that was considered the ultimate of elegance in the first years of the nineteenth century. As A. J. Downing put it, "In the case of large landed estates, the capabilities of Landscape Gardening may be displayed to their full extent."

Downing's description of these older properties is perhaps the best record that has come down to us of landscape gardening in the pre-Romantic era. The English tradition of landscape gardening, as popularized since the mid-1700s by Capability Brown, was mimicked by elite owners in the Hudson River Valley. By the early nineteenth century the tenets of landscape gardening were commonly understood. As can be discerned from descriptions of these local examples, the development of park-like grounds became a critical component of the Hudson River Valley's earliest landscape gardens.

Parkland had also been a key element of the English practice.[34] There, the idea evolved over many centuries from its medieval origins as royal hunting preserves—the original "deer parks." The physical character of the English park included closely grazed turf and protected—and therefore, often mature—native specimen trees. The trees were pruned by grazing to a line about five feet off the ground so that, for those on the ground, views through the park were unimpeded. The short turf allowed easy access on foot or horseback. This trimmed and tidy condition fitted in well with imagery that celebrated idealized pastoral landscapes of shepherds and classical architecture, as associated with the painted landscapes of Claude Lorrain (d. 1682) and Gaspard Poussin (d. 1675). When landscape gardening became the vogue, owners annexed a portion of their hunting land and made the appropriate embellishments to incorporate parkland into the ornamental garden composition.

In the Hudson Valley, devoid of ancient game preserves, the long metamorphosis from deer park to ornamental parkland was telescoped into the early years of the nineteenth century and was often achieved by simply using former farmland or by carving out park-like landscapes from woodland.

In 1841, discussing the older Hudson River Valley estates of Clermont, Massena and Montgomery Place, Downing commented on the retrofitting of nature to create the earliest landscape "parks":

These places owe almost their entire beauty to nature, as nearly all the fine trees, groves and woods, are the natural growth of the soil. ... Here, just so much of the natural growth of timber has been retained, as to clothe the estate with a truly noble garniture, and the proportions of meadow, or lawn and wood, as well as the arrangement and situation of the latter, have been so judiciously managed, that ... much of the effect of the finest park, carefully laid out, and planted in the modern style of landscape gardening, is produced, mainly by retaining and preserving the materials of which nature has been so extremely prodigal.

In truth, developing attractive parkland from unmanaged woods was not an easy task, but clearly those who undertook such alterations were motivated by the ideal of an English deer park, without having to undergo the long history of park development.

❧ "In Complete Fairy-Land" and a Visit to Landor's Cottage

In 1812, Washington Irving (1783–1859) America's most popular author of romantic themes, sailed up the Hudson River to northern Dutchess County to visit an acquaintance, John R. Livingston, at Massena. He stayed for a week, dined twice with Chancellor Robert Livingston at Clermont (Idele), and once with "old Mrs. Livingston [Montgomery]" at Chateau de Montgomery. In a letter that followed, Irving reminisced of his experiences "in complete fairy-land," where "fine grounds" and country lifestyle were "exactly after my own heart."[35]

While it would be inappropriate to highlight one moment or one person as introducing romanticism to the Hudson River Valley, the activities of New York native Washington Irving would make a compelling case. His heightened romantic attitudes regarding the Livingstons and their properties were reflective of the new values that he, better than any of his contemporaries, transmitted to the wider American society, beginning with the *Letters of Jonathan Old Style* (1802) and the *History of New York by Diedrich Knickerbocker* (1809). Washington Irving expressed the romanticism of his time by, as he put it, "addressing myself to the feeling and fancy of the reader more than to his judgement."

In 1815, a few years after his sojourn on the Hudson, Washington Irving went to England for an extended stay. His travels took him on several "picturesque tours," visiting such storied landscapes as the Wye Valley in western England and the Welsh and Scottish Highlands, following in the wake of William Gilpin on familiar itineraries. In the Wye Valley, Irving found "scenery similar to the glens of the Hudson Highlands" and he called the gentle upper Wye "not unlike the Mohawk River [Valley]." The Wye Valley (Herefordshire) in general impressed Irving as "very like America."[36] This was the home of the picturesque improvers; the River Wye passed beneath Uvedale Price's Foxley estate.

Irving's travels exposed him to the English fashion of landscape gardening. He visited such famous landscape gardens as Hagley and The Leasowes, near Birmingham. In an essay entitled "Christmas Eve," published in his acclaimed work *The Sketch Book* (1819), Irving spoke of visiting an old-fashioned English country estate, commenting that the "grounds [were] laid out in the old formal manner of artificial flower-beds, clipped shrubbery, raised terraces, and heavy stone balustrades, ornamented with urns, a leaden statue and a jet of water." Irving called this "obsolete finery," but noted that the elderly "squire" had proudly preserved his old garden against "the boasted imitation of nature in modern [landscape] gardening." For the old conservative owner the new taste in gardening had political implications, namely "republican notions [that] smacked of the leveling system. The squire was glad of any argument to defend his clipt [sic] yew trees and formal terraces, which had been ... attacked by modern landscape gardeners." Irving wryly observed, "I could not help smiling at this introduction of politics into gardening." Elsewhere in *The Sketch Book*, in an essay on "Rural Life in England," Irving concluded that "the taste of the English in the cultivation of land, and what is called landscape gardening, is unrivaled." Irving pursued an enthusiastic discussion of the subject, maintaining that success came to those who "have studied nature intently, and discover an exquisite sense of her beautiful forms and harmonious combinations ... her coy and furtive graces." Irving then turned to "park scenery," wonderfully evoked in his elegant prose:

Figure 36. *Portrait of Washington Irving,* by John Wesley Jarvis, 1809. Cosmopolitan and imbued with romantic sensibilities, Washington Irving led America away from the realities of colonial and revolutionary life to a lighter celebration of America's quirky past and unsurpassed natural landscapes. Courtesy of Historic Hudson Valley.

Amounting to a new way of "seeing," Irving's vision resided ultimately in his imagination, but a like-minded public responded to his artistic perception. Irving was a popular success and a literary hero, and by the close of his career was called by one American critic "our favorite author."[38]

The poetic invention of history, and nostalgia for New York's Dutch colonial past, proved to be key ingredients of Irving's Hudson River Valley writings. Also crucial was a heightened understanding of nature, embraced as the creation of God and as a generator of romantic sentiment. "No, never need an American look beyond his own country for the sublime and beautiful of natural scenery," said Irving, celebrating his native land in *The Sketch Book*. Yet he did more; he went on to define that "scenery" by giving physical substance and emotional meaning to the Hudson's varied, majestic riverscape. Even today, Irving's Hudson is synonymous with our perception of scenic beauty there. For Irving's readers there was no mistaking this Hudson River Valley for the landscape of tidy, Puritan New England or the unfathomable expanse of the unsettled West. After Washington Irving, the Hudson was understood as a distinct place, and "our favorite author" contributed importantly to that distinction.

All of this provided underpinning for landscape gardening, reflecting "the genius of place." Irving made the past present, viewed now as a charming picture of life in harmony with nature. A hardscrabble Dutch homestead was, in Irving's interpretation, "a lingering haunt of poetry and romance, [where] a drowsy, dreamy influence seems to hang over the land, and to pervade the very atmosphere, [and] the descendents [of] the original Dutch settlers ... walk in continual reverie."

Nowhere were reveries more intense than in the garden. Another romantic author, Edgar Allan Poe (1809–1849) (Figure 37), described a landscape garden in his story "Landor's Cottage," offering a period representation of the perfect garden, evoked by a poet, appreciated as art. Edgar Allan Poe was America's great, dark romantic, but he seems to have spent some of his more cheerful moments in gardens. He also spent some time in the Hudson River Valley, first as a West Point cadet in

Vast lawns that extend like sheets of vivid green, with here and there clumps of gigantic trees, heaping up rich piles of foliage: the solemn pomp of groves and woodland glades, with the deer trooping in silent herds.

Though hidden, the influence of man's art in these landscapes was apparent. For Washington Irving, landscape gardening was best directed to idealize nature by producing an enhanced, but still natural, appearance. When a man-made element was included, it should be "some rustic temple or sylvan statue, grown green and dank with age." Steeped in the New World, it mattered little to Irving whether garden ornaments were Roman or Gothic, their original associations having long ago lost meaning, but now these simply added "an air of classic sanctity to the seclusion."

"Rip Van Winkle" and "The Legend of Sleepy Hollow," from *The Sketch Book*, are the best-known of Washington Irving's Hudson Valley writings. In these stories he mixed fanciful history and local landscapes in so convincing a way as to suggest a new interpretation of Hudson River life. Even twenty years after his death, a popular guidebook commented, "We somehow feel the reality of every legend he has given us."[37]

the early 1830s, and later in his career when he rented a romantically shrouded cottage at Fordham, in New York City.

Poe felt the power of landscape gardening. He wrote of the ultimate design amateur, a wealthy man named Ellison who, with a large inheritance and good taste, pursued nirvana by creating a landscape garden for his own delight. After several rewrites, Poe finally took his readers to the landscape garden of his imagination at fictitious Landor's Cottage (Figure 38).[39] This description can be read as the ideal of Poe's generation— a designed landscape of considerable bliss. Otherworldly, the landscape at Landor's Cottage was certainly without formality, but neither did it duplicate nature. Instead, Landor's Cottage was a design grounded in organic forms, naturally occurring features and romantic sensibilities.

In the story, Poe is an anonymous traveler walking along a rural road in the Hudson River Valley on a foggy morning. At a road junction he is drawn to an intriguing byway off to his right. The roadway is without identification, but it is beautifully surfaced with smooth, emerald-green grass. It was not like other rural roads:

> It was grass, clearly, but grass such as we seldom see out of England, so short, so thick, so even, and so vivid in color. Not a single impediment lay in the wheel-route, not even a chip or dead twig. The stones that once obstructed the way had been carefully placed—not thrown—along the sides of the lane, so as to define its boundaries with a kind of half-precise, half-negligent, and wholly picturesque definition. Clumps of wild flowers grew everywhere, luxuriantly, in the interspaces.

Poe is drawn onto the grassy lane:

> I entered this road, and now, arising, I continued in the same direction. ... The little vale into which I thus peered down from under the fog-canopy could not have been more than four hundred yards long. ... All, in a word, sloped and softened to the south; and yet the whole vale was engirdled by eminences, more or less high. ... To the north—on a craggy precipice— a few paces from the verge, up sprang the magnificent trunks of numerous hickories, black walnuts, and chestnuts, interspersed with occasional oak; and the strong lateral branches thrown out by the wal-

nuts especially, spread far over the edge of the cliff. ... The general floor of this amphitheatre was grass of the same character as that I had found in the road; if anything, more deliciously soft, thick, velvety, and miraculously green. It is hard to conceive how all this beauty had been attained. The expanse of green turf was relieved, here and there, by an occasional showy shrub, such as the hydrangea, or the common snowball [*Viburnum opulus*], or the aromatic seringa [lilac]; or, more frequently by a clump of geraniums blossoming gorgeously in great varieties. ... Besides all this, the lawn's velvet was exquisitely spotted with sheep—a considerable flock of which roamed about the vale, in company with three tamed deer, and a vast number of brilliantly-plumed ducks.

Drawn on by this menagerie, Poe came to a stream, calling it a "rivulet":

> I have spoken of two openings into the vale. From the one to the northwest issued a rivulet, which came, gently murmuring and slightly foaming, down the ravine ... after a series of sweeps, it turned off at right angles and pursued a generally southern direction—meandering as it went—until it became lost in a small lake of irregular figure that lay gleaming near the lower extremity of the vale.

Poe moved closer to the lake and noticed:

> A light birch canoe that lay placidly on the water, was reflected in its minutest fibers with a fidelity unsurpassed by the most exquisitely polished mirror. A small island, fairly laughing with flowers in full bloom, and affording little more space than just enough for a picturesque little building, seemingly a fowl-house, arose from the lake not far from its northern shore, to which it was connected by means of an inconceivably light-looking and yet very primitive bridge. From the southern extreme of the lake issued a continuation of the rivulet, which, after meandering for perhaps thirty yards, finally passed through the depression in the middle of the southern declivity, and tumbling down a sheer precipice of a hundred feet, made its devious and unnoticed way to the Hudson.

Figure 38. Sketch Showing the Landscape at Landor's Cottage, by Dahl Taylor. Edgar Allan Poe, in "Landor's Cottage," wrote of a "little vale ... sloped and softened ... engirdled by eminences ... exquisitely spotted with sheep." He imagined a "small lake" ornamented with a canoe and an island for ducks. "From the southern extreme of the lake issued a continuation of the rivulet, which made its devious and unnoticed way to the Hudson." Close to the river "stood a dwelling house ... of poetry ... Its marvelous effect lay altogether in its artistic arrangement as a picture. ... Here was art undoubtedly ... The greatest care had been taken to preserve a due medium between the neat and graceful on the one hand, and the picturesque on the other. There were few straight, and no uninterrupted lines ... Everywhere was variety in uniformity. It was a piece of composition." Poe's imagery was personified at many of the Hudson Valley landscape gardens created during the Romantic period.

Close to the river, Poe came to a house, the domicile of this landscape garden dreamscape:

> At one turn, the [rivulet] sweeping backward, made an almost circular loop, so as to form a peninsula, which was very nearly an island. ... On this peninsula stood a dwelling-house ... its *tout ensemble* struck me with the keenest sense of combined novelty and propriety—in a word, of poetry. In fact, nothing would well be more simple—more utterly unpretending than this cottage. Its marvelous effect lay altogether in its artistic arrangement as a picture. I could have fancied, while I looked at it, that some eminent landscape painter had built it with his brush.

Poe, an urbanite who had limited direct experience with landscape gardening, was enchanted:

> Here was art undoubtedly. ... all that seemed to have been done, might be done here, with such natural "capabilities" (as they have it in the books on Landscape Gardening)—with very little labor and expense. No, it was not the amount but the character of the art. ... an artist, and one with a most scrupulous eye for form, had superintended all these arrangements. The greatest care had been taken to preserve a due medium between the neat and graceful on the one hand, and the picturesque on the other. There were few straight, and no uninterrupted lines. The same effect of curvature or of color appeared twice, usu-ally, but not oftener, at any one point of view. Everywhere was variety in uniformity. It was a piece of "composition."

If the landscape at Landor's Cottage wasn't fully natural, even while it was "picturesque," it was because of this matter of "composition." Poe asserted that "we are justly instructed to regard nature as supreme. ... Who shall presume to imitate the color of the tulip, or to improve the proportions of the lily-of-the-valley?" Still, nature is messy. Poe admitted that a "natural landscape ... will always [have] many excesses and defects" and "be susceptible to improvement." The purity of nature's component parts—the tulips and lily-of-the-valley, for example—was not questioned, but there was no art in nature, because nature wasn't man-made. Picturesque landscape gardens were man-made, attempting paradise on earth. For Poe, it is through the designer's artistic imagination that nature becomes a garden "to the eyes which were to behold it on earth." Poe's purpose is to show that landscape art can gratify man's aesthetic pleasure. We do not imitate nature, but rather adjust it to "the constitution of the human mind."

The garden Edgar Allan Poe experienced and described in "Landor's Cottage" was romantically induced, as were the Livingstons' properties for Washington Irving. Together, Poe and Irving led their generation into romance and the connotations of romantic for garden and landscape design. Gardens had radically new agendas, only half-existing in reality. Essential, too, was the heightened imagination of those who experienced the garden—the romantic Americans who created them, and those who visited them as evocative places. ❧

CHAPTER 4

HYDE PARK
(VANDERBILT)

While Washington Irving lived in Europe, from 1815 to 1832, romantic themes influenced landscape gardening along the Hudson. Estate owners brought increased sophistication to their efforts, and this was an era of improved technical skills. In 1806 a Philadelphia nurseryman, Bernard McMahon, published *American Gardener*, whose 600-plus pages of gardening advice included 16 pages devoted to landscape design of what McMahon called "pleasure grounds," the first such essay in the New World. Many of the trained gardeners like McMahon were foreign-born, and they were becoming more numerous. There was better access to nursery-raised plant material and sound horticultural advice.[40] On the land, as one generation followed another, improvements often benefited from earlier efforts.

This was the case at one of the most important and interesting examples of landscape gardening undertaken while Washington Irving was abroad—the ongoing development at Hyde Park. Today, Hyde Park is presented as the early-twentieth-century home of the "Gilded Age" Frederick Vanderbilts (Figure 40), but in fact the property had a long history and reached a crescendo more than two decades before Frederick Vanderbilt was born. John Bard had provided the start in the colonial period, arranging the agricultural and milling infrastructure, while his son, Samuel Bard, took the first steps towards an identifiable residential landscape (see page 33). The grounds of Samuel Bard's Federal-era house were impressive, but his design achievements were old-fashioned, reflective of a transitional mix of old and new ideas (Figure 41).

Figure 39. Engraving, Portrait of David Hosack, not dated. David Hosack was an esteemed fifty-nine-year-old medical doctor when he purchased the Hyde Park estate in 1828. He had been a friend of Samuel Bard and he knew Hyde Park well. Courtesy of the American Antiquarian Society.

In 1828, a few years after Samuel Bard died, about 550 acres of the Bards' original Hyde Park were sold to Doctor David Hosack (1769–1835) (Figure 39). Although the property was sold out of the Bard family, its continuity was assured because David Hosack was the Bards' heir in all but name. As a physician, Hosack was a close colleague of Samuel Bard, and he had visited Hyde Park often. Building on the Bards' earlier efforts, Hyde Park achieved the status of a premier country seat with David Hosack. [41] It was the most famous Hudson River property in the Romantic period, proclaimed by Andrew Jackson Downing "one of the finest specimens of the modern style of Landscape Gardening in America." For Downing, the term "modern" referred to the English "Natural" style as defined in the age of Lancelot "Capability" Brown.

David Hosack was a mature and sophisticated urbanite, fifty-nine years old when he purchased Hyde Park. He was a proud New Yorker, a substantial patron of the arts, and a prominent man of his times. His library at Hyde Park was one of the largest private collections in the United States. He also kept an impressive picture gallery at Hyde Park, including early works by Thomas Cole and others of the first generation Hudson River School.

As related to gardening, David Hosack had a documented interest in horticulture and landscape design. Hosack's medical training in England included studies in botany, a topic for which he had special affinity. In 1801 he directed the development of the earliest botanical garden in New York City, the famed Elgin Garden, located on the site of today's Rockefeller Center in midtown Manhattan. The Elgin Garden was used for the cultivation of medicinal plants, but it was also appreciated as an artistic place. It remained under Hosack's direct guidance until it was disassembled in 1811, when some of its remaining plants were moved to Hyde Park. In 1822 the New York Horticultural Society was founded; within a year David Hosack became its president. Six years later, as the new owner of Hyde Park, Hosack retired from his medical practice and in a letter assured a friend that "agriculture and horticulture will now occupy the residue of my life." [42]

While friendship and professional interests linked David Hosack to Samuel Bard, and while Hyde Park retained conti-

Figure 40. Vanderbilt Mansion (Hyde Park). Today's house was built for Frederick W. Vanderbilt in the last years of the nineteenth century. It is the fourth house to stand on this same spot, and all were formal, classical designs. Photograph courtesy of National Park Service, W D Urbin.

nuity between the Bards and Hosack, it is important to recognize critical differences. From his marriage in 1825 to a wealthy widow, Magdelena Coster, Hosack had considerable financial resources. At Hyde Park he was an eager patron of landscape gardening and able to pursue it on an expansive scale. A year after acquiring the property, it was reported that about $100,000 had been spent on landscape improvements, a figure that would equal millions of dollars in today's currency.

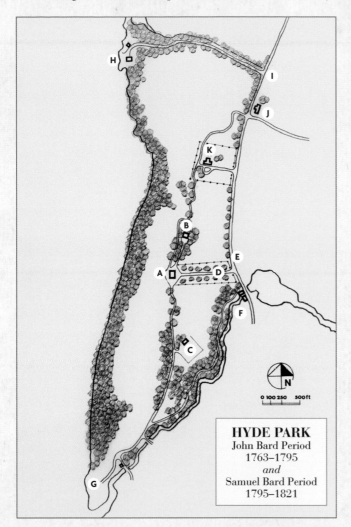

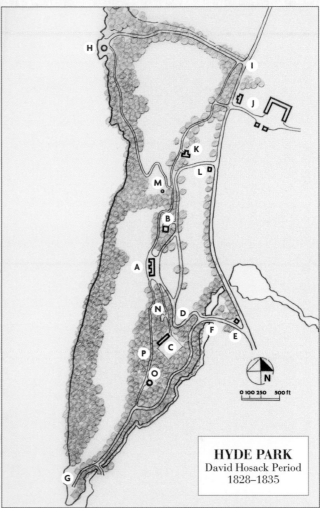

Figure 41 (above left). Plan Showing Hyde Park Landscape in the Bards' Period (1763–1821), by R. M. Toole. Samuel Bard built his house (A) on the edge of the escarpment overlooking the Hudson Valley. He isolated the stable (B) and a kitchen/flower garden (C) away from the house. His entrance drive (D) came straight into the house from the public road (E). The Crum Elbow Creek (F) was heavily used for milling operations. The Hyde Park landing was the primary access (G). The old Bard Rock landing (H) had direct access to the public road (I) and the Bards' old Red House/farm complex (J). In about 1814 a separate cottage residence was developed (K).

Figure 42 (above right). Plan Showing Hyde Park Landscape in Hosack Period (1828–1835), by R. M. Toole. David Hosack's new house (A) was on the site of Samuel Bard's. The stable (B) and old

kitchen garden (C), now an ornamental flower/botanic garden and greenhouse complex, remained. The redesigned main entrance drive (D) with its classical-style gatehouse (E) and bridge over the Crum Elbow Creek (F) was a dramatic change. Ornamental improvements were also made to the creek along the road to the old landing (G). Bard Rock (H) was reserved for a decorative summerhouse. The road out to the public road (I) and the Red House/farm complex (J) remained. The cottage grounds (K) were melded with the parkland, and a new north entrance and gatehouse were developed (L). The grounds were enhanced with several features, including Euterpe Knoll (M), an elaborate shrubbery (N), and the (not located) L'isle des Peupliers. A classical pavilion (O) dominated the escarpment walk (P) that traced the terrace edge and led to Bard Rock.

More important than lavish development was the pervasive influence of romanticism on David Hosack's designed landscape at Hyde Park. Here was epitomized the swing from an eighteenth-century focus on the supremacy of intellect, reason and geometry, to a nineteenth-century concern for emotion, sensibility, and deference to Nature, a shift that distinguished landscape design in America's Romantic period. For David Hosack this shift occurred when the practical concerns of the Revolutionary War years—his parents' generation—gave way to the relatively relaxed concerns of the 1820s. With Hosack, romantic sentiment crystallized appreciation for Hyde Park. In 1829 one visitor, writing in *The New York Farmer and Horticultural Repository*, mused:

> The natural scenery along the whole [shore] line to the distance of about a quarter of a mile from the verge of the river, is highly picturesque, and in no direction can the eye be turned through this romantic situation, without the mind's eye being impressed with the strongest emotions of reverence of the great Creator.[43]

In Hosack's era, another writer described the Hyde Park landscape as a "rural paradise,"[44] while a third called it a "terrestrial paradise"[45]—effusive praise unlikely to have been heard during the Bards' ownership.

By 1830, Hyde Park had gone from a colonial-period wilderness to a refined landscape garden (Figure 42). In turn, the esoteric practice of landscape gardening had gained a heightened aesthetic purpose. There remained some preference for formality. As will be shown, there was a certain polish

Figure 43. *View in the Grounds at Hyde Park*, engraving from *Landscape Gardening* by A. J. Downing (1844). This was, and remains today, the distinctive view from Hyde Park, looking northwest. A. J. Downing said that the views from Hyde Park, "including as they do the noble Hudson, and the superb wooded valley which stretches away until bounded at the horizon by the distant summits of the blue Catskills, are unrivalled in picturesque beauty."

to Hosack's Hyde Park, appropriately serving the austere elegance of its architecture and classical garden features. Refined and genteel, this was a provincial hybrid that reflected the era's appreciation for romantic nature filtered through a somewhat antiquated taste. Hosack's landscape was in a sense "genteel," because many of its themes were borrowed from earlier, classical influences, rather than emerging from native and natural sources. There was a certain detached, aloof, even Old World feel to Hosack's landscape at Hyde Park, somewhat in contrast to "the genius of the place" represented in the Hudson Valley of 1830. It must be concluded that Hyde Park was an example of A. J. Downing's Beautiful design style, rather than the Picturesque.

One of the Old World influences documented at Hyde Park was the involvement of André Parmentier (1780–1830). Parmentier was a recent Belgian immigrant, having arrived in America in 1824. He operated a nursery in Brooklyn and was one of the notable early foreign-born landscape gardeners to practice professionally in the United States. David Hosack had known him from the time of his arrival. Parmentier was from a family of distinguished horticulturists. Skilled and experienced, he was well positioned to serve as a consultant on landscape gardening. Although his background is little understood, he outlined some design ideas in a brief essay entitled "Landscapes and Picturesque Gardens," published in Thomas Fessenden's *The New American Gardener* in 1828, the year David Hosack purchased Hyde Park.

In discussing landscape design Parmentier used standard rhetoric:

> Gardens are now treated like landscapes, the charms of which are not to be improved by any rules of art … to understand this style of garden requires a quick perception of the beauties of a landscape.

His reliance on a purely natural look seemed fitted to the Hudson River Valley with its distinctive sense of place and its particularly attractive and even sublime natural effects. Still, Parmentier was a mature practitioner when he arrived in America, with ingrained attitudes on domestic propriety and tasteful design. These he no doubt transmitted to his New World clients and their New World landscapes. In fact, it is perhaps for this reason that he was so eagerly consulted; he was an early celebrity designer. Unfortunately, Parmentier died suddenly only six years after his arrival in America and within eighteen months of the start of Hosack's Hyde Park project.

The specifics of Parmentier's role in Hosack's design work at Hyde Park are somewhat unclear. Still, its importance was confirmed by A.J. Downing, who wrote in the 1st edition of *Landscape Gardening* that "the plans for laying out the grounds [at Hyde Park], were furnished by Parmentier." On first review this attribution seems too broad, ignoring as it does the earlier work of John and Samuel Bard from which Hosack began, and also Hosack's own role. While direct evidence and details of Parmentier's Hyde Park work are nearly nonexistent, Downing's words are emphatic and come from a knowledgeable commentator who understood the terms he was using.

In clarifying this situation, David Hosack's new "plans" did generally incorporate the Bards' improvements and at least some of the earlier landscape design decisions, the house site most notably. But, for A. J. Downing, what mattered was the aesthetics of landscape gardening, and in this respect Hosack and Parmentier radically altered Hyde Park. Given the documentation and the traditional role played in this era, Hyde Park after Hosack's tenure probably can be most accurately described as a collaborative effort, but Parmentier's work as professional designer at a critical moment was significant. In turn, Hyde Park was one of Parmentier's better-known commissions, and portions of the work he influenced are preserved.

Despite Parmentier's role, Hosack's contribution as client and owner at Hyde Park seems to have been decisive, and it was certainly important in carrying out the goals and design schemes determined during Parmentier's brief consultation. Hosack was actively involved, as a contemporary noted in 1830:

> He rises early, and soon repairs to the point [on the grounds] where his presence is most required, allowing himself little relaxation either of mind or muscle. He never suffers his talents to be hid in a napkin, nor his wealth hoarded under a miser's key.[46]

At Hyde Park, owner and professional designer no doubt worked harmoniously within the framework established by the Bards. Hosack and Parmentier were left to modify, expand and embellish the landscape, especially that part of Hyde Park lying between the public road (Albany Post Road) and the river, a landscape of about 200 acres. A visitor in 1834 described her tour to "both sides of the high road; the farm on one side, and the pleasure grounds on the other."[47]

Hosack got an early start on his project. By late autumn 1828 he and Parmentier had begun planning. The placement of drives and footpaths, fence lines and new plantings ("new plantations," Downing later called them), were the most important design contributions resulting from Hosack's consultation with Parmentier. If Parmentier's design work was largely completed early in 1829, this would have left two full seasons for construction to continue under his supervision before Parmentier died late in 1830.

At the start, in March 1829, with ice still on the Hudson, Hosack wrote saying that he would be upriver from New York City in a month to "determine the amount of work to be done in the present year." The design implications are apparent when Hosack related his wish to "reserve and cultivate" ground around a separate cottage residence that had been developed on the open terrace north of Samuel Bard's 1790s house. This suggests Hosack's desire to integrate this intrusive property into his unified, park-like scheme. Hosack specifically mentioned "removing fences."[48] As Parmentier stated in his essay "Landscapes and Picturesque Gardens," "fences ... should be concealed so as not to appear as boundaries to the establishment, and present to the eye a disagreeable interruption in the prospect."

By autumn 1829 improvements were reported to be "in progress on every part of the farm."[49] Samuel Bard's thirty-year-old house underwent major alterations, but it remained a classical design. Hosack commissioned Town and Thompson, preeminent New York City architects of this period, to handle the architectural work. The formal composition of the house was expanded by adding symmetrical wings to the original rectangular core. The fenestration was simplified. While an improvement, the house apparently struck some as a rather awkward pile, less than the purity of the Greek Revival, then the fashion, and "without any pretensions to architectural beauty," as Charles A. Murray summarized in his *Travels in North*

Figure 44. Photograph Showing the View from Hyde Park (Vanderbilt Mansion National Historic Site), 2009, by Steve Benson. The famous Hyde Park view remains, although overgrown and offering only glimpses of the Hudson. Hyde Park's links to the Romantic period are further obscured by the design alterations by the property's most recent residents, the Gilded Age Vanderbilts.

America (1839). From the site's perspective it is notable that classical architecture remained, as it had for Samuel Bard, the central feature of Hyde Park's designed landscape.

Besides the alterations on the main house, Town and Thompson supplied designs for gatehouses. One was at Hosack's new main entry gate, and the other was at a north entrance. These gatehouses were Greek Revival designs. The north gatehouse was described by an admiring visitor as "much and deservedly admired for its architectural beauty."[50] In addition, Town and Thompson may have provided plans for a reconstructed stable building as well as designs for some of the garden structures, although this is not known with certainty.

The stiff, straight approach drive from the Post Road that led to the east front of Samuel Bard's house was removed. It was replaced with a new approach drive that was wholly different in form and effect. For Parmentier and Hosack, Samuel Bard's straight approach must have seemed very old-fashioned. The direct and continuous view of the flat house façade was by then considered tasteless. Instead, an approach drive that introduced an expansive and varied landscape and the setting of the house, treating the house as only one feature of the larger residential landscape composition, was now the ideal.

At Hyde Park the new entry scheme, nearly a half mile in length, amounted to a considerable undertaking. Though little is known about the project, the results are well preserved and may be studied on the ground. Using the natural topography as the basis for the design, the new driveway was clearly meant to present a varied and interesting experience for those entering the site. Parmentier had defined the design concept in his essay "Landscapes and Picturesque Gardens," when he stated that "the road which leads to [the house] may give a good idea of the extent of the proprietor's domains, and care should be taken that the road is proportioned to this extent." He added that the approach drive should be "gently serpentine."

Hyde Park's new drive began at the new main gatehouse (at the site of today's main entrance). In order to acquire this entry point, Hosack purchased a small parcel of land fronting the public road southeast of Crum Elbow Creek. This entry point required that the approach drive cross the creek. Rather than an inconvenience, Hosack saw this as an aesthetic opportunity. For the Bards, Crum Elbow Creek was primarily a source of power for several mills. Hosack did not completely demolish the mills. Instead, he cleaned up the area and made it part of the entry

experience. An "elegant wooden bridge"[51] was constructed. The road then ascended the far bank through a series of dramatic switchback curves and, turning towards the northwest, opened out onto the terrace and parkland that surrounded the house. Today the entrance sequence remains unchanged, although the house itself, the bridge and the entrance were all replaced at the end of the nineteenth century.

Arrival at the house was from the left (south) without the perfunctory, head-on view of one façade, as had been the case with Samuel Bard's straight avenue. There were no river views from the new drive, as these were reserved for theatrical presentation after passing through the house to the western front. One visitor in 1836 recalled, "dismounting at the door [I was] invited ... into the house and ... followed ... to the other side of the house, where might be seen a picture more glorious than ever mortal pencil designed."[52]

In addition to the new approach drive into Hyde Park from the public highway, the drive from the river landing at the southern end of the property was realigned to follow along Crum Elbow Creek, which became a focus of Hosack's and Parmentier's ornamental landscape development. This is not surprising, since the Crum Elbow had highly prized scenic qualities and the old drive—functional, ascending from the landing along the ridge line, ever so slowly revealing views of the river—lacked drama. On the new route the new wooden entrance bridge was seen from below as a feature. One visitor called it a "very sweet composition."[53] Extensive improvements along the Crum Elbow included construction of small dams and rock work to form pools and artificial cascades. The vegetation was judiciously thinned and pruned and augmented with new plantings. In this way the former mill stream was now redefined and described by one visitor as a "copious stream ... noisy as the Arno itself, filling the hanging gardens and groves on its borders with murmurs."[54] Another visitor called it a "never tiring scene."[55]

Samuel Bard's original kitchen gardens south of the house evolved under Hosack from a partially utilitarian garden to one of considerable ornament. In Hosack's time vegetable gardening seems to have been restricted to the farm complex east of the public road. Near the house, an earlier greenhouse (conservatory) and other horticultural facilities were upgraded and the garden beds were rearranged. Flower beds were noted as located "around the conservatories,"[56] and these were described as "parterres,"[57] suggesting some refinement in the layout of this enclosed area. The quality of these garden features was attested to by several visitors. One said, "the conservatory is remarkable in America ... the flower garden all that it can be."[58]

The nearly level ground between the flower garden and the house was laid out with elaborate shrub borders set out along meandering walks. This extensive "shrubbery," as it was called, extended over almost three acres and was described by A. J. Downing in *Landscape Gardening* in his treatment of ornamental landscape embellishments. This narrative came after Hosack's death when the plantings had reached maturity:

> The shrubbery at Hyde Park, the residence of the late Dr. Hosack, which borders the walk leading from the mansion to the hot-houses [in the flower garden] ... [is] a fine example of this mode of mingling woody and herbaceous plants. The belts or borders occupied by the shrubbery and flower-garden there, are perhaps from 25 to 35 feet in width, completely filled with a collection of shrubs and herbaceous plants; the smallest of the latter being quite near the walk; these succeeded by taller species receding from the front of the border, then follow shrubs of moderate size, advancing in height until the back ground of the whole is a rich mass of tall shrubs and trees of moderate size. The effect of this belt on so large a scale, in high keeping, is remarkably striking and elegant.

Downing specifically cites these types of plantings with "polished beauty," that is, the Beautiful, as opposed to the Picturesque design mode. In fact, the deliberate design of the Hyde Park shrubbery relates it to planting themes practiced in England by the mid-eighteenth century. The careful layering of the plants, as described by Downing, is a technique well documented in English practice. While not unique, the Hyde Park shrubbery was one of the finest such horticultural displays recorded in the Hudson River Valley in this period. The shrubbery has disappeared, and only level lawn and several old trees occupy this portion of today's site.

It is likely (but uncertain) that André Parmentier's influence included the layout of the shrubbery, as well as other horticultural and planting schemes at Hyde Park. This was Parmentier's expertise, and he had definite theories on ornamental plant design. He believed in using massive shade trees close to a house to evoke longevity and complement the architectural massing. Hyde Park's famous old trees, spaced out along the top

of the terrace, fit the need perfectly. Away from the house, Parmentier recommended lighter foliage trees, for example fruit trees, planted along the edge of woodland. There the flowers and fruit would be "of great beauty and interest." Shrubs, shade trees and fruit trees could have been supplied from Parmentier's considerable inventory in his Brooklyn nursery.

David Hosack was also a skilled plantsman, and he planned to write a descriptive catalogue of his Hyde Park collection. If actually undertaken, the catalogue has not been located and we are left with the fleeting impressions of visitors to attest to Hosack's famed display of plantsmanship. From the greenhouse, "among the rich display of rare shrubs and plants, were the *Magnolia grandiflora* [bull bay], the splendid *Strelitzia* [bird of paradise], the fragrant farnesianna [*Acacia farnesiana*], and a beautiful tree of the *Ficus elastica* or Indian rubber." In the shrubbery were "trees, shrubs, and flowers; among which stand ... the *Magnolia glanca* [a.k.a. *M. virginiana*, sweet swamp bay], bearing large white flowers."[59] Another visitor noted that "the flower beds are perfectly splendid" and recognized "the fringe tree [*Chionanthus virginicus*] and *Althaea frutex* [*Hibiscus syriacus*] covered with flowers."[60]

Hosack actively sought plants for his collection at Hyde Park. In January 1831, for example, he wrote to nurseryman Jesse Buel:

> If you should receive anything new in fruits—shrubbery or that you may consider a useful addition to my collection, I shall be glad to receive them in the spring before I publish my catalogue. I expect a visit from a Committee of the Lyceum of Natural History. ... I am therefore desirous of rendering my collection worthy of their notice.[61]

Besides the carriage drive system, footpaths provided alternate circulation throughout Hyde Park's pleasure grounds. The footpath system was important, since it determined the viewpoints from which the landscape composition was experienced. The escarpment walk was the most important of these routes. The panoramic views from the terrace, ennobled by the splendid trees, remained Hyde Park's signature feature. Another important path descended the escarpment at a break in the steep slope north of the house. From this point the path dropped dramatically through a ravine and along a tidal cove to Bard Rock, an early river landing that by this date had been given over to ornamental purposes.

Figure 45. Engraving Showing Classical Pavilion at Hyde Park, from *Landscape Gardening* by A. J. Downing (1841). Downing said that this was "a highly finished form of covered seat, which are occasionally introduced in splendid places where classic architecture prevails" —a reference to Hyde Park.

In 1832, David Hosack commissioned a young artist named Thomas Wharton to complete a portfolio illustrating the Hyde Park landscape. The artist also described the landscape in his diary. Wharton was mightily impressed with Hyde Park, showing enthusiasm over scenery that was "most magical ... there is a weird and almost spiritual purity ... that sometimes seems hardly to belong to earth." Along the escarpment walk and elsewhere, he found "seats scattered here and there from which you can survey at leisure ... the exquisite beauty of the river scenery below."[62] In addition to incidental seats, the landscaped grounds included several prominent features. All were designed in the classical style. The first of these was a temple-like shelter at Bard Rock. This structure is shown on two of Thomas Wharton's drawings. In one view the Bard Rock pavilion is a domed and columned structure set dramatically against the river scene. It was similar to a "Grecian Pavilion, roofed with a dome" described by Wharton as located on the terrace on a "raised spot near the main walk." This second structure seems to be the pavilion shown on an early map of the property. It was located along the escarpment walk south of the house, the "main

Figure 46. Drawing Showing "Euterpe Knoll," by T. K. Wharton, 1839. The open prospect, with Bard Rock and its pavilion clearly seen to the west, highlighted a colossal urn that must have been visible from the Hudson River. Courtesy of the New York Public Library.

walk" to the river landing. Downing called it "a temple … high finished … introduced in splendid places where classic architecture prevails. There is a circular pavilion of this kind at the termination of one of the walks at … Hyde Park." (Figure 45)

Besides the nearly identical classical pavilions, there were at least two special garden features at Hyde Park in Hosack's lifetime. One of these was called the "Euterpe Knoll," which Wharton sketched (Figure 46), and the other was a "L'isle des Peupliers," which he described. The "Euterpe Knoll" was located north of the house close to the edge of the escarpment. At this point the path to Bard Rock breaks from the escarpment walk and leads downhill into a ravine. Beside this path intersection, a knoll juts out into the slope. Here was placed "a tasteful vase of colossal proportions, and dedicated to the goddess of Lyric Poesy." The "Island of Poplars" (L'isle des Peupliers) was described by Wharton as "a grassy knoll covered with tall poplars [Lombardy poplars] … with a bust on a pedestal." The subject of this bust and the location of this evocative if imported feature was not revealed, but the composition was said to be "in imitation of Rousseau."[62] This is a reference to Jean Jacques Rousseau, the early romantic philosopher who died in 1778 and was buried on a small island, his classical tomb ringed with slender poplars, on an artificial lake in the landscape garden at the Ermonville estate, outside Paris. Rousseau was the idol of romantics everywhere, and this emblematic garden feature strongly hints at David Hosack's garden sentiments in the early 1830s.

Hosack was an ambitious and successful American patron of the fine art of landscape gardening. He had just enough time before his death in 1835 for his achievements, and he left Hyde Park, according to A. J. Downing, to serve as "one of the most instructive seats in this country." Wrote Downing in *Landscape Gardening*, five years after Hosack's death:

> Nature has indeed done much for this place, as the grounds are finely varied, beautifully watered by a lively stream [Crum Elbow Creek]. … But the efforts of art are not unworthy so rare a locality; and while the native woods and beautiful undulating grounds are preserved in their original state, the pleasure grounds, roads, walks, drives, and new plantations, have been laid out in so tasteful a manner as to heighten the charms of nature. Large and costly hot-houses were erected, and elegant entrance lodges at two points on the estate, a fine bridge over the stream, and numerous pavilions and seats commanding extensive prospects. ☙

CHAPTER 5

MONTGOMERY PLACE

It is indicative of the close personal relationships that flourished throughout the Hudson River Valley in the 1830s that one of the pallbearers at David Hosack's funeral in December 1835 was Edward Livingston of Montgomery Place (Figure 47). By this date Edward had retired from public life to spend his last summer at the property he inherited in 1828 from his sister, Janet Livingston Montgomery (see page 43).

Edward Livingston's later years held many distractions. He was away from Montgomery Place for long periods, first as President Andrew Jackson's Secretary of State (1831–33), and then as Ambassador to France (1833–35). It was only in his last year that he could concentrate on ornamental landscape gardening at Montgomery Place. In October 1835 he wrote to a friend, "We are all very well and very busy, planting, cutting down, leveling, sloping, opening views, clearing walks, and preparing much work for the ensuing spring to embellish."[63] Two months later Edward reported he had been "extremely active in the improvement of my grounds, in the planting of trees and laying out gardens."[64] Edward seems to have contemplated extensive landscape development, and he was happy to have the work started. Much of the focus was in the Sawkill Valley that traced the northern boundary of the property.

Figure 47. *Portrait of Edward Livingston*, by Charles Bird King, not dated. Edward was the youngest brother of Chancellor Robert R. Livingston. He lived for many years in Louisiana before returning to the Hudson Valley after inheriting his sister's Chateau de Montgomery in 1828. Edward renamed the property Montgomery Place and began extensive landscape gardening there before his death in 1836. Courtesy of the Redwood Library and Athenaeum, Newport, Rhode Island.

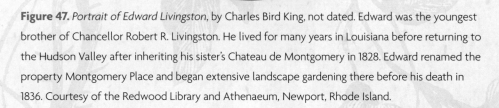

Figure 48. *Portrait of Louise Davezac Livingston,* attributed to Theobald Chartran, c. 1872. After her husband's death, Louise Livingston remained at Montgomery Place with her daughter, Coralie, and Coralie's husband, Thomas Barton. This threesome can be credited with the notable landscape gardening that was described by Andrew Jackson Downing in 1847. Courtesy of Historic Hudson Valley.

As with David Hosack's Crum Elbow Creek, the Sawkill had powered several mills since the colonial period. Over time this use became less crucial and, by the early 1840s, much of the Sawkill had been given over to ornamental purposes.

Edward Livingston died in the "ensuing spring" of 1836, but the "we" he mentioned as being "very busy" remained at Montgomery Place—his wife, Louise Livingston (1781–1860) (Figure 48), and their daughter, Cora Livingston Barton (1806–

1873) (Figure 49), who had married Thomas Pennant Barton (1803–1869) in 1833. Thomas Barton was from the Philadelphia area and was the son of the noted naturalist Benjamin Barton. The Bartons were in their thirties when Edward died. With Louise Livingston's active involvement, they eagerly took up Edward's ambitions for landscape gardening. This triumvirate must be credited with the landscape development that occurred in the next decade, in the heart of the Hudson Valley's Romantic period (Figure 50).

The Barton/Livingston alterations to the house (Figure 51) and their ambitious landscape gardening are difficult to detail year-to-year from the documentation that remains, but these activities were summarized by A. J. Downing in a lengthy article published in *The Horticulturist* in October 1847. By this date Montgomery Place had been transformed into one of the Hudson Valley's most evocative and complex landscape garden compositions. Of its 400 acres, a substantial portion was given to what Downing called "pleasure grounds and ornamental purposes," all acclaimed "second as it is to no seat in America:"

> Around Montgomery Place, indeed, this air of quiet and seclusion lurks more bewitchingly than in any other seat whose hospitality we have enjoyed. Whether the charm lies in the deep and mysterious woods, full

Figure 49. *Portrait of Coralie Livingston Barton,* attributed to Jacques Guillaume L. Amans, c. 1840. Cora was actively involved in making landscape design decisions. Her death in 1873 ended the forty-five-year-long tenure of Edward Livingston's family at Montgomery Place. Courtesy of Historic Hudson Valley.

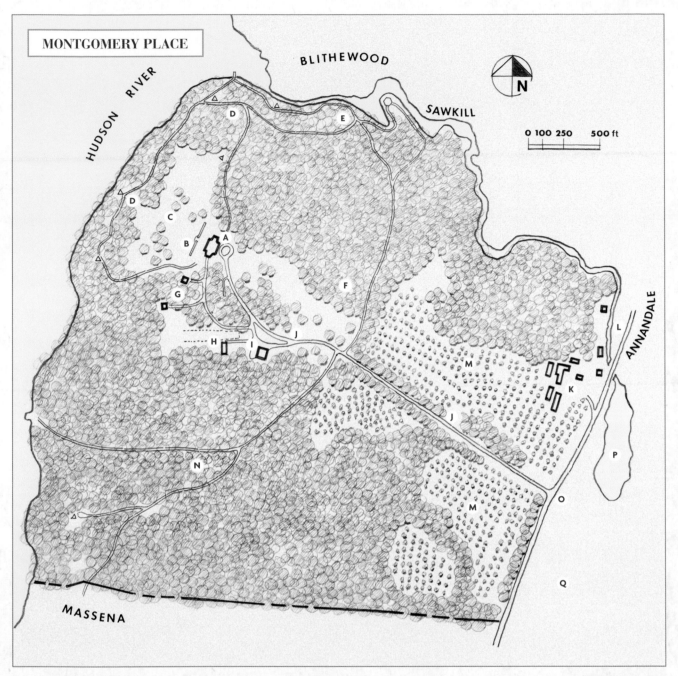

Figure 50. Plan of Montgomery Place, by R. M. Toole. Montgomery Place was designed on an expansive scale, creating a sense of isolation and unity that A. J. Downing said distinguished it as a landscape garden composition. The plan shows the house, where the flower garden was maintained (A), the West Terrace (B), West Park (C), and the "Morning Walk" with its shelters and seats overlooking the Hudson (D). Along the northern boundary were the Sawkill Valley and the so-called "Wilderness" (E). Elsewhere were the arboretum (F), the gardener's cottage and icehouse (G), the kitchen garden and greenhouse (H) and the stable (I). The long straight driveway (J) led to the public road. There were a separate farm complex (K) and a "hamlet group" of cottages and workshops close to Annandale (L). Orchards (M) and the so-called "South Woods" (N) occupied peripheral acres. Carriage drives through the south woods led to the river landing and neighboring Massena. River Road and the entrance gate (O) were located close to an old mill pond (P). Other estate acreage was located east of the public road (Q).

of the echo of water spirits ... or whether it grows out of a profound feeling of completeness and perfection in foregrounds of old trees, and distances of calm serene mountains ... certain it is that there is a spell in the very air, which is fatal to the energies of a great speculation.

Downing's familiarity with Montgomery Place seems to have grown over several visits in the early 1840s. The property was not specifically mentioned in the 1st edition of *Landscape Gardening* (1841), but was included in the 2nd edition (1844) with a brief description of its woodland edges, the interest of its "shadowy walks of great length and variety," and "numerous, tasteful rustic seats, arbours and root-houses ... a stately Conservatory, and flower-garden."

In 1845, Downing's nursery supplied Louise Livingston with a substantial quantity of plant material, including thirty-six ornamental trees, twenty-two fruit trees, about seventy-five shrubs, and eighteen perennials.[65] It is not clear what role Downing had in determining the plants that were ordered or their design use, but in any event Downing was now a family friend. He and his wife accepted periodic invitations to visit Montgomery Place. The 3rd edition of *Landscape Gardening* (1849) included a lavish treatment of the property, illustrated with two engravings from the 1847 article. Some exaggeration was creeping into the story. Downing called this "one of our oldest improved country seats, having been originally the residence of Gen. Montgomery, the hero of Quebec." In fact, the general was dead for a quarter century before Montgomery Place was first developed by his widow. But Downing was certainly on firmer ground when he noted Montgomery Place's scenic "grandeur" and "dignified and elegant seclusion" as its chief assets. Downing paid special attention to the "Wilderness," being the valley of the Sawkill that Edward Livingston and his family had actively devel-

Figure 51. Montgomery Place. This was another classical house (c. 1802) brought to a crescendo with the alterations of A. J. Davis in the early 1840s, which included the decorative east portico and north pavilion featured here. Courtesy of Historic Hudson Valley.

Figure 52. Engraving Showing the House at Montgomery Place from the East, from *The Horticulturist*, October 1847. This view shows the innovative open porch designed for the north pavilion of the house by A. J. Davis. Davis drew this scene for A. J. Downing's use in the publication of "A Visit to Montgomery Place," in 1847.

oped in the previous decade. Downing called it "highly picturesque" and "threaded with dark, intricate, and mazy walks, along which are placed a variety of rustic seats." He concluded that Montgomery Place was "nowhere surpassed in America, in point of location, natural beauty, or the landscape gardening charms which it exhibits."

By 1847, Montgomery Place was a mature landscape having undergone nearly fifty years of consistent family stewardship overlaid on the colonial-era Van Benthuysen farm. Downing's treatment in *The Horticulturist* found "numberless lessons here for the landscape gardener." Portions of the landscape were original to the initial layout of the property, such as the long, straight, entrance avenue and the direct connection to the south towards the river landing and Massena, John Livingston's estate. First laid out in 1797, Massena was so closely connected with Janet Montgomery Livingston's Chateau de Montgomery that their grounds intermingled. Towards Massena, Downing described "rich oak woods" where a series of excellent carriage roads had been created that amounted to "The Drive," being a "sylvan route" through mature forests, ideal for horseback or carriage excursions.

Elsewhere, Downing found great repose in the more recent work. He took his reader on a tour through the landscape along what he called the "Morning Walk," starting on the west side of the house at the lawn terraces overlooking the river. He described the scenery in suitably superlative terms, with the wide river enlivened by several islands, and the Catskill Mountains beyond, "a spectacle of rare beauty." Downing then guided the reader west across the lawn to a "rustic gabled seat,"

where began "a long walk, which was the favorite morning ramble of guests." This footpath followed the Hudson shoreline for about a half mile to the mouth of the Sawkill. There, "half-way along this morning ramble, a rustic seat, placed on a bold little plateau, at the base of a large tree, eighty feet above the water ... invites you to linger and gaze at the fascinating river landscape here presented."

A little farther on, a side path led back up to the house from the north on "a flight of rocky steps ... at the top of these is a rustic seat with a thatched canopy, curiously built round the trunk of an aged tree." Ignoring this side path, the Morning Walk continued, soon descending to the river shore where yet another "little rustic pavilion" was located (Figure 53). From there, a boat could be taken out onto the river. Beyond, the walk entered the embowered Sawkill Valley. Here, Downing spoke of "the depth and massiveness of its foliage ... thick, dark and shadowy," imparting a distinctive sense of place. The topography along the Sawkill varied, from steep-sided ravines to broader bottomland and hollows in the woods. The Sawkill was a substantial stream dropping to the Hudson over several waterfalls. A. J. Downing called these "cataracts ... all striking enough to be worthy of the pencil of the artist, and ... a feast of wonders to the lovers of the picturesque" (Figure 54). The banks of the Sawkill were accessible on a series of footpaths set out with numerous small garden buildings and seats. Downing described one as a "porch [where] the roof is prettily thatched with thick green moss." Elsewhere he crossed a "rustic bridge." In one spot he spoke of a "rustic barrier," or railing, protecting the steep edges along the path.

The natural drama of the Sawkill and the references to "rustic" features would suggest that the "Wilderness" was an interpretation of what Downing called landscape gardening in the Picturesque design mode. However, the aesthetic character of the Wilderness, as well as other areas at Montgomery Place, was a more complex topic. While he never discussed the property as representative of one design mode over another, Downing addressed the issue vaguely, saying, "the Wilderness is by no means savage in the aspect of its beauty; on the contrary, here as elsewhere in this demesne, are evidences, in every improvement, of a fine appreciation of the natural charms of the locality." There is a hint here, supported by several illustrations dating to this era, that the Livingston women preferred their "Wilderness," or at least its man-made accoutrements, to be delicate and well maintained, and rather genteel given the setting.

The garden's many little buildings recall the French influence and the French use of what was called "*fabrique.*" The term referred to a plethora of decidedly decorative, not rustic, garden structures, seats, pavilions and such, intended to

Figure 53. *One of the Rustic Seats* at Montgomery Place, engraving from *The Horticulturist*, October 1847. This was one of the spots described by A. J. Downing as the site of "rustic seats, formed beneath the trees, in deep secluded thickets, by the side of the swift rushing stream, or on some inviting eminence, [which] enables one fully to enjoy [the views]."

Figure 54. Photograph Showing the Cataract on the Sawkill, 2009, by Steve Benson. Waterfalls were natural landscape features. At nineteenth-century Montgomery Place, this example in the Sawkill Valley took on heightened aesthetic purpose as an evocative garden component. The Sawkill is preserved, recognized today as a living link to the region's romanticism.

evoke light-hearted gaiety. In the hands of patrons with French connections, this taste may be expected to have been indulged, and at Montgomery Place, this seems the case. In fact, Montgomery Place, given its authentic French heritage, might be the best example in America of this important design theme.

As a case in point, consider the grandly named "Lake," which was reached next on Downing's tour along the Sawkill. The Lake, actually a small, former mill pond in a widened opening along the Sawkill, was given a mock grandeur and near mystical air, well-evoked in Downing's account. The Lake featured a small boat—called "Psyche's Boat"—decorated with a "giant butterfly" attached to the prow "that looks so mysteriously down into the depths below as to impress you with a belief that it is the metempsychosis of the spirit of the place, guarding against all unhallowed violation of its purity and solitude." The Lake and Psyche's Boat were shown on one of the engraved illustrations that accompanied Downing's article (Figure 55).

The Lake's shore also featured what Downing called "a rustic temple" set beside a "graceful" weeping willow tree on a small peninsula jutting into the water. Downing's illustration shows the willow, but the temple does not seem to be a "rustic" structure, at least as we understand that term today. It was a lightly constructed symmetrical pavilion of vaguely classical design. Elsewhere at Montgomery Place,

Figure 55. *The Lake* at Montgomery Place, engraving from *The Horticulturist*, October 1847. This drawing looks up the Sawkill, with the lake in the foreground. It shows the shelter that stood on a little peninsula surrounded by weeping willows. On the lake is what Downing called "Psyche's Boat," ornamented with the image of a butterfly. Tidy upkeep and the evocative, sequestered setting led Downing to conclude that "the wilderness is by no means savage in the aspect of its beauty."

the Gothic Revival garden structures, and even the cruder wooden seats and shelters, appear as formal designs and symmetrical in their overall arrangements (Figure 56). In one letter Cora Barton discussed the design of a tool house, stating "we want no rustic work."[66]

As at Hyde Park, landscape gardening at Montgomery Place, even in the Wilderness, retained considerable refinement and polish rather than closely mimicking vernacular themes or being indistinguishable from raw nature. As Downing wrote to a friend in the autumn of 1846, "Mrs. Barton & her mother had made great improvements in their place since last year—and I was particularly delighted with the excellent keeping of the grounds."[67]

While the accessories were elegant and the upkeep tidy, Downing left no doubt that at Montgomery Place the visitor was in the realm of nature. Rambling through the Wilderness, Downing mused:

> The memory of the world's toil gradually becomes fainter and fainter, under the spell of the [Sawkill's] soothing monotone; until at last one begins to doubt the existence of towns and cities, full of busy fellow beings, and to fancy the true happiness of life lies in a more simple existence, where man, the dreamy silence of thick forests, the lulling tones of babbling brooks, and the whole heart of nature, make one sensation, full of quiet harmony and joy.

Continuing his tour up the Sawkill, Downing walked past the Lake to another "cascade." Downing noted that the animated scene had been screened moments before so that the Lake's "spirit of repose" was not compromised by the "foamy, noisy little waterfall." Downing considered this a nice design touch.

Before reaching yet another waterfall, Downing brought the reader back up from the Sawkill on a footpath that led out of the ravine and back to the east side of the house, where an elaborate flower garden had been established. Originally, the flower garden area may have been used as a courtyard fronting the east side of the house. It was an enclosed area "surrounded and shut out from the lawn by a belt of shrubbery," but the

date when the area was given over to floral purposes is unclear. This could be the "gardens" mentioned by Edward Livingston late in 1835. Then, before 1840, a large, elegant greenhouse (Downing called it the Conservatory) was erected. According to Downing this impressive Gothic-style building was designed by English architect/artist Frederick Catherwood. It seems to have been located east of and facing the house, with the intervening ground being the flower garden (Figure 57).

The flower garden beds were free-form in design, as Downing described it, "surrounded by low edging of turf or box, and the whole looks like some rich oriental pattern or carpet of embroidery." The bed pattern would have been seen from the east side of the house. The garden also featured a "fanciful light summer-house, or pavilion, of Moresque character," and several classical urns and vases were placed along the walks. Downing concluded, "If there is any prettier flower-garden scene than this ensemble in the country, we have not yet had the good fortune to behold it." Elsewhere he wrote that the Montgomery Place flower garden was "one of the most perfect flower gardens in the country."

In 1845, Downing became directly involved with the flower garden, providing Louise Livingston and Cora Barton with plant material, but possibly also doing a drawing of its layout and suggesting some alterations. At one point Downing investigated the garden's correct dimensions, but its design cannot be attributed to him because the garden was in existence earlier, at least since 1840. In the 1847 piece in *The Horticulturist*, the flower garden was described as "gay and smiling. Bright parterres of brilliant flowers bask in the full daylight." Later in 1857, the gardens were said to be the "especial pet of Mrs. Barton" and the surrounding "arbors, overgrown with *Aristolochia sipho* [*durior*], the Dutchman's pipe, exceed anything of the kind we have seen."

Finally, mention may be made here of Montgomery Place's arboretum located east of the flower garden and begun by Thomas Barton in 1846. It was under development for many years thereafter. Downing called the arboretum "so laudable an undertaking."[68] In 1849 its arrangements were entrusted to Hans Jacob Ehlers (1804–1858), one of a small number of professional landscape gardeners working in the Hudson River Valley in this period. In 1857 a piece in *The*

Opposite: Figure 56. *Shore Seat* at Montgomery Place, by A. J. Davis, c. 1841. This was one of several drawings prepared by architect A. J. Davis in the Livingston/Barton period. It may be considered an example of *fabrique* that seems to have been prevalent at Montgomery Place. Note that despite the use of natural tree branches, twigs, and embellishments like an "old root or rock" as a roof ornament, this is a symmetrical building with an overall formal character. Courtesy of The Metropolitan Museum of Art.

Horticulturist called the arboretum "the most successful effort yet made among us ... executed at considerable cost of time, labor and money."

Louise Livingston died at Montgomery Place in 1860 on the eve of the Civil War. In that same year Benson J. Lossing, in his chronicle *The Hudson, from the Wilderness to the Sea* (1860), reported on Montgomery Place, "of all the fine estates along this portion of the Hudson, this is said to be the most perfect in its beauty and arrangements." ᕯ

Figure 57. *The Conservatory* [and Flower Garden] at Montgomery Place, engraving from *The Horticulturist*, October 1847. The flower garden stood between the east side of the house and the elaborate Gothic-style conservatory shown here. Downing said, "the walks are fancifully laid out, so as to form a tasteful whole; the beds are surrounded by low edgings of turf or box, and the whole looks like some rich oriental pattern of carpet or embroidery." On its north and south sides the garden was "shut out from the lawn, by a belt of shrubbery." Downing claimed he had never seen a "prettier ... ensemble."

CHAPTER 6

BLITHEWOOD

The historical distinction of Montgomery Place as the "most perfect" example of landscape gardening on the Hudson was matched by the neighbor on the north side of the Sawkill. This property was originally Mill Hill, discussed earlier as the second residence of John Armstrong and his wife Alida Livingston, who developed it in their customary practical way in the late 1790s (see page 38). After several intervening owners, Mill Hill was purchased in 1836 by a newcomer on the Hudson, Robert Donaldson (1800–1872) who, with his wife Susan Gaston (1808–1866), restyled the property in the romantic way, calling it "Blithewood"

for the lighthearted symphony of bird life emanating from the surrounding woods.

In April 1836, on their first trip up the river as owners, the Donaldsons met their Montgomery Place neighbors, Cora and Thomas Barton. Similar in age, they came from different backgrounds, but each in their way was an aficionado of landscape gardening. At Montgomery Place the owners had landscaped over the work of their predecessors, sometimes responding with elegant high fashion. New to the neighborhood, the Donaldsons at Blithewood represented no less than the genesis of a fresh approach.

Figure 58. *Portrait of Robert Donaldson,* by Charles R. Leslie, c. 1820. Robert Donaldson brought patronage and avant-garde taste to the art of landscape gardening on the Hudson. He commissioned the era's pioneering designer of eclectic architecture, A. J. Davis, and befriended A. J. Downing, who dedicated his second book, *Cottage Residences* (1842), to Robert Donaldson, calling him "Arbiter Elegantiarum." Donaldson's early enthusiasm for the Picturesque in architecture and landscape gardening led to his development at Blithewood, at Annandale-on-Hudson. Courtesy of Richard Hampton Jenrette.

During their years at Blithewood, Robert Donaldson was the leading light of a diverse group of Hudson Valley gentleman farmers who propelled landscape gardening to its romantic crescendo. Blithewood was a set piece, created singularly in a relatively brief period. Donaldson's landscape gardening was championed by Andrew Jackson Downing, who heralded Blithewood on the frontispiece of *Landscape Gardening* (Figure 59) and dedicated his second book, *Cottage Residences* (1842), to Donaldson, calling him "Arbiter Elegantiarum." For Downing, Blithewood was "in many respects the finest on the Hudson ... under the influence of fine and correct taste."[69]

Donaldson's reputation is enhanced by his role as an early patron of Alexander Jackson (A. J.) Davis, the New York architect largely responsible for America's post-classical architecture. Davis's pioneering Gothic Revival work joined other motifs, such as the Italianate, Oriental, Swiss and Egyptian styles that would be the eclectic vogue until late into the nineteenth century. To some extent these separate architectural styles suggested separate landscape treatments, at least close to the house. Italianate might prompt Downing's Beautiful mode, while a Swiss abode must use the Picturesque design mode. With good reason A. J. Davis is recognized now as America's most important Romantic-period architect, and some of his most significant early works were commissioned by Robert Donaldson.[70] In turn, in 1838, Donaldson brought together A. J. Downing, whom he knew from his horticultural interests, and A. J. Davis, initiating what is possibly the most fruitful artistic collaboration in American history. These were "collaborators in the picturesque," as one historian called the relationship.[71] Davis enriched Downing's evolving interests in architectural design and drew many of the wonderful architectural drawings that were made into engravings to illustrate Downing's books. In turn, Downing provided Davis with day-to-day promotion, and Downing's publications were a vehicle for Davis's lasting legacy.

Figure 59. *View in the Grounds at Blithewood*, engraving from *Landscape Gardening* by A. J. Downing (1841). This illustration, from a drawing by A. J. Davis, epitomizes landscape design in the Hudson Valley's Romantic era. It was the featured frontispiece of A. J. Downing's *Landscape Gardening*. The view shows the ornamental veranda that A. J. Davis added to what had been a Federal-style house when converting it to Robert Donaldson's *cottage ornée*. Note the classical urns.

Figure 60. Watercolor Showing House, by A. J. Davis, 1834. This was A. J. Davis's design for Robert Donaldson's house at Beacon (never built). It was a spectacular Gothic-style rendition set close to the majestic Hudson Highlands, depicted in the background. While a grand edifice, the site was a paltry twenty-two acres. Donaldson turned down the idea and quickly moved to the previously established Blithewood, where 125 acres awaited his ambitions for landscape gardening. Courtesy of The Metropolitan Museum of Art.

By 1841, Davis had become acquainted with Mrs. Livingston and the Bartons next door to the Donaldsons at Montgomery Place, and thereafter provided myriad architectural services at that property. This work included additions to all four sides of the old Federal-style house and designs for several outbuildings and many of the garden structures described by A. J. Downing along the "Morning Walk" and at the flower garden (see Figure 56). United by these properties, A. J. Davis and A. J. Downing forged a close working relationship through the mutual patronage and support of Robert Donaldson, Louise Livingston and the Bartons.

Donaldson's career can be quickly summarized. He was originally from North Carolina, but after his marriage to Susan Gaston the couple lived in New York City, where he was called a "man of leisure," having inherited considerable wealth. Donaldson's leisure pursuits included landscape gardening, which he knew from earlier European travels, his readings and from visits along the Hudson, notably to David Hosack's Hyde Park. After a few years in New York City, Donaldson decided to make a permanent home in the Hudson Valley, involving himself in the rural pursuits and "a taste for rural improvements" that so challenged and amused wealthy gentlemen of his generation. In 1832 his wife wrote to her father that Robert was "disposed to select a site for a country house & to employ himself in landscape gardening."[72]

Initially, Donaldson purchased a twenty-two-acre undeveloped site at today's Beacon, near the northern end of the scenic Hudson River Highlands. The property was later called "Wodenethe," meaning "woody promontory." A. J. Davis was called on to design a house for the site, and he responded with one of the earliest and most expansive Gothic Revival residences yet proposed in America. The design was published in Davis's 1838 book, *Rural Residences*, wherein he called the rambling, irregular pile "suited to scenery of a picturesque character, and to an eminence commanding an extensive prospect" (Figure 60). The house illustration suggested its Hudson Highlands setting. The estimated cost was $12,000, more than three times the next most expensive house included in *Rural Residences*, an indication of Donaldson's architectural ambitions. The picturesque site and Gothic Revival architecture were early indications of Donaldson's interest in the Picturesque mode of landscape gardening, a taste that can be observed consistently in his activities at Blithewood. A. J. Davis stoked Donaldson's interest, and in *Rural Residences* he provided an indication of what he considered an appropriate Picturesque landscape design. The overwhelming importance was a strikingly dramatic, scenic setting, the more sublime the better (as at Donaldson's Highlands' site). In the Highlands, a spectacular overview was contrasted with shadowy wooded backdrops. In *Rural Residences*, Davis's watercolor drawings show ancient trees overhung with vines, varied, unclipped shrubbery, and native wildflowers growing at the edges of wooded groves. Closely cropped lawn near the house gave way to rougher meadows farther off. Natural-appearing water edges, complete with felled logs and a variety of indigenous vegetation are also shown by Davis close to his picturesque houses.

In 1835, Robert Donaldson abandoned the Highlands project, never building Davis's grand, gothic proposal. He moved on to a new opportunity on the much larger, 125-acre estate, Mill Hill. Here, a new house was not needed, so Donaldson had A. J. Davis romanticize the Armstrong's old Federal-style house into a unique *cottage ornée*—an ornamental cottage—the sort of modest dwelling well-fitted to Picturesque design themes. In 1836, Davis also designed a new gatehouse for Blithewood, later used as a gardener's cottage (Figure 61). This modest, gothic-inspired structure struck a chord as reflective of both the Hudson's forested backdrops and its "democratic" lifestyles. Today it is considered the first of America's earliest picturesque houses, a prototype widely copied into the Victorian period. Donaldson and Davis pioneered the style at Blithewood.

Donaldson's property eventually incorporated numerous other outbuildings designed by A. J. Davis. These included a greenhouse, rustic arbors (part of an elaborate flower garden), an ornamental tool house, a fanciful water tower, and miscellaneous garden shelters and pavilions. A new hexagonal gatehouse was added in 1841. There was even a hermitage, although no record of an actual hermit survives.

In the first edition of *Landscape Gardening* (1841), A. J. Downing included a description of Blithewood, calling it:

one of the most tasteful villa residences in the Union. The lawn or park, which commands a view of surpassing beauty, is studded with groups of fine forest trees, beneath which are delightful walks leading in easy curves to rustic seats, summer houses, etc. disposed in secluded spots, or to openings affording the most lovely prospects.

Figure 61. Watercolor Showing the Rustic Cottage at Blithewood, by A. J. Davis, 1836. With the main house visible to the west, this gatehouse, later used by the gardener, captured the essence of the picturesque cottage. Courtesy of Avery Library, Columbia University.

At an unknown date, but with its principal features in place, A. J. Davis drew a plan of Blithewood that documented its arrangements (Figure 62). He also prepared several watercolor drawings illustrating the landscape. The plan shows the house and the array of outbuildings, carriage drives and footpaths. Open fields are differentiated from wooded areas. Much of the layout was for purely ornamental purposes, but the farm, a gentleman's farm, was integral to the design, serving Donaldson's domestic needs and agrarian interests.

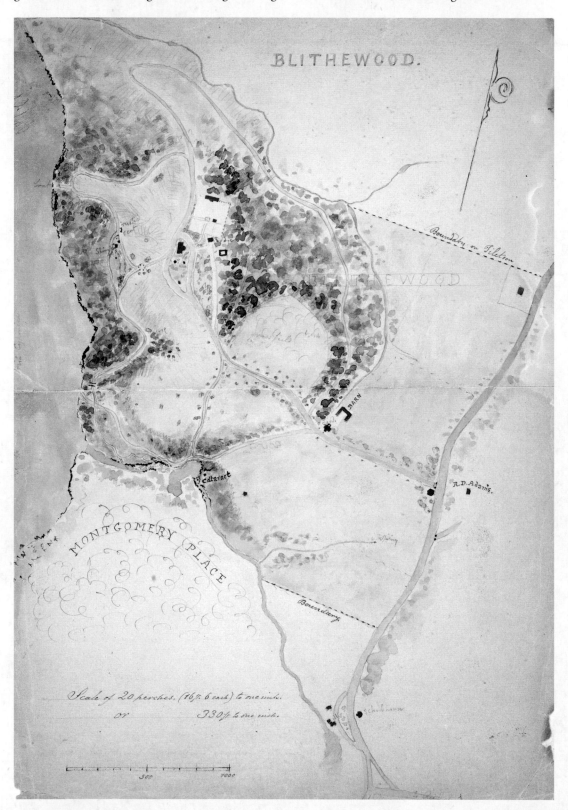

Figure 62. Map of Blithewood, by A. J. Davis (c. 1840s). This is one of the best site plans to survive showing a Picturesque landscape garden. It was prepared by A. J. Davis and included most of the elements present at Blithewood by the late 1840s. Courtesy of Avery Library, Columbia University.

Figure 63. Watercolor Showing Paths and Thatched Shelter at Blithewood, by A. J. Davis, 1840. This sketch illustrates picturesque aspects along the Sawkill. Montgomery Place is across the ravine to the right. The footpaths were rigorous, but offered planned views of the many waterfalls seen from rustic overlooks. Courtesy of Avery Library, Columbia University.

In A. J. Downing's reporting on the landscape, "Maltese vases" were "disposed in such a manner as to give a classic air to the grounds," suggesting some artificial effects reflective of what Downing might call the Beautiful design mode. But despite this comment, a comprehensive look at Donaldson's landscape shows that the Beautiful mode was restricted. Downing himself augmented his earlier characterization in the 2nd edition of *Landscape Gardening* (1844) with a description of the property's "wild and picturesque" aspects (Figure 63). It seems Blithewood was kept in a way consistent with what Downing called the Picturesque mode of design, reflecting a fully natural, rural, even unkempt appearance, as compared with the Graceful or Beautiful approach which, as described by Downing, accentuated classical design, high polish and refinement, all traits found more readily at the older Montgomery Place and Hyde Park. Interpreting this aspect of historic landscape gardening can be the most problematic of tasks, but important to understanding the design's response to romanticism, the picturesque aesthetic, and sensitivity to the genius of the place.

In this respect, commentary from Hans Jacob Ehlers, the professional landscape gardener described earlier as working at Montgomery Place, is of great interest. Ehlers described Blithewood as being too rustic and unembellished, too Picturesque in its design. Ehlers said the Blithewood house was masked in foliage, leaving it like "a privy, rather than the mansion of the proprietor ... walks resemble ditches, hardly fit for cattle to walk in."[73] Ehlers's observations were from one who clearly preferred a more highly kept landscape. A. J. Downing may have agreed, suggesting in 1847 that Donaldson improve the quality of his lawns, saying he favored a "finely kept lawn" over whatever (a wildflower meadow?) had been Donaldson's preference. Downing wanted more finish and he

strongly advised Donaldson, "If I were you I should have a horse roller going after every shower & would mow regularly every fortnight. Try it one season & see if the beauty of the effect produced is not worth all the flowers in the world!"[74] The outcome of this debate is left uncertain, but the illustrations and arrangements of Donaldson's landscape reflected attention to local scenery and Picturesque design themes. Donaldson's sensibilities no doubt prevailed.

Coincident with A. J. Downing's death in 1852, Donaldson seems to have grown tired of his Blithewood project. In his mind the landscape was complete and he needed to find a new challenge. Donaldson sold Blithewood in 1853, moving to an established property, Edgewater, and its 1820s Greek revival mansion on the banks of the Hudson at Barrytown. He told A. J. Davis that he had "no thought of trying to make a Blithewood."[75] In his fifties, Donaldson was retiring from expansive landscape gardening.

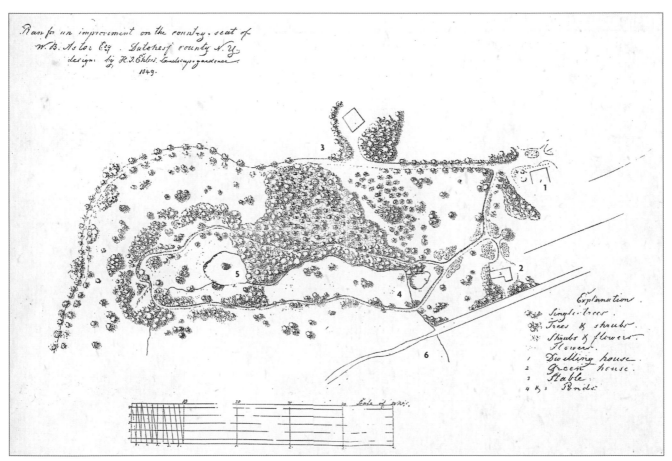

Figure 64. Plan of a Portion of Rokeby, by H. J. Ehlers, 1849. North is to the bottom of the plan, which shows the area east of the house (1). The entrance drive is shown approaching the house from the east and passing a stable (3). A "Green house" (2) is fronted on the south by several large "island" plant beds set out with shrubbery and flowers. A looping path extended along the Mudderkill Creek, shown in the lower center with a pond in which there is a small island shown as a single tree (5). Another, smaller pond is identified farther west (4). The straight farm access road is on the north at the bottom of the plan (6). Courtesy of Rokeby.

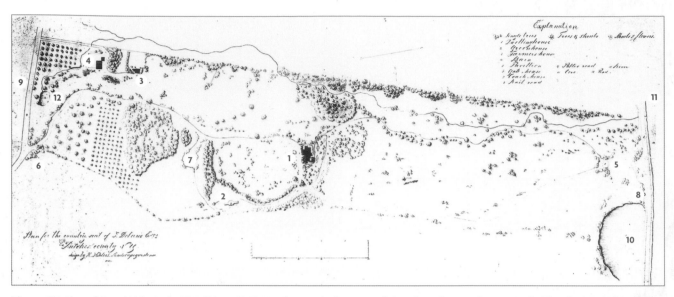

Figure 65. Plan of Steen Valetje, by H. J. Ehlers, 1849. North is to the bottom of the plan. The map key is entitled "Explanations." It reads as follows (larger numbers have been added): Dwelling house (1), Greenhouse (2), Farmer's house (3), Barn (4), Pavilion [icehouse?] (5), Gatehouse (6), Coach house (7), Railroad (8), Public Road (9), Cove (10), River (11), Pond (12). An extensive orchard, planted in a rectilinear grid in the autumn of 1848, is shown on the right (north) side of the entrance drive. The Rhinebeck Town line formed the south property line (top of plan). The Steen Valetje Creek runs along the town line to the Hudson River. Courtesy of Rokeby.

Figure 66. Aerial Photograph Showing Steen Valetje, by Marcia A. Toole. The house, set back from the river with the sinuous approach drive passing through extensive parkland, recalls Rokeby, where H. J. Ehlers, who designed Steen Valetje, also worked. The plan is innovative for its placement of the outbuildings. A stable is seen in the lower right, convenient but hidden in an interior wooded area. Elsewhere a farmer's cottage and gatehouse were placed as features. The Steen Valetje Creek ran through the south (left) woodland.

As a designed landscape Blithewood lingered, maintained for several decades as Donaldson created it. Finally, in 1899, an enormous "Gilded Age" mansion was constructed in a classical Georgian style close to the site of the Donaldsons' cottage, which was demolished. Today the site, much altered with only faint traces of its romantic arrangements remaining, is accessible as part of the Bard College Campus.

A footnote might be added here regarding Hans Jacob Ehlers.[76] He was an immigrant, trained in gardening and arboriculture in Germany. He arrived in New York City circa 1841–42, when he was already middle-aged. In uncertain circumstances he made his way to Rokeby, the former "La Bergerie" (see page 39). In 1842, Rokeby was still home to the elderly widower John Armstrong, although by this date the property was owned by his daughter Margaret Armstrong and her husband William B. Astor.

Over several years in the late 1840s, "H. J. Ehlers, landscape gardener," as he signed his name, directed the Astors' landscape improvements at Rokeby (Figures 64 and 67). He also laid out and supervised the development of an adjoining property, called Steen Valetje (meaning "little stony brook") for the Astors' daughter and son-in-law, Laura and Franklin Delano, before 1852 (Figures 65 and 66). In these years Steen Valetje bore a close resemblance to Rokeby in its layout and upkeep, and Ehlers became a familiar personality in the riverfront neighborhood. In 1849, Thomas Barton hired him to take charge of his arboretum development at Montgomery Place.

It was related to his work for Thomas Barton that Ehlers's critical comments regarding Blithewood were documented. It seems Ehlers had some confrontation with Robert Donaldson, who apparently did not like

Figure 67. Photograph Showing a Rustic Shelter at Rokeby, 2009, by Steve Benson. A propped-up survivor of the picturesque aesthetic, this old summerhouse (as it was called), probably dating to the late nineteenth century, is a relic of a bygone era at an old family estate. Ephemeral built features seldom last, but reconstruction using varied documentation can recreate the past in an authentic way (see Figure 141).

Ehlers's work. In response, Ehlers's contemptuous comments about Blithewood and Donaldson reflected deep disregard. No doubt looking for support for his criticisms of Blithewood, Ehlers addressed Thomas Barton, saying, "You are a witness to their truth," implying Barton's agreement.

As to Ehlers's own design approach, it seems to have favored an embellished, polished look, more in keeping with Downing's Beautiful/Graceful mode than Donaldson's Picturesque preferences. Ehlers's surviving plans for Rokeby and Steen Valetje include myriad flower beds cut into lawn areas. This was a fashionable European conceit. The beds often produced a cluttered and highly floral effect, oblivious to the expansive scale and rustic character of the Hudson Valley. While imported fashion can be presumed to have influenced Ehlers, he does seem to have appreciated a landscape's natural assets. For example, he treated standing specimen trees as landscape features, setting them off as destinations along his footpaths. He also laid out paths and small bridges along a stream, the Mudderkill, in a park-like setting east of the Rokeby house. ❧

CHAPTER 7

SUNNYSIDE

Hyde Park, Montgomery Place and Rokeby were large ancestral estates that underwent landscape improvements over several generations. By comparison, Blithewood, Steen Valetje and others were new, somewhat smaller properties where more modest landscape gardening reflected themes particular to the Romantic period. In fact, it was a diminutive development—that of Washington Irving at his little farm at Tarrytown—that left the most lasting impression.

In 1832, Washington Irving returned from his long sojourn in Europe (see page 46). He was welcomed by the New York City press, "crowned with the purest literary renown."[77] Irving was by then synonymous with American romanticism, having long since laid its literary foundations with the first of the fanciful Knickerbocker tales in

1809. Irving's syntheses of romantic notions, and his articulation of a romanticism custommade for the young United States ("binding the heart of the native inhabitant to his home," as Irving put it), were lasting contributions to American letters.

Almost immediately on his return, Irving set about creating a home for himself. Sunnyside was the result. One of America's most important historic sites, it is open to the public under the management of Historic Hudson Valley.

At Sunnyside, ahead of all others, romantic-induced domesticity was on display. The home of a celebrity, it was also a place that spoke to the aspirations of a broader range of Americans, those who could not dream of owning a large estate property such as Hyde Park or Montgomery Place. Sunnyside was a tangible example of the

Figure 68. Engraving, *Washington Irving & Dog*, by Felix O. C. Darley, July 1848. Sketched about fifteen years after beginning the Sunnyside development, Irving, at age sixty-five, is shown relaxing in the landscape. Courtesy of Historic Hudson Valley.

"democratic" homes and landscapes that would have special relevance for the future. While great works of landscape gardening were usually achieved on great acreage, its practice had much to offer smaller properties. A. J. Downing addressed this topic in *Landscape Gardening* and entitled his second book *Cottage Residences*. Downing concluded that these were:

> a class of residences likely to become more numerous than any other in this country—the tasteful suburban cottage ... [where] on grounds of half a dozen acres, a more intense degree of pleasure, than the arrangements of a vast estate [can be achieved].

These thoughts were exemplified at Washington Irving's Sunnyside and other *cottage ornée*-style properties that previewed American suburbia. The early- and mid-nineteenth century appeal of domestic modesty and coziness of setting, especially for owners of moderate means but high sensibilities, was a romantic sentiment that met wide acceptance and became a core value of the American dream.

Elegant cottage dwellings—the *cottage ornèe*—had been fashionable in England since at least the 1790s.[78] Experiencing the concept in England, Irving foretold of his future home in *The Sketch Book* (1819). In the essay "Rural Life in England," Irving praised "the creative talent with which the English decorate the unostentatious abodes ... the rudest habitation" transformed into "a little paradise" by the landscape gardener who "seizes at once upon [a property's] capabilities," so that:

> The sterile spot grows into loveliness under his hand; and yet the operations of art which produces the effect are scarcely to be perceived. The cherishing and training of some trees; the cautious pruning of others; the nice distribution of flowers and plants of tender and graceful foliage; the introduction of a green slope of velvet turf; the partial opening of a peep of blue dis-

Figure 69. The House at Sunnyside. Washington Irving's quintessential cottage (he called it his "elegant little snuggery") is preserved, embowered in romance and wisteria. Courtesy of Historic Hudson Valley.

tance, or silver gleam of water; all these are managed with a delicate tact, a pervading yet quiet assiduity, like the magic touchings with which a painter finishes up a favorite picture.

Washington Irving wrote down these artistic thoughts nearly twenty years before his own "sterile spot grew into loveliness" in his hands, but even in 1819, in the context of English landscape gardening, Irving's description of the *cottage ornée* amounted to enlightened but long-established taste. In fact, garden design in England had by 1815 taken on a renewed appreciation for refinement and decoration, quite unlike the subtle effects of nature suggested in Irving's prose. By 1819, horticultural exhibit, fussy display and geometric layouts were again the garden fashion of the English Regency period, Washington Irving's milieu during his stay abroad. Still, despite current English fashion, Irving praised the natural-appearing compositions championed by the late-eighteenth-century picturesque improvers, and these he interpreted within the genius of his own romantic sentiment. For

Irving, the themes of the picturesque improvers found fertile ground in the Hudson River Valley.

During the colonial period, Sunnyside had been part of a tenant farm on Philipsburg Manor. After four previous owners, Irving purchased the old house in 1835. Several small land acquisitions followed, resulting in a twenty-acre property, a fraction the size of David Hosack's Hyde Park or the Livingstons' Clermont or Montgomery Place.

When Irving first saw the property, it included a small stone house, sequestered directly on the shore of the Hudson (Figure 70). A painting of the original house shows its workaday grounds surrounded by a picket fence, with other fence lines forming yards to the side and rear. It was described by Irving's brother as littered with "old outhouses, fences and rubbish."[79]

The old house stood beside a small cove backed by a steep wooded hillside. A little brook emptied into the cove. The brook paralleled a long sinuous road, later called Sunnyside Lane, which descended from the public highway (today, U.S. Rt. 9) down through a wooded glen to the river. There was a small jetty that served as a public wharf. A diminutive farm

Figure 70. *Old Cottage Taken Previous to Improvements*, by George Harvey, c. 1835. The painting shows the vernacular colonial farmhouse (c. late seventeenth century) and fenced landscape before Washington Irving's alterations. Courtesy of Historic Hudson Valley.

complex was located east of the house. Small orchards, the fenced kitchen/flower garden, and small arable fields and pastures occupied higher ground to the north, east and south. A farm pond formed by damming the brook was set against a wooded bank. The glen and brook, adorned with mature forest trees and rocky outcrops, were a rugged contrast to the agricultural land use. It was an altogether picturesque scene (Figure 71).

Early on, Washington Irving's widowed brother, Ebenezer, wrote that his brother "proposes enlarging the house, preserving its present old Dutch style, and making it an inviting and comfortable nook for the family."[80] "Preserving its present old Dutch style" does not accurately describe the changes Irving made

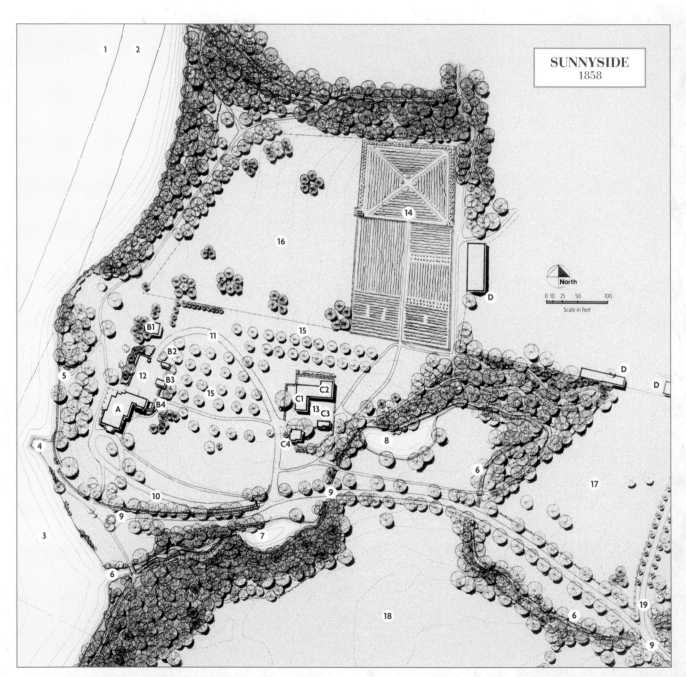

Figure 71. Plan of Sunnyside (1858) by R. M. Toole. This period plan is based on the existing site conditions and the historic surveys and other historic documentation, written and pictorial. Sunnyside was originally a small farm in a picturesque setting. Washington Irving built on the diminutive scale and sheltered aspect to create an intimate designed landscape.

to what had been a simple vernacular dwelling. Irving's work altered the building's exterior into a fantasy. Architectural critics have tried to classify Irving's cottage design, but in fact it is unique. For Irving, to be original but fitting was a hallmark of tasteful design. An imported architectural style—the Italianate or Gothic coveted by others—would not do for Irving, and so this house is an American example of great distinction and significance. Stepped gables, ornamental chimney pots, intri-

cate Dutch weathervanes, miniscule dormers and the sheltered entrance porch embowered in vines were devices intended to produce a familiar yet highly evocative building that belonged only to the Hudson River Valley (Figure 72). Quite appropriately its design is attributed not to an architect but to an artist, George Harvey (c. 1800–1878), an English-born painter.

By early October 1835 the house remodeling was reported "in a considerable state of forwardness."[81] The following April, even before the house was finished, Irving wrote to his sister describing the spring landscape work: "I have been out of doors from morning until night ever since I have been up here, setting out trees &c. &c."[82] Thus began the landscape gardening that was to provide an ongoing interest for the rest of Washington Irving's life.

There were several employees on the property to help with the work. This staff included a gardener and hired hands whose numbers varied over time and the seasons. Periodically Irving hired others to help with landscape tasks and special projects. There was no doubt as to the supervision of this activity. Irving later wrote, "[I] was pretty much my own architect; projector [planner] and landscape gardener, and had but rough hands to work under me."[83] In 1841, in a letter to his niece Sarah, Irving commented:

> My afternoon was taken up with superintending the improvements about the place, trimming and setting trees and clearing out paths. I have been working about the grounds and especially about the old fallen

KEY TO SUNNYSIDE PLAN

BUILDINGS:

A. House

B. Outbuildings

  B1. Icehouse

  B2. Wood/Coal Shed

  B3. Root Cellar

  B4. Privy

C. Farm Group

  C1. Barn

  C2. Cow Barn/Pig Shed

  C3. Shed

  C4. Gardener's Cottage

D. Neighbor's Structures

SITE COMPONENTS

1. Hudson River

2. Railroad Embankment (1848)

3. Cove (high water line shown)

4. Landing

5. Spring

6. Brook/Glen

7. Ice Pond (1847)

8. Farm Pond

9. Sunnyside Lane (public road)

10. Approach Drive (private)

11. Service Drive

12. Service Yard

13. Farm Yard

14. Kitchen/Flower Garden

15. Orchard

16. North Pasture

17. East Pasture

18. South Pasture

19. Entrance to Neighbor

Figure 72. Engraving Showing the Sunnyside House, from *Landscape Gardening* by A. J. Downing (1841). The engraving was made from a drawing by architect A. J. Davis. The house is shown before vines had grown on the walls. Note the damaged Lombardy poplar tree to the right center, a remnant of the older landscape.

chestnut tree. ... I have new paths leading to and from it along the brook, and it is really one of the prettiest places in my whole grounds.[84]

Two weeks later, another long letter to Sarah included the following:

The trees and shrubs and clambering vines that have been transplanted within the last year or two have now taken good root and begin to grow luxuriantly. If vegetation goes on at this rate we shall before long be buried among roses and honeysuckles and ivy and sweet briar.[85]

Irving made major alterations to the riverfront of the house, which he described to his niece in 1841. When purchased, Irving said the river edge was in a "state of nature," much of it a thicket of brush and weed trees that screened his views. The narrow beach and bank frequently eroded in times of storm and high tide. Irving cleared this unkempt river edge of all but the better trees, graded it to a smooth surface ("finished off," as he described the process), and surfaced it with grass. Paths and steps were laid out leading from the house down to the river. These alterations imparted a decidedly polished treatment to what was originally a more natural river edge (Figure 73). Irving set out "seats" at carefully selected vantage points along the river and approvingly concluded that the work "adds greatly to the appearance of the cottage from the water."[86] The south, east and west sides of the cottage were surrounded by lawns, with the fenced yards and garden plots of the old farm removed. Irving rejected the necessary inconvenience of using sheep to graze the lawns. He maintained separate fenced pastures for animals, and used the scythe to keep his turf and ungrazed areas trimmed. On the small lawn terrace west of the cottage, the grass was kept carpet-like. Irving planted flowering shrubs and maintained flower beds close to the cottage He planted "seeds of all kinds"[87] and boasted of living in "the midst of birds and blossoms and flowers."[88]

While visible from the river, the cottage was set low to the water. It was not meant to be a bold feature, as were the

Figure 73. *Sunnyside from the Hudson*, unknown artist, after 1860. The view shows the intrusion of the railroad after 1848. The cove, at this point a backwater, is seen to the right. The cottage front was cleared of scrub vegetation, with the lawn reaching down to the water's edge. The large tree in the foreground was an American elm that remained into the 1940s when the house and property were preserved and opened as a house museum. Courtesy of Historic Hudson Valley.

Figure 74. *In the Glen,* by T. Addison Richards, 1855. This sketch was one of several used in an article published in *Harper's New Monthly Magazine* in December 1856. The view shows the picturesque garden effects maintained only a few hundred feet from Irving's cottage. Paths and seats were laid out in the area. Courtesy of Historic Hudson Valley.

Federal-style houses at Hyde Park, Montgomery Place and The Hill, but rather to meld with nature's verdant backdrop, overhung by trees and draped in vines, as at Blithewood. Irving finished the cottage with muted colors and trained a variety of vines on the house. These included the English ivy (*Hedera helix*), sweetbriar (*Rosa rubiginosa*), trumpet creeper (*Campsis radicans*), climbing roses and white flowering clematis, which together, as Irving said, nearly "buried" the cottage after 1841.

Irving developed an extensive system of footpaths at Sunnyside. These were crucial to the landscape design, because they directed one's movement and so defined the sequence from which the landscape garden was experienced. Washington Irving was a prodigious path builder. The interconnected system of paths led away from the house in all directions. One segment went along the river shore and up the glen from the beach (Figure 74). Another extended across the steep wooded glen above the pond, forming a loop arrangement, and from there intersected with a perimeter walk along the east side of the kitchen/flower garden. Paths led through the woodland belts kept around the open pastures and fields. These in turn connected with the neighbors' path systems north, east and south of Sunnyside. Reflecting his sensibilities, Irving surfaced his paths with dirt, which he "dug out and walked hard," unlike the neighbors' "smooth gravel walks."[89] A. J. Downing highlighted these dirt paths when he reported on Sunnyside in *Landscape Gardening*, saying that "the charming manner in which the wild foot-paths, in the neighborhood of this cottage, are conducted among the picturesque dells and banks, is precisely what one would look for here."

The varieties of trees in the wooded areas at Sunnyside were those typical of the northern hardwood forest association. Irving mentioned oaks, maples and the tulip tree (*Liriodendron tulipifera*), and noted that "my place abounds with fine [American] chestnut [*Castanea dentata*], black-walnut [*Juglans nigra*], and butter-nut trees [*Juglans cinerea*]."[90] The American elm (*Ulmus Americana*) and sycamore (*Platanus occidentalis*) were present along the shore. In addition, previous owners intro-

duced several tree varieties—for example, black locust (*Robinia pseudoacacia*), European larch (*Larix decidua*), horse chestnut (*Aesculus hippocastanum*), and the old-fashioned Lombardy poplar (*Populus nigra italica*).

Gentleman farming was fundamental to Sunnyside's decorative landscape. The colonial- era farm had functioned on much larger acreage. Still, Washington Irving retained a creditable farm operation, and this was important to the property's authenticity as a rural place. Farm operations at Sunnyside changed over time, but seem to have been consistently active and varied. Irving kept saddle and coach horses, cows, pigs and poultry, including turkeys, geese, ducks and chickens. A wide range of vegetables was grown, and Irving set out an orchard. He maintained a pigeon coop, spread manure over the fields, cut ice from the pond, and erected an elaborate arrangement of fences. At one point, three dogs (and their litters) were in residence. Farm operations were amended to meet aesthetic criteria, to combine, as Irving described it, "the useful and the beautiful in rural life."[91]

Sunnyside's intricate and intimate grounds were, of course, the antithesis of a typical agricultural landscape. An efficient farm would have large, cleared pastures and plowed arable fields, with minimal "wasted" ground and few intervening trees. In contrast, the three pastures for animals at Sunnyside varied from 1½ to 6 acres in size and were park-like glades, studded with specimen trees and with thick woodland belts between them. Working with the natural forms, Irving arranged his farm as an ensemble of separate areas, each with its spatial character and sense of place. The woodland belts sheltered the path system, segmented the landscape, presented the fields to view and formed an irregular quilt on the land.

The fenced kitchen garden was also a decorative and practical element. Within the 1½ acre, rectangular garden enclosure was a geometric arrangement of walks that linked with Sunnyside's overall path system. The kitchen garden was located at the site's highest elevation, in the northeastern cor-

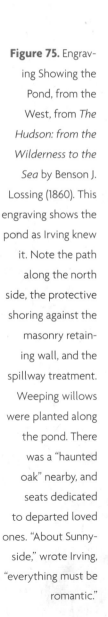

Figure 75. Engraving Showing the Pond, from the West, from *The Hudson: from the Wilderness to the Sea* by Benson J. Lossing (1860). This engraving shows the pond as Irving knew it. Note the path along the north side, the protective shoring against the masonry retaining wall, and the spillway treatment. Weeping willows were planted along the pond. There was a "haunted oak" nearby, and seats dedicated to departed loved ones. "About Sunnyside," wrote Irving, "everything must be romantic."

ner of the property. This isolated setting was removed from sight and did not intrude on the landscape's natural forms and appearance.

Blending use and visual consideration, Irving's landscape garden had dual functions. The picturesque icehouse served as a garden feature, and the original farm pond, essential for agriculture, was also ornamental (Figure 75).

For Washington Irving, Sunnyside was "quaint but unpretending"[92] and a place to "ruralize."[93] He wrote his sister Sarah in 1840:

> [My neighbors] are generally in opulent, or at least easy circumstances; well bred and well informed. We have frequent gatherings ... delightful little parties ... occasionally excellent music ... picnic parties, sometimes on the banks of the Hudson. You would be delighted with these picturesque assemblages, on some wild woodland point jutting into the Tappan Sea [sic]. Country life with us at present is very differ-ent from what it was in your youthful days [c. 1800]. It has a politer tone.[94]

Andrew Jackson Downing visited Sunnyside. He supplied Irving with some plants from his Newburgh nursery, and Washington Irving in a letter referred to Downing as "a friend."[95] Downing, a much younger man, seems to have been enthralled with Irving's stature. In *Landscape Gardening* he commented on Irving's "characteristic taste" and quoted from one of his "elegant essays," "Rural Life in England" from *The Sketch Book*. Downing held up Irving's words as an inspiration and concluded that "Washington Irving's cottage is even more poetical than any chapter of his *Sketch Book*":

> There is also a quiet-keeping in the cottage and the grounds around it, that assists in making up the charm of the whole; the gently swelling slope reaching down to the water's edge, bordered by prettily wooded ravines through which a brook meanders

Figure 76. Photograph Showing Entrance at Sunnyside, Tarrytown, 2009, by Steve Benson. Sunnyside melded the art of landscape design with the natural assets at hand in an especially alluring way. The entrance off Sunnyside Lane skirts a wild brook and its picturesque wooded banks (left). Ahead, the scene opened to the expansive Hudson experienced from the refined cottage grounds.

pleasantly; and threaded by foot-paths ingeniously contrived so as sometimes to afford secluded walks, and at others to allow fine vistas of the broad expanse of river scenery.

Downing concluded that Sunnyside "is, in location and accessories, almost the beau ideal of a *cottage ornée*."

Washington Irving presented Sunnyside as an idyllic, lyrical landscape, fundamentally removed from its utilitarian past. This led to some basic incongruities. The cares of a workaday world were integral to life on the old Dutch tenant farm, but were consciously excluded at Sunnyside. Then, too, the landscape design was decorative, without a hint of the ruder aspects of unkempt rusticity. Irving was not reviving the past. He did not recreate a vernacular scene or the rectilinear basis of old Anglo-Dutch gardening, but instead returned to the site's natural assets and Sunnyside's vernacular, stage-set appearance, infusing romance, following the principles of the English picturesque improvers, in a fully American idiom.

Sunnyside was a remarkably effective designed landscape. America's "choice little place," as one critic called it, was an evocative visual whole. A set piece, its design distinction was apparent in A. J. Downing's summation that Sunnyside (and several other cottage properties in the Tarrytown area) "show how fast the feeling for something more expressive and picturesque, is working progress among us." Sunnyside epitomized this aesthetic achievement in American life. Irving's contribution was not as a horticulturist, where he was an enthusiastic amateur, but as designer and tastemaker, where he was unrivaled. Irving's sensibilities were so affecting, so well-known and emulated that they can be seen as representing the best of American landscape gardening in the pre–Civil War decades. ❧

Figure 77. Cigar Box Cover Showing Sunnyside (Hoyt, Barbour & Co., Louisville, Kentucky) c. 1850. Illustrations of Sunnyside were widely circulated in the mid-nineteenth century as Washington Irving's home became a national domestic icon. This cigar box top was typical. Courtesy of Historic Hudson Valley.

CHAPTER 8

KNOLL (LYNDHURST)

During the late 1830s, as Washington Irving settled into Sunnyside, his neighbors to the north, elderly General William Paulding (1770–1854) (Figure 78) and his son, Philip Rhinelander Paulding (1816–1864), began construction at their country estate "Knoll."

Knoll, called by its post-Paulding owners "Lyndhurst," is today operated as a museum property by the National Trust for Historic Preservation. It has long been recognized for the Pauldings' choice of architecture and architect. Lauded as America's finest domestic example of the Gothic Revival style, the house was the masterwork of A. J. Davis, who undertook the commission a few years after the start of his association with Robert Donaldson at Blithewood.

In June 1841, Washington Irving took a carriage ride to what he called the Pauldings' "mansion." There he commented on the riverfront veranda, calling it the "piazza," which he was seeing for the first time. He praised it as "noble" and thought the entire house would "be both picturesque and convenient."[96]

As at Sunnyside, the Knoll property was initially part of a large tenant farm on the Philipsburg Manor. After the Revolutionary War the land was subdivided. In 1785 a local farmer, Glode Requa (d. 1806), purchased a 296-acre lot, a strip of land fronting on the Hudson River and extending about a mile and a half inland. In 1817 this farm was inherited by two brothers, who split the parcel down the middle, each

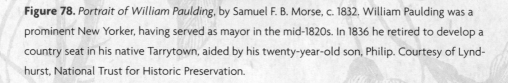

Figure 78. *Portrait of William Paulding*, by Samuel F. B. Morse, c. 1832. William Paulding was a prominent New Yorker, having served as mayor in the mid-1820s. In 1836 he retired to develop a country seat in his native Tarrytown, aided by his twenty-year-old son, Philip. Courtesy of Lyndhurst, National Trust for Historic Preservation.

retaining river frontage and a mix of orchards, woodlots, pastures and arable land to the east. The old Post Road bisected the property (Figure 79).

In October 1836 one brother, Daniel Requa, sold his farm to General William Paulding. The land included the farmhouse complex and a 115-acre agricultural parcel east of the public road, and a 68-acre parcel between the public road and the river. Except for the wooded banks and ravines along the Hudson River, the land west of the public road was largely open fields and was to be the residential setting for A. J. Davis's Gothic house.

The Paulding family was of old Dutch stock from one of Tarrytown's earliest settlers. General William Paulding was born at his father's homestead near the old dock in Tarrytown. A cousin, John Paulding, was one of the heroic captors of the British spy Major André during the Revolution. William's brother, James Kirke Paulding, collaborated with Washington Irving on essays for the magazine *Salmagundi* in 1807–08. After the Revolutionary War, William lived in New York City where he was practicing law by 1797. An orator and a politician, William represented New York City in the 12th United States Congress (1811–1813). Later he served as mayor of New York City, from 1824 to 1826, and again from 1827 to 1829.

In 1836, at age sixty-six, elder statesman William Paulding was retired, building a country residence in his ancestral neighborhood. His interest was shared and encouraged by his youngest son, Philip. Then in his early twenties, Philip lived with his parents and studied law. He was involved with the development of the Tarrytown property from the beginning, providing the youthful energy and enthusiasm for new ideas

vital to the innovative, romantically charged design work at Knoll. He also seems to have taken the lead in the day-to-day management of the property, responsibilities that would have included landscape improvements. The stylish manifestations of romanticisms represented by the house architecture and the Knoll landscape had an easy appeal to Philip. He was a sensitive patron of the Gothic Revival, and the picturesque sentiments played out in the Pauldings' house construction, interior design, furnishings, and landscape gardening.

The house construction, begun in 1838, required a four-year effort. Important landscape design decisions were made early on. Notably, the house location was selected. This was a dramatic, barren field set 135 feet above the Hudson River and commanding broad views over the Tappan Zee. The house was to stand in baronial splendor as a piece of Gothic sculpture. A. J. Davis's watercolor drawings show the house design as executed on its open site (Figure 81). The *porte-cochere* and main entry door were on the east, and services were discreetly handled on the north side of the house at a hidden, basement level. A stable area was developed away from the house to the southeast, screened by the lay of the land, older trees and new plantings. An approach drive, which Philip Paulding called "the lane," was installed from the public road. No doubt river access was also established at this date, of use in off-loading the Sing-Sing marble and other building supplies needed for the house construction.

Initially, there is the sense that Knoll's potential for landscape gardening was made difficult by the exposed character of the grounds. One commentator complained that:

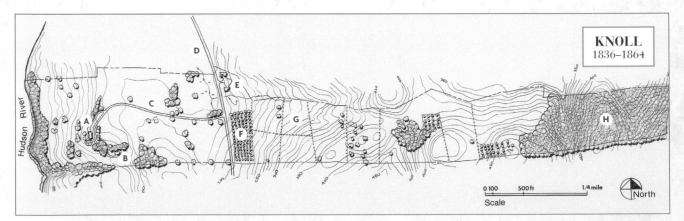

Figure 79. Plan of Knoll (1836–1864), by R. M. Toole. The long, narrow configuration of older riverfront properties is well reflected at the Pauldings' 180-acre parcel that reached 1.5 miles inland. The residential grounds occupied the 70 acres west of the public road. (A) house, (B) stable, (C) entrance drive, (D) public road, (E) Requa farmhouse, barn and kitchen garden, (F) orchards, (G) fenced fields and (H) woodlot.

South of the village [Tarrytown], among other things, I noticed a Gothic pile of marble, of such dimensions that I was at a loss whether to name it a cottage or a palace, and wished only that some enchanter's wand would call up around it a few old oaks and elms.[97]

Several accounts assert that conditions would be much improved, as one said, "when the estate is put in complete order, and the lawns and shrubberies in growth."[98] Still, the absence of old trees attested to the skill needed to integrate the new work with the conditions at hand in 1838. It seems the Pauldings, and by extension, A. J. Davis, celebrated the Requa's agricultural landscape as a muse. The open ground that prompted the name "Knoll" was also treated as a primary landscape feature, in acceptance of the genius of the place. The prominent, perch-like setting was called by one visitor "a bold bank of the Hudson," from which the house "commands ... the noblest prospects"[99] (Figure 82).

A.J. Davis, on his periodic site visits during house construction, can be presumed to have offered his advice and comments on aspects of the landscape layout, consultation inherent in the integrated nature of

Figure 80. Lyndhurst. Considered the preeminent Gothic-style house in America, the original landscape development was in the complementary Picturesque design mode. Courtesy of Lyndhurst, National Trust for Historic Preservation.

the design project. Davis had great interest in landscape design issues, and he felt the primacy of the landscape deeply. His allegiance to romantic themes in architecture attested to the essential fusion of site and building. It was fundamental to his thinking. While no drawn plan of Knoll survives from this early period, and the extent of Davis's influence over landscape gardening at Knoll is undocumented, his very presence suggests at a minimum the informed, but informal, role he is known to have provided elsewhere. It is possible that his influence on Knoll's landscape layout was decisive, but the record does not prove this.

Certainly, important landscape design decisions were made during A. J. Davis's period of consultation. For Davis, and for the Pauldings, careful consideration of the landscape—its layout and appearance—was a deliberate process. Davis stayed involved with the project and maintained a friendship with Philip Paulding, who shared Davis's enthusiasm for the picturesque aesthetic implicit in the work. It can be said with certainty that, given the romantic viewpoints, the development at Knoll proceeded in close visual harmony with the natural situation.

Sometime in 1840, before the house was completed, A. J. Davis wrote a brief description of the Paulding site for A. J. Downing's use as Downing prepared the 1st edition of *Landscape Gardening*. Downing had not visited the property. Davis's narrative provided the earliest evidence that landscape improvements, following a conscious landscape design approach, had begun. Davis noted the site's "agreeable diversity," where, from the house:

Figure 81. Watercolor Showing the Original House at Knoll from East, by A. J. Davis, 1838. The house was a Gothic-Revival edifice set on a true knoll, as shown here in the architect's rendering. To the west the Hudson River is fully exposed in a panorama that extended from the Palisades, left, to the Village of Nyack, seen here to the right of the house. Courtesy of the Metropolitan Museum of Art.

Figure 82. *Panorama of the Hudson River* (detail showing Knoll & Sunnyside), by William Wade, 1845. In this artist's view of the Hudson's eastern shore, Washington Irving's Sunnyside is shown set low on the river, an embowered *cottage ornée*. It is overlooked by the Pauldings' Knoll, with the house set majestically in its austere, exposed setting. Each property is expressive of the genius of the place. Courtesy of Historic Hudson Valley.

a wide terrace, with stone parapets ... on three sides of the building, leading to a remarkably picturesque lawn of rock and clump; surrounded by plantations of the greatest variety of shrub and evergreens, yet young, but which age will still improve.[100]

The "terrace" was a formalized level lawn area lying south and east of the piazza (veranda). As designed by A. J. Davis, its limits were traced by a raised stone curb, marked at the corners with ornamental "stone parapets." Although shown on all the drawings, including those of later additions, there is no evidence that this stonework was ever installed.

Davis's mention of the "remarkably picturesque lawn of rock and clump" referred to the parkland along the river, west of the house, where large exposed bedrock formed landscape features. A ravine provided topographic interest along the south side of the property. "Plantations of the greatest variety" referred to wooded areas in the ravine, along the river, and on the sloping ground below the house, as well as to new plantings set out around the new house. The existing vegetation was enhanced with new trees placed in groves and singly, and shrubbery "yet young."

The drama of the knoll, as an exposed platform on which the house stood with enhanced monumentality, was especially evident in the arc of open ground to the west. From this raised viewpoint, a wild, boundless landscape of immense scale was dramatically presented. Trees were retained and planted east and immediately north and south of the house, but sparingly in the arc towards the west. The outcroppings of rock were highlighted in the middle ground. Native eastern red

cedars (*Juniperus virginiana*), a narrow, sculptural evergreen that did not intrude on the river prospects, were planted (or retained) around the rocky outcrops, providing interest and scale (Figure 83). Along the river bank and up into the deep ravine that followed the south property line, native woods were apparently retained. Several large scarlet oaks (*Quercus coccinea*), black oaks (*Q. velutina*), and sycamores (*Platanus occidentalis*) remain in these wooded areas. On the north boundary, despite the narrow property, the undulating meadows of Knoll melded with the neighboring fields of the old Requa farm, so that a unified effect was preserved with only a fence line distinguishing the separate ownerships. In this way the Pauldings "borrowed" the adjoining landscape as part of the consistent rolling foreground to views northwest over the wide Tappan Zee towards Hook Mountain and Haverstraw Bay, and beyond to the Highlands, seen twenty-five miles away on a clear day. This expansive prospect was certainly the site's most spectacular, but the southwest view from the house toward the Palisades was more intimate and well-arranged. This orientation looked out onto a more irregular, smaller-scaled foreground landscape. Some garden improvements seem to have been initiated in the middle ground at an early date. Paths were laid out in this area, passing through the rocky ground and a grove of older trees and crossing over to the neighboring property to the south, towards Sunnyside, as well as leading down to the river edge.

While the immediate house area was very open, stands of trees were planted nearby and these, together with the few existing trees, were intended as backdrops, providing future shelter for the house on its eastern side. Many of these are seen as semi-mature trees in photographs taken in the 1860s and '70s, and were exactingly delineated on a survey plan prepared in 1873 (Figures 84). The designed landscape at Knoll was essentially unadorned parkland, exhibiting a wild, natural appearance. The design was a romantic evocation that exploited the site's natural variety, but aimed for a simple, dramatic look. Ultimately, the Tappen Zee encompassed all, integrating architecture and farm with nature in a coherent and vastly scaled visual whole. In this way the garden experience was fused with the experience of the wider regional setting.

The approach drive from the public road was also a primary design element. Entering at a spot that avoided wet ground, the driveway curved in a wide arc, looping to the edge of the steep grade fronting the river before turning south and approaching the house obliquely along the edge of the knoll. While documentation regarding Knoll is limited, there do not seem to have been ornamental outbuildings or built garden features dotting the landscape as at Montgomery Place, Blithewood and elsewhere. Could it be that the Pauldings were uninterested in the derivative aspects of this type of embellishment? Was the more natural, truly Picturesque style, highlighting, for example, "a picturesque lawn of rock and clump," accepted as a worthy substitute? As far as it is known, there were no floral features at Knoll. It may be that flowers were restricted to the kitchen garden, as was done elsewhere in this period.

Figure 83. Photograph Showing View to the West from Lyndhurst, by Rogers, c. 1870–73. The view looks towards the Hudson River about thirty years after the Pauldings' initial development. The cedar trees were associated with several rocky outcrops that seem to have been kept as foreground features in the otherwise open parkland down to the river. Today there are no views of the river from this location because of the growth of vegetation. Courtesy of Lyndhurst, National Trust for Historic Preservation.

These clues suggest that Knoll was an early example of the no-frills, fully natural Picturesque that would be the epitome of Hudson Valley landscape gardening in the decades to come. No illustrations better represent this than the starkly rendered drawings of the house by A. J. Davis (Figure 81). Taken together, they show the landscape that existed during the Paulding period. It was a landscape design carefully and consciously composed to evoke an idealized, inherently American sense of place.

At its inception, the quality of the Pauldings' work was widely praised. A July 1843 article entitled "The Architects and Architecture of New York," published in the New York City periodical *Brother Jonathan*, described Philip Paulding as "quiet, gentlemanly and unpretending," and asserted that at his country seat:

> the same fitness and beauty of proportion are found to pervade every part. ... There is, too, something aristocratic, in the best sense of the word, (which we take

to be 'gentlemanly') in those gorgeous windows of enameled glass; the lofty halls ... the gothic sculptures ... lawns and terraces, —all these are found in the estate of Mr. Paulding, and they will remain a perpetual monument of a pure and cultivated taste.

William Paulding's old political nemesis, Philip Hone, did not appreciate the Gothic Revival house, but concluded that "the situation, the prospect, and the form of the grounds [at Knoll] are all admirable."[101] Andrew Jackson Downing, working closely from A. J. Davis's description, called the property "Paulding's Manor" (to the Pauldings' chagrin) and said that the house was:

> Situated on a promontory ... it commands noble prospects from three of its sides; of the Tappen Zee, Haverstraw Bay, and the lofty and striking Palisades. ... the surface of the grounds is bold and well varied; and when the ornamental plantations arrive

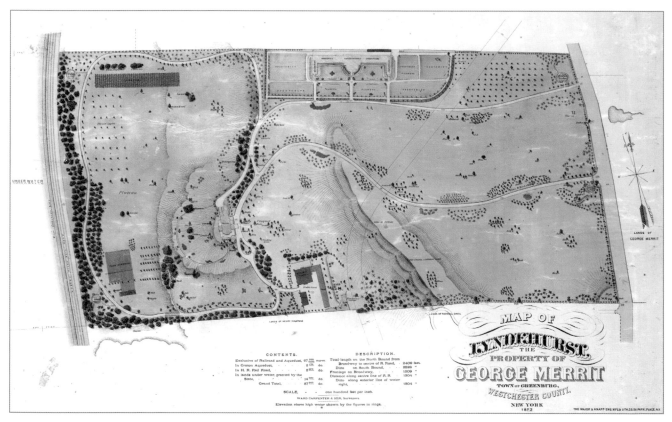

Figure 84. Plan of Lyndhurst in the Merritt Period, by Ward Carpenter, surveyor, 1873. An unusually detailed plan shows the extensive changes undertaken at Knoll after the Paulding period. Notable at the renamed "Lyndehurst" is the large greenhouse complex that extended across the north side of the property (top). Also, the clumped tree plantings along the driveway and cultivated crops (including vineyards) along the river are examples of the lavish landscape developed in the post–Civil War period. These embellishments altered the simple Picturesque composition of the Pauldings' original work. Courtesy of Lyndhurst, National Trust for Historic Preservation.

Figure 85. Photograph Showing East Side of the House at Lyndhurst, by Rogers, c. 1867. This photograph depicts the large addition added by George Merritt to the north (right) side of the original house (compare Figure 81). Older trees on the north, east and south sides of the house, planted by the Pauldings, are also shown. The emerging maturity of several linden trees apparently inspired Merritt's renaming the property "Lyndhurst." Courtesy of Lyndhurst, National Trust for Historic Preservation.

at maturity, the effect of the building will be greatly heightened. ... the Arcaded piazza, and wide terrace with stone parapets, affording shelter and shade, as well as an agreeable promenade.

The Picturesque design era at Knoll was fleeting. After the house was completed, in 1842, William and his wife Maria lived there with Philip for nine years. In 1851 Philip married, but remained on the property. Two children were born, and Philip settled down as a gentleman farmer for a time, active in the Westchester County Society of Agriculture and Horti-culture. In 1852 he is documented as exhibiting a prize pig in a local fair. General William Paulding, age eighty-three, died early in 1854 and Philip Paulding inherited Knoll. Then, early in 1856, Philip's wife, taking their two young children, left the

property after a marital dispute. The Pauldings' life at Knoll can be said to conclude at this point, less than five years before the Civil War. Within several months Philip had leased the house and river front. He had financial problems and lived the remaining eight years of his life at the old Requa farmhouse east of the public road. In these years, tenants occupied the Gothic house and riverfront site. It was eventually sold to a wealthy merchant, George Merritt, in 1864. Philip died a few months later.

Late-nineteenth-century commentators reported on the conditions at Knoll after Philip Paulding's death. These accounts are telltale in describing the Picturesque landscape gardening and the changing fashion that was then impacting landscape design in America. The descriptions were offered as a contrast to the extensive "improvements" of the wealthy new owner, George Merritt. Thirty years after Philip Paulding's death, the intentional Picturesque landscape design at Knoll was seen as having been simply unimproved. For example, a local historian, writing in 1886, said the land around the Pauldings' house out to the public road was "meadows ...while the part on the west, between the house and the river, consisted of hills and ravines lying wild in a state of nature."[102] The "meadows ... hills and ravines" in a "state of nature" was a fitting, if unwitting, description of Philip Paulding's Picturesque landscape at Knoll.

The later history of this property is of interest for the total redesign of the landscape that occurred after the Civil War (Figure 84). George Merritt named the property "Lyndenhurst" (also spelled Lyndehurst and today, Lyndhurst) in consequence of some fine specimens of linden trees (*Tilia cordata*) planted during the Paulding years. Several of these remain to this day. Undertaking extensive development, Merritt nearly doubled the house size, creating today's mansion. In less than five years Merritt also built a number of cottages and a large greenhouse on the sixty-eight-acre riverfront parcel and implemented a major new landscape design scheme. These changes virtually obliterated and redefined the pastoral, natural-appearing landscape maintained earlier by the Pauldings. While A. J. Davis was recalled for the house additions and alterations, and no doubt offered opinions on the landscape, he was not directly involved in the landscape makeover.

This work was under the supervision of Ferdinand Mangold, a German master gardener who had immigrated to the United States in 1852. Together, George Merritt and Ferdinand Mangold embellished the site and redefined its landscape aesthetic, replacing Picturesque landscape gardening with an obviously

Figure 86. Photograph Showing the Grounds at Lyndhurst, 2009, by Steve Benson. Today, the landscape at historic Knoll features specimen trees from the elaborate Victorian-era plantings of George Merritt's ownership. Romantic-era Knoll, its house so distinguished by an exposed, heroic setting overlooking a vast Hudson River panorama, now commands only limited views to the river.

artificial scheme that included elaborate ornamental displays and the arboretum-like exhibition of plant materials. The Merritt-era landscape belonged to the Victorian aesthetic. It was, when fully developed in the mid-1870s, possibly the most expansive and finest example of J. C. Loudon's "Gardenesque" style of design ever built in America. It is remembered that A. J. Downing had included the Gardenesque in his Beautiful design mode as a contrast to the Picturesque. It was a decorative approach that appealed to the newly wealthy barons of industry and commerce intent on opulence and status. George Merritt fit this description. Knoll was redesigned, and renamed, for the "Gilded Age." ❧

CHAPTER 9

MILLBROOK AND KENWOOD

Blithewood, Sunnyside and Knoll illustrate that the late 1830s and early 1840s were critical years of change in landscape gardening along the Hudson. The quality of the new work was determined by the attributes of the sites, featuring Hudson River frontage. The knowledge, sophistication, and what A. J. Downing called the "taste" of wealthy patrons were also critical factors to the production of evocative landscape design effects. Sunnyside and Knoll were not unique, as an investigation of two other sites, Millbrook and Kenwood, both associated with A. J. Davis, will attest. While neither has survived to the present day, both are seen as typical of many others, illustrating the fate of ephemeral works of nineteenth-century landscape gardening on the Hudson.

Close to Sunnyside and Knoll was Millbrook, at Tarrytown. In 1839, Henry Sheldon, an urbane silk merchant and friend of Washington Irving, commissioned A. J. Davis to design an elegant Gothic Revival cottage on the property. It was highlighted in the 1st edition of *Landscape Gardening* (1841) (Figure 87). Unlike Knoll, the house was a wooden structure, a larger version of Donaldson's prototypical Gothic cottage at Blithewood. A. J. Downing called Sheldon's house another example of the "Rural Gothic mode, worthy of the study of the amateur." Downing apparently visited Millbrook in October 1840. He concluded that it was "one of the best specimens of this kind of residence on the river." The Millbrook cottage was set close to an attractive stream that led to the Hudson, and considerable landscape gardening was undertaken by Shelton with this stream as a focus, as described by a local historian:

> No pains have been spared in laying out the adjoining grounds and plantations. ... A small stream running through a deep and woody glen has been obstructed in various places by rock work, and thus forms several artificial cascades. Some close walks, winding by the stream, conduit to a large fall situated at the glen's mouth. The scenery about the falls is extremely fine embracing a lovely view of the Hudson River.[103]

Figure 87. Engraving Showing Millbrook, from *Landscape Gardening* by A. J. Downing (1841). Built during the late 1830s, when picturesque domestic architecture was first becoming popular, A. J. Downing cited Henry Sheldon's house as "another example of the Rural Gothic mode" and concluded that it and "numerous other cottages now building, or in contemplation ... show how fast the feeling for something more expressive and picturesque, is making progress among us." As was typical, A. J. Davis, who designed the house, provided Downing with the drawing or watercolor used for this engraving.

Philip Hone, the New York City tastemaker and diarist, visited Millbrook in September 1839. He commented that Henry Sheldon had "ornamented the grounds, and among other improvements converted a tumbling, noisy brook into a series of cascades, and made a succession of shady walks and rural seats, enough to turn the brain of a romantic seeker after the beauties of nature."[104] In 1840, in one of his earliest letters to A. J. Davis, A. J. Downing also praised this stream treatment, saying, "Mr. Sheldon has made quite a gem of [it] ... along the stream or inlet on the south portion of his grounds."[105]

The planned view of the Hudson River from the lawn terrace fronting Henry Sheldon's cottage was highly regarded. It balanced man's vernacular imposition into the natural world in a way that created a heightened landscape effect. Riverside buildings in the view were apparently modified by Sheldon to serve as romantic "eye catchers" in the larger river scene. A local historian reported that "the old Van Weert mill has been transformed into a Swiss cottage and boat house." Washington Irving weighed in, noting in a letter "the superb view which it [Sheldon's house] commands."[106]

All this has now disappeared beneath highways and suburban land use. So, too, have numerous other landscape gardens created in the southern Hudson Valley during the 1830s, '40s and '50s. Their owners were seldom prominent historic personages, and the properties have not been preserved as historic sites. But they were indicative of their times and so helped define their era. As at Henry Sheldon's Millbrook, several of the most notable of these "lost landscapes" were unabashedly Picturesque designs reflective of the fully natural, artistically austere, even stark qualities evident at Knoll. It was a landscape garden aesthetic now understood as indicative of the Hudson Valley's Romantic period.

This trend can be pleasantly followed to another of A. J. Davis's projects, at a property south of Albany called Kenwood. This was the home of Joel Rathbone (1806–1863), a successful businessman who retired in 1841 at age thirty-five to the pleasure of creating a country seat. Rathbone's house was another Gothic Revival edifice, and the landscape was one of the more notable garden achievements along the Hudson in this accomplished era. Unfortunately, the results did not last long. Rathbone's landscape declined rapidly without its master's hand after the property was sold in 1858. Kenwood became a religious and educational center. In 1867 the house was demolished. Extensive new construction followed. While the property's gatehouse survives (Figure 90), today's Kenwood reflects little of its residential past and landscape gardening.

But the history was impressive. A. J. Davis's involvement with Kenwood began in 1840 when he was commissioned to design Rathbone's house (Figure 88). As at Knoll, this was an early Gothic design with a regional reference, quickly praised by A. J. Downing as "one of the finest specimens of the Gothic, or Pointed style of architecture in this country." As to the landscape, Downing visited at an early date, possibly the summer of 1841. Then, as late as the summer of 1844, he and his wife were guests at Kenwood, suggesting there had been an ongoing involvement that may well have influenced Rathbone's landscape decisions.[107] Downing's published comments on Kenwood appeared in the 1st edition of *Cottage Residences* (1842) and were then edited and included in subsequent editions of *Landscape Gardening*. Downing made it clear that Kenwood was impressive for its extensive Picturesque-style designed landscape.

In 1842, Downing was working closely with A. J. Davis. Davis had provided drawings and examples of residential architecture that helped illustrate Downing's flourishing writings. Davis's collaboration allowed Downing to write more creditably on architectural matters. In response, Downing provided promotional help, mentioning "A. J. Davis, Esq., Architect" in the first line of his article on Kenwood. While enamored of Davis's Gothic work, Downing kept returning to Kenwood's landscape gardening, which was his expertise. He made it clear that the house design would have been less impressive if not for the natural attributes of the site, "supported by the corresponding intricacy and variety of the trees and foliage around it, which are here in admirable keeping with the picturesque outlines of the edifice."

Indeed, Kenwood was the perfect romantic and picturesque ensemble. The property had a long and notable history that gave Rathbone's project instant lineage, including Native American heritage, an attribute much prized by romantics and often lacking at other Hudson Valley properties. Kenwood was the famed "Lower Hollow" of the colonial period, where a substantial stream, the Normanskill, came to the Hudson, thundering through a deep gorge just to the west of Kenwood. By 1630 a Dutchman, Norman Bradt, had settled the flats at the mouth of the gorge, but his presence was preceded by a large Native American village, *Tawacentha* ("Place of the Departed Spirits"). The Indian name referred to the adjacent hillsides, where Kenwood's acres sheltered numerous native burials. In 1847 one reporter romantically described these as "sacred sepulchers."[108] A later history claimed that remains were discovered during construction of

Figure 88. Watercolor Showing Kenwood House, by A. J. Davis, 1842. The stepped gable above the *porte-cochere* was A. J. Davis's gesture to Albany's Dutch heritage, but this is otherwise a fine Gothic-style edifice set in a dramatic, elevated landscape with wooded ravines framing the house grounds opening to river views towards the southwest. Courtesy of Avery Library, Columbia University.

Rathbone's farm and that one lay, as a sort of memorial, beneath the lawn terrace fronting the Kenwood house. In this period, a blend of facts and fiction contributed to the romantic allure of Kenwood.

Kenwood's forested ravines were described by A. J. Downing as a "wild and densely wooded hill, almost inaccessible ... of considerable extent, commanding an extensive view of the Hudson." The forested areas were so characteristic of the property that:

> The preference was given [by Rathbone] to this site, as its natural picturesqueness and intricacy seemed to be admirably in keeping with the style of building. ... There is great variety of surface, caused by the undulations of the ground, upon this area, which will eventually, if proper advantage is taken in this circumstance, cause the demesne to appear of large extent.

Downing left no doubt that Rathbone's landscape was in the Picturesque design mode, something of a wooded version of the Pauldings' Knoll. The forested conditions meant that considerable acreage needed to be carefully and selectively cleared of vegetation in order to sculpt out the house site, lawns and meadows. At the time of his visit, Downing felt that Rathbone's clearing work had been done with "great taste" and respect for the property's "natural expression," a reference to the *genius loci*:

> It is found much easier to produce, in a short time, a satisfactory effect by thinning out and improving a suitable natural wood, than by planting and raising up new growths of sylvan

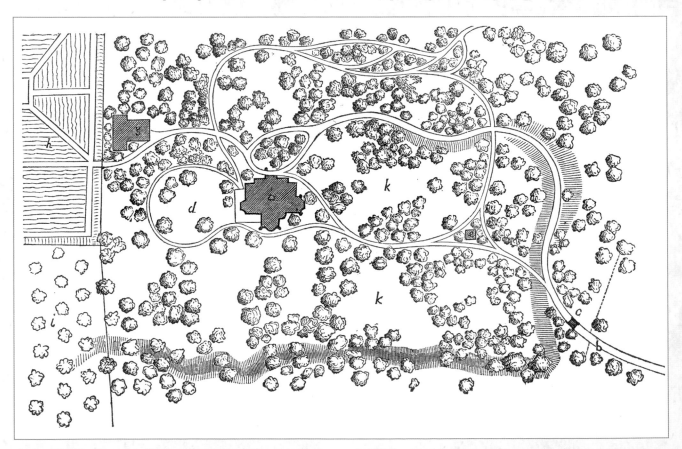

Figure 89. Plan of Kenwood, from *Cottage Residences* by A. J. Downing (1842). The plan (north is to the top) shows the approach drive from the gatehouse on the public road (lower right), at "b," crossing the rustic bridge at "c," and from there to the house on a sinuous route through a wooded ravine, ending at a looped arrival. The stable and kitchen gardens lay beyond to the west. Parkland, cleared from former woodland, surrounded the house, "k." There were river views to the southeast.

accessories where none are already existing. ... [Difficulty] lies in thinning out and opening the wood judiciously—in seizing on the finer portions to be left, and selecting such as may with greatest advantage, be cleared away.

For A. J. Downing, Kenwood's "greatest charm" was "its quiet, secluded shades, full of wildness, only sufficiently subdued by art to heighten its natural beauty." Some of the layout and design features of Kenwood were described by Downing, and he included with the text a site plan, possibly first drawn by A. J. Davis, that showed the grounds close to the house (Figure 89). The published site plan seems to have been drawn initially as a proposal or an illustrative sketch. A later, more accurate,

surveyed drawing of the property shows changes made in the arrangements as it evolved over time.

Downing began his written tour of Kenwood with the entrance road, which was cut into a steep slope leading to the public road along the river. The surviving Gothic-style gatehouse matched the house, extending the architectural design theme to the property's entrance (Figure 90). Once inside the gate, the drive crossed a stream where a "pretty rustic bridge" was erected, "constructed of the roots and stems of the trees felled in opening the road." The roadway was overlooked by "a rustic pavilion or summer-house, on a knoll." Downing included a sketch of this pavilion (Figure 91). It was a truly rustic affair, built around a large live tree, with rough logs forming columns holding up a thatched roof. No

Figure 90. Photograph Showing the Gatehouse at Kenwood, 2009, by Steve Benson. Laid out in the early 1840s, the driveway from the public road entered the site on an angle, a decidedly Picturesque arrangement. While long ago developed as a religious institution, Kenwood's Gothic-style gatehouse remains from the site's residential origins.

Figure 91. Engraving Showing Rustic Pavilion at Kenwood, from *Cottage Residences* by A. J. Downing (1842). This decidedly picturesque feature, with its thatched roof and construction around a large tree trunk, was sited on a knoll near the house. Of Kenwood, Downing concluded, "the greatest charm of this residence ... will be the novelty and contrast experienced in coming directly from the highly artificial and populous city [Albany] ... to its quiet, secluded shades, full of wildness, only sufficiently subdued by art to heighten its natural beauty."

historic image of the bridge of "roots and stems" survives, but Downing's description evokes a highly Picturesque crossing.

The house was approached off an egg-shaped loop focused on the *porte-cochere* and the Dutch stepped gable, as at Sunnyside, that could belong only on the Hudson. All around was embowered parkland. Towards the river was the open lawn terrace, "enlivened by groups of flowering shrubs and plants." No separate floral features were described, but these may have been included in a portion of the kitchen garden. Given the extensive and varied scenery close at hand, footpaths led away from the house in all directions, and these were important in determining the experience of moving through the landscape. Downing admired:

> The long and intricate walk, which may be led at pleasure a long distance beneath the shady, embowering branches of tall beeches, stately maples, and melancholy pines, now threading little dells filled with mosses and ferns, and dark with forest verdure, and again emerging into sunny glades, opened among the forest trees here and there.

At age fifty-two, Joel Rathbone sold Kenwood and eventually moved to Europe. By 1865 he was dead, and much of the Kenwood landscape was already altered. A history of Albany County, published that year, remembered that "Kenwood, which [Rathbone] laid out and beautified, and where for many years he resided, furnishes ample evidence of his cultivated and exquisite taste. ... [he was] a man of noblest virtues."[109]

CHAPTER 10

LOCUST GROVE

With David Hosack at Hyde Park, Washington Irving at Sunnyside, the activities of A. J. Davis and A. J. Downing, and the eager romantics Robert Donaldson, Philip Paulding, Henry Sheldon and Joel Rathbone, landscape gardening was of interest to some remarkable men along the Hudson. In the region's golden age, Locust Grove, today a not-for-profit museum property in Poughkeepsie, further testifies to the era's passion for landscape gardening and to the credentials of its Romantic-period, mostly amateur practitioners.

Samuel F. B. Morse (1791–1872) is certainly one of the most famous Americans to have been involved in landscape gardening. At his death Morse was called "perhaps the most illustrious American of his age." Morse perfected the telegraph, work that revolutionized communication after its formal demonstration on May 24, 1844, when this transmission sent from Washington, D.C., was received at Baltimore: "What hath God wrought!" The telegraph earned Morse great fame and wealth in his lifetime. He responded by developing his home, Locust Grove, and by pursuing landscape gardening along the banks of the Hudson River.

Although renowned as the inventor of the telegraph, Morse was also one of America's important early artists, and this was a critical connection in investigating his landscape gardening.

Morse's background in the arts mirrored the frustrating period before America established its cultural identity.[110] He escaped the limited opportunities available in the United States by visiting England in 1811 to study with English masters and fellow expatriates. It was during this stay that Morse was exposed to landscape design. He appreciated landscape painting's special relationship to landscape gardening, and his broad artistic interests led him to investigate landscape gardening in considerable detail.

Morse's study of Thomas Whately's important work, *Observations on Modern Gardening* (1770), was an influence on his artistic theories (see page 5), but he was also widely informed and familiar, for example, with the writings of Uvedale Price and Richard Paine Knight, the picturesque improvers. While Morse pursued his painterly art, he also studied artistic theory and positioned himself as a promoter of art appreciation in the young United States.

Morse returned home to modest artistic success, primarily as a portrait painter. In 1825 he moved to New York City, where he obtained an important commission for a portrait of the Marquis de Lafayette, then on a triumphal visit to America. In this period Morse also painted an occasional landscape (Figure 93). In 1826 he was influential in founding the National Academy of Design, and he served as its first president. Seeing, as he put it, "an opportunity of doing something for the Arts in this country,"[111] Morse produced a written discourse on landscape gardening as part of his *Lectures on the Affinity of Painting with the Other Fine Arts*, which he delivered to numerous audiences after its initial presentation in the spring of 1826. Morse's lectures discussed all the arts, but his inclusion of landscape gardening was exceptional as one of the earliest and most interesting treatises on the topic to survive from this formative American period. In turn, Morse's documented understanding of landscape gardening is important to a consideration of his home, Locust Grove.

Morse's lectures offered a unique analytic discourse on the position of landscape gardening as related to the other fine arts, written by an intellectual and sophisticated American. He stressed the crucial theoretical foundation on which the study of any art is predicated. The result was a unique contribution to the history of landscape gardening in America. Morse's lectures prefigured the work of the writers on landscape gardening who would come later, notably A. J. Downing, who was an eleven-year-old boy when Morse first delivered his systematic, learned talk to a New York City audience.

Figure 92. The House at Locust Grove. The Italianate style, with the deep *port-cochere* and piazza (veranda), provided shelter at the house and altered the geometry of the earlier Federal-style edifice. Courtesy of Locust Grove.

Morse began his lectures by describing three "perfect fine arts—poetry, music and landscape gardening." These he considered "perfect" because they did not obtain their effects from a mixture of other arts. Morse described landscape gardening as:

The Art of arranging the objects of Nature in such a manner as to form a consistent landscape ... the art of hiding defects by interposing beauties; ... of contriving at every point some consistent beauty so that the imagination in every part of the theatre of his performance [i.e., the landscape] may revel in a continual dream of delight. [The landscape gardener's] main object is to select from Nature all that is agreeable, and to reject or change every thing that is disagreeable.

The objective of landscape gardening, as with all the fine arts, was to "please the imagination," and the practitioner must:

... possess the mind of the Landscape Painter, but he paints with the objects themselves ... it is not the laborer who levels a hill, or fills a hollow, or plants a grove that is the landscape gardener, it is he alone who with the "prophetic eye of taste," sees prospectively the full grown forest in the young plantation, and selects with a poet's feeling passages which he knows will affect agreeably the imagination.

In discussing design theory Morse favored landscape gardens that revealed what he called nature's "original character" over any artificial intrusion, championing the Picturesque as understood by Downing. "Nature is full of objects that naturally affect the imagination," wrote Morse. Landscape gardening was "not arbitrary nor dependent on mere authority, but ... [has its] origin deeply rooted in the principles of nature." Morse went on to provide some practical ideas and even included a "before" and "after" sketch of a fictitious residential landscape improved by the principles of landscape gardening.

Figure 93. Engraving Showing Landscape and House, from painting by Samuel F. B. Morse, from *Rural Residences*, by A. J. Davis, 1837. A. J. Davis's book was America's first pattern book for picturesque architecture. Samuel F. B. Morse illustrated the book's title page, emphasizing Davis's theme that the house was only a feature of the larger, unified landscape composition. The image shows Morse's and Davis's sensitivity to the fine art of landscape gardening. Courtesy of The Metropolitan Museum of Art.

Morse remained actively involved with the arts until in 1837 when, at age forty-six, he was rejected for an important commission to paint a historical subject at the Capitol rotunda in Washington, D. C. After this disappointment Morse turned his full attention to the telegraph (he had been mulling over the idea for several years) and gave up painting altogether.

For Morse, technological invention proved far more lucrative than life as a struggling artist. After a frantic decade of perfecting and demonstrating the telegraph's potential, Morse was in the position to acquire a farm property on the Hudson River and to practice the art form he had considered so carefully as a younger man. The development of Locust Grove can rightly be called one of Samuel F. B. Morse's most important artistic works, given the place of landscape gardening in the arts in this historic period.

The history of the Locust Grove landscape is fascinating. In October 1846, then a widower with grown sons living in rented quarters in New York City, Morse wrote to his brother of his interest in securing a permanent home. Speaking of his twenty-three-year-old son, Morse wrote: "Charles has little to do. ... He is desirous of a farm and I have made up my mind to indulge him. ... I shall go up the river in a day or two and look in the vicinity of Po'keepsie."[112] A year later, with the income from the telegraph more secure, Morse visited the Poughkeepsie area again and wrote to his brother that he had been "informed of a place for sale, south of the village two miles, on the bank of the river. ... I have this day concluded a bargain for it. There are about one hundred acres. I pay for it $17,500." Morse called the property "far superior" and laced his description with references to landscape gardening:

I am afraid to tell you of its beauties and advantages. It is just such a place as in England could not be purchased for double the number of pounds sterling. Its "capabilities," as the landscape gardeners would say, are unequalled. There is every variety of surface, plain, hill, dale, glen, running stream, and fine forests, and every variety of distant prospect. . . I will not enlarge [on the description]: I am congratulated by all in having made an excellent purchase.[113]

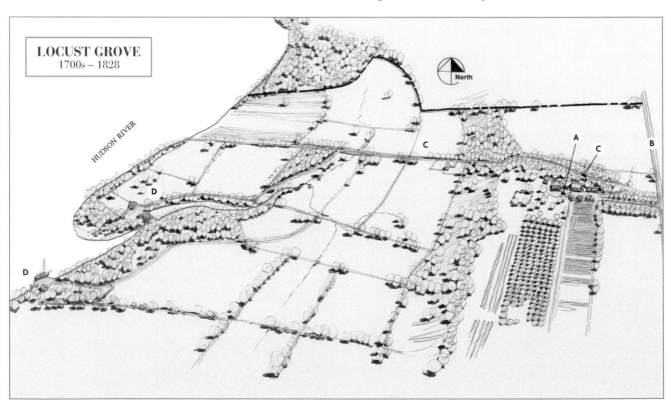

Figure 94. Bird's-Eye View of Locust Grove (1700s–1828), by R. M. Toole. Samuel F. B. Morse's Locust Grove was developed from a large colonial farm owned initially by Henry Vanderburgh, who moved to the area in about 1712. Later, a farmhouse and farm complex (A) and adjacent fields were developed on the elevated "fertile plain" on the east side of the property along the public road (B). From the house site above the bluff, a rough road (C) led down through a ravine to the river where a sawmill and dock (D) were located. By the end of the eighteenth century, much of the land was cleared and arranged in a pattern of open fields.

Figure 95. Photograph Showing Samuel F. B. Morse and Family at Locust Grove, c. 1858. Seated in the driveway on the south side of the porte cochere of the remodeled house at Locust Grove are Samuel F. B. Morse, at the center, flanked by his second wife, Sarah (left), and two of their young children, Cornelia (b. 1851) and William (b. 1853). On the right is Morse's daughter from his first marriage, Susan, and far right, Sarah's mother. Susan's husband, Edward Lind, stands behind his wife, with Morse's son by his first marriage, Finley (b. 1825), standing to the left. Courtesy of Locust Grove.

The parcel was the northern portion of a 700-acre colonial-period farm that had been reduced to 250 acres when purchased by an Irish immigrant named John Montgomery in 1830. Montgomery built an austere Federal-style house close to an old farmhouse. Morse acquired the house and 100 acres of Montgomery's larger property and renamed it Locust Grove.

Morse appreciated the *genius loci*. The site's physical form would be decisive in determining its landscape development. The primary physical feature was a bluff paralleling the Hudson, rising about 100 feet on a precipitous slope about a half mile from the river. At the top of the bluff was a nearly level plateau. Here, the 1830 Montgomery house stood close to the edge, from which a broad panorama opened across the Hudson Valley. The raised plateau had fertile soil and was the center of horticultural activities, including the house grounds, kitchen and flower gardens, and orchards. The riverfront, below the bluff, had been farmland. This area—the foreground of the panoramic views as seen from above—was highly varied, with topography generally falling towards the river but shaped by a stream that crossed the site diagonally, forming a substantial ravine. A smaller brook, which included an attractive waterfall, joined the larger stream near the center of the property. All this runoff reached the Hudson at a cove that had been a river landing in the colonial period. Above the cove, the rocky frontage on the river was punctuated by numerous ridge lines and small hills that gave accent and third-dimension to the land.

After moving to Locust Grove, Morse called the property a "delightful retreat." "The farm ... gains in my affections at every day's residence. ... [The house and] grounds can be gradually improved as means and inclination dictates."[114] From the evidence, it is clear that Morse undertook landscape gardening from the first. In the autumn of 1847, he asked his brother for help, "should [you] chance upon any practical works on Landscape Gardening, with numerous designs, you may get it for me."[115] As an early example of his landscape gardening, Morse built a pond in 1848 located below the little waterfall on the small brook close to where it joined the site's primary stream. The area, Morse said, was developed with great care and he described his daily involvement:

> ... selecting and marking carefully those trees which were to be removed and charging not to cut a single twig that I had not selected and marked. The shade of the trees was calculated and essential for my purpose.[116]

These and similar projects seem to have continued at an ongoing, steady pace for the first five or six years of Morse's residency at Locust Grove.

On August 10, 1848, Morse remarried. He was fifty-seven years old, and his wife, Sarah, was twenty-six. A new family grew to occupy Locust Grove. In July 1849 a son, Arthur, was born, followed by Cornelia in 1851, William in 1853 and Edward, born in 1857 when Morse was sixty-six years old (Figure 95).

Early on, Morse's intended use of his country seat changed when his older son, Charles, who had been "desirous of a farm," married and moved away. Morse commented, "farming is pleasant to talk and think about but it requires a different sort of mind from Charles' to make farming profitable."[117] Morse also sensed that his 100-acre property was not a viable economic entity. In March 1850 he wryly wrote a friend, "I have indeed a farm out of which a farmer might obtain a living, but to me it is a source of expense." In truth, farming had been much reduced in acreage after each of Locust Grove's previous ownerships, a typical situation as the riverfront properties were subdivided. Under these circumstances profitable farming was increasingly difficult. Over time Morse seems to have come to terms with this reality. Locust Grove would be a gentleman's farm, and Morse would involve himself in the property's farm-related activities as a hobby, working with a salaried farmer and gardener.

The owner's change of heart about Locust Grove, from commercial farming to *ferme ornée*, resulted in telltale land transactions. In the spring of 1850, Morse purchased nineteen acres along his south boundary. It was all woodland, and this addition provided a critical buffer on Morse's south boundary line, helping to define his riverfront as a separate place. Notably, no additional farmland was added in this transaction. A year later, Morse complemented the earlier move by selling about one-third of the Locust Grove property (43-plus acres), located along the north property line. This was a substantial parcel of open farmland, awkward for the landscape gardener and separated from the main Locust Grove riverfront by a straight, east-west farm road and adjoining wall/fence lines. With these land transactions Locust Grove was reconfigured into a seventy-six-acre whole where farming was deemphasized and the landscape became a canvas for ornamental improvements.

At the same time Morse directed his attention to his Federal-style house, which he derisively said had "no pretensions to taste."[118] In 1850 he contacted a long-time acquaintance; architect A. J. Davis, then at the height of his career. With Davis's help, Morse sketched his ideas for an extreme makeover. The exterior was remodeled in the Italianate style, transforming it into what one drawing identified as a "Tuscan Villa." A substantial *porte-cochere* was added on the east, while the west was dominated by a tower, called the "campanile," and on the south, by a wraparound veranda or piazza (Figure 96). Services were isolated on the north side of the house. The tower and veranda dominated the level lawn terrace at the bluff edge.

Figure 96. Photograph Showing Locust Grove House from the Southwest, c. 1870. This important photograph shows the lawn terrace near the end of Samuel F. B. Morse's lifetime. Morse is seated (with white beard) on the right, with family members and friends clustered nearby. Note the flower beds on the lawn and vines on the veranda and climbing the walls of the tower. Courtesy of Locust Grove.

The terrace performed as would an Italian "belvedere," being a dramatic overlook towards the river. With the encouragement of his architect, Morse further developed the terrace theme when he raised the ground around the house by about three feet, using a geometrically formed turf bank that traced the house on the south and west sides. The turf banks provided the substantial platform on which the house stood with heightened monumentality.

In front of the house, the bluff was cleared across its entire width. Vegetation was retained only on the flanks to frame the view. Only occasional specimen trees were retained for scale and foreground interest on the sloping bluff face. As the land dropped away, the woodland understory vegetation thickened. The bluff face was an organic composition in constant need of management. Periodically, clearing operations were undertaken to return the desired look.

A. J. Davis visited Morse in Poughkeepsie for the first time in April 1851, spending three days there. He sketched a crude map of the property, entitling it "Morsestan" (Figure 97), but despite this gesture to the landscape there is no evidence that Davis had direct or professional responsibility for any site-related projects. Still, there were landscape design improvements occurring at this time. Certainly Davis can be presumed to

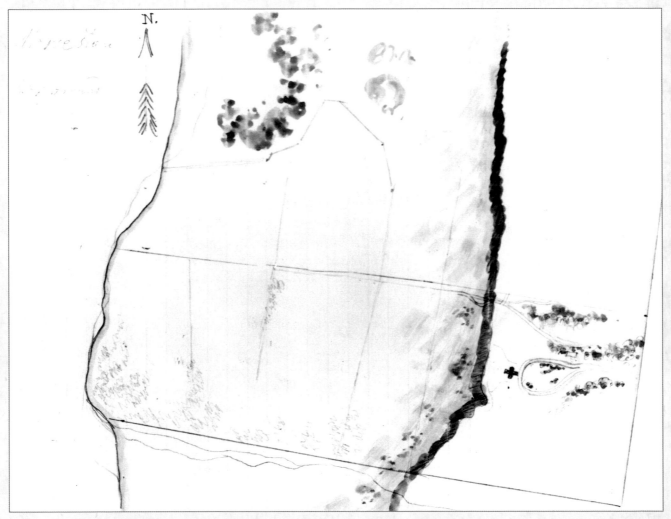

Figure 97. Map of Locust Grove, by A. J. Davis, c. 1851. Inscribed "Morsestan / Plot of ground," this rough drawing shows the Locust Grove property with the house on the far right, fronted by a looped arrival drive. The old Livingston house is shown on the north side of the drive. The so-called Grade Road is shown to the north. The escarpment (bluff) is indicated with the thick black line, and the river frontage extended from there to the river (far left). In this area Davis shows the Grade Road, the wall lines that crossed the property, and the stream that formed the south boundary line. Courtesy of Locust Grove.

have discussed all matters of the property's development with Morse when he visited. This was customary practice, given the close link Davis felt between architecture and landscape design. Davis came to Locust Grove to see the construction in August and in October 1851, and again in the spring of 1852. Then, at the end of the summer of 1852, he wrote, "curious to hear how you find your new house, and what you are doing to make the grounds beautiful."[119] Morse immediately responded, updating Davis on the landscape work. Unfortunately, his letter has not survived, but Davis's subsequent reply confirmed that carefully considered landscape gardening was underway:

> Of course your landscape gardening is going on according to Whately, [Humphry] Repton, [John Claudius] Loudon & Downing, and is immediately to exhibit the most finished illustration of Natural Beauty—the art modestly retiring with the background!

Then, focusing on a landscape issue close to the house, Davis continued:

> Allow me to suggest that you terrace the north side of the house, and so trellis and plant as to balance or symmetrise with the south veranda. Also, that the plantations so approach the house that portions [of the house] only may be seen from any one point, peeping from forth the verdure, and so playing upon the imagination that an idea of great extent of accommodation and an infinite variety of picturesque beauty be presented to the exercised mind.[120]

Two photographs from late in Morse's residency and several contemporary engravings illustrate the completed scene. The photographs, from about 1870, show numerous curvilinear flower beds cut into the lawn (Figure 96). In one view, a circular bed is shown centered on the campanile tower, flanked by at least eight other beds on the north and south. These flower beds were planted seasonally using bulbs, annuals and tender exotics that were over-wintered in a nearby greenhouse. These types of bedded-out displays were very typical of taste in the post–Civil War, Victorian period.

East of the house was the entrance driveway and park, with agricultural activities relegated to the south. The entrance park featured a variety of specimen trees, including several maples, spruce and oaks. Closer to the public road, the straight entrance driveway was lined with rows of black locust trees (*Robinia pseudoacacia*), a typical colonial-era planting that remained from the pre–Locust Grove history. These trees inspired the property's name.

Locust Grove had a long background as a farm, having undergone active development for over a hundred years before Morse's purchase. Remnants from the past were incorporated into Morse's arrangements. Most conspicuous near the house was the old colonial-era farmhouse, which was somewhat dilapidated at the time of Morse's purchase. It was retained and restored as valued accommodation for the hired help, and also as a landscape feature emblematic of the property's past.

Around the old farmhouse, the original ensemble of outbuildings and fenced yards was tidied-up. The stable/carriage house complex, offset northwest of the house, attested to the concern to isolate services and enhance amenity in the house grounds. Away from the house, paths extended along the terrace edge, and rustic seats and features, like urns, were set out on the lawns. A fountain was installed east of the house, centered on the *porte-cochere*. Morse constructed a rustic summerhouse, seen in a later photograph and noted in later diary accounts. It was located along the bluff edge south of the house. From this position a path and flight of rough steps, constructed of logs, were installed leading down the face of the bluff to the riverfront. Below the bluff, a second farmhouse, barn, and perhaps other farm-related outbuildings were constructed before Morse's purchase. This utilitarian complex was retained, but also screened from view.

After Morse's land sales in 1851, the farm road that descended to the river formed Locust Grove's north property line. The original arrangement of fields in the riverfront was established during the active farming decades that preceded Morse's ownership. He altered this old layout. After 1830, and especially during the Morse period, the largely cleared landscape was partially returned to woods (compare Figures 98 and 100). By the close of the Morse residency, only about 30 percent of the riverfront remained open, used as pastures and mown meadows. There were no plowed fields in the riverfront. Morse understood that open land, defined by this wooded boundary, established landscape interest and revealed the inherent variety of a three-dimensional composition. In deciding on this arrangement of wooded versus open ground, Morse effectively created a landscape garden, experienced as a foreground to the western views, and in its details for those following the intricate system of carriage drives that threaded the riverfront landscape.

The stone walls and fence lines that delineated the original fields were important landscape design elements. A map drawn in about 1851 showed four such demarcation lines running north-south in the riverfront. An 1850 deed described these as "cross walls" (Figure 97).[121] The layout of these walls, as modified by Morse, was a deliberate design decision. The two cross walls closest to the river had been constructed in low areas, and so they were not seen in the panoramic view from the house grounds. These hidden walls were preserved. In contrast, the wall closest to the house was located on the exposed east-facing side of a ridge line, fully open to view from the house. In response, sometime after 1851, Morse had this wall dismantled and erected a new wall, probably using the same stones, set several hundred feet farther to the west where it was tucked on the west side of the ridge and hidden from view.

The most interesting of Locust Grove's old fieldstone walls was along the south side of the property running east-west. This wall marked an old survey line established in the eighteenth century. It was a harsh, straight wall, laid out with no concern for the land's natural form. It dipped arbitrarily into a steep ravine and crisscrossed a brook that paralleled it. No doubt unhappy with this awkward wall line, Morse's 1850 purchase of a 300-foot-wide strip of woods south of this wall (discussed earlier) made the old line obsolete as a demarcation. In response, Morse altered the old wall line to an arrangement more sensitive to the land's configuration, removing sections that were especially egregious and respecting the brook's alignment instead of the old wall. Morse's alterations to these earlier wall lines were instances where landscape gardening provided aesthetic improvements to the earlier utilitarian layout.

Figure 98. Photograph Showing Western View from Locust Grove, 1902. This view records the riverfront landscape garden about thirty years after Morse's death. It is the earliest known illustration of the area and shows Morse's designed landscape generally unchanged except for the maturing look of the tree growth in what had been, for Morse, a more open scene. Courtesy of Locust Grove.

Farm fields were maintained within the wall and fence lines. Immediately below the bluff was the "lower flat," about six acres of open ground. The woodland edge that defined this grazing field curved around rocky ground in the northwest corner of the field. A wooded knoll was maintained in the center. On the south, Morse located a fence line along the stream that formed a natural field edge on this side. From above, the arrangement provided a heightened sense of three-dimension and depth of field, a testimony to Morse's subtlety as a landscape gardener.

The most expansive of the agricultural fields in the riverfront was a six-acre meadow maintained on a large rounded hill, later called the "Great Green Hill," that occupied the field closest to the river. East of the Great Green Hill, between it and the lower flat, was a complex area of about six acres bisected by the site's major stream. The landscape here included steep, rocky portions where woodland may have been in place even before Morse's purchase. Generally unsuited to growing crops, or even mowing, this area was otherwise marginal pasture. Under Morse it served the visual concerns of landscape gardening, with grazing severely restricted. Only one small field was left in this central location, the rest being allowed to return to woodland.

Grazing was also reduced in certain areas of the immediate riverfront. This was a sizable area of twelve or thirteen acres and included a headland sixty feet above the river. Except along the immediate shore line and on the rocky slopes, this area seems to have been open ground before Morse's ownership. Afterward, a wide wooded edge was maintained, with trees cleared only in the low gap that was a central feature of the scene from the house. Native vegetation grew along the immediate river edge to screen the railroad (built in 1850) from view.

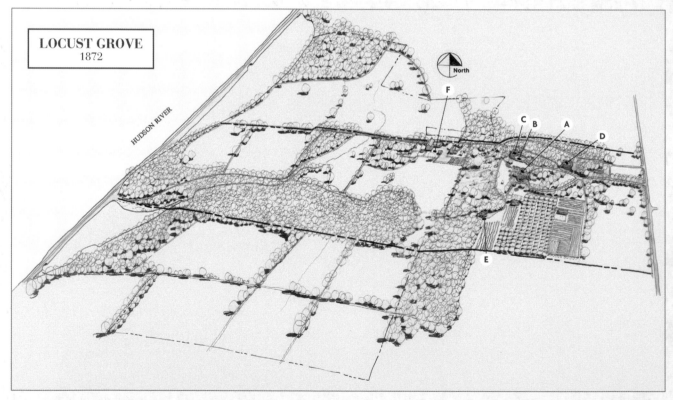

Figure 99. Bird's-Eye View of Locust Grove (1872), by R. M. Toole. Landscape gardening followed Samuel F. B. Morse's purchase of the property in 1847. The Federal-style house (A), built in 1830, was remodeled and the lawn terrace west of the house was enlivened with flower beds and a greenhouse (B). A stable and coach house were screened to the north (C). The old farmhouse (D) was preserved, but the adjoining farm complex was removed. A rustic summerhouse (E) was sited along the bluff to the south. The panoramic view west was a composed "picture," with the riverfront farmland carefully arranged in an artistic composition (compare to Figure 94). A new farm complex was hidden below the bluff (F). The railroad was constructed along the shoreline in 1848–49.

The visual unity of the landscape garden design Morse created in the riverfront was a hallmark of the property in this period. Working on a large scale—most importantly, from the generally fixed vantage point of the upper lawn terrace and house—Morse formed the landscape into a park-like scene, freely borrowing the neighbor's field, the Hudson River and the pastoral backdrop on the western shore to extend and complete the panorama. One writer, in 1914, called it "a picture" where "the whole scene is a unit for the boundaries are distinctly marked"[122] (Figure 98).

While many of the elements of this composition were in place in 1847, Morse enhanced the scheme before 1852 and then maintained it without further changes. The design principles and quality of the work may be evaluated in light of Morse's achievements as an accomplished and learned artist. Discussing painting in 1826, Morse said:

A picture then is not merely a copy of any work of Nature, it is constructed on the principles of Nature.

While its parts are copies of natural objects, the whole work is an artificial arrangement of them similar to the construction of a poem or a piece of music.[123]

Or of a landscape garden, for indeed these thoughts have direct application to landscape gardening as Morse understood it at Locust Grove. Certainly these scenes were "picturesque," as that term was applied in common usage—"like a picture." In addition, Morse's appreciation of the riverfront evolved from its natural situation and its history as farmland, a testimony to the Picturesque design mode as defined by A. J. Downing. The riverfront was a complex design, melding natural elements (native woodland, flowing water, exposed rock, undulating land forms) with vernacular agriculture, forming a pastoral whole. While the land's physical character largely determined the landscape design, the composition of open and wooded areas produced a visually varied and unified arrangement. Morse's reliance on the natural attributes of his landscape led to his claim that it was "as beautiful a landscape prospect as the noble Hudson

Figure 100. Photograph Showing the Western View at Locust Grove, 2009, by Steve Benson. Today, the central view from the house and raised terrace is overgrown (compared with Figure 98). Locust Grove retains only a narrow view to the Hudson River. Restoring visual links to the river is a basic challenge at many of today's historic sites.

affords,"[124] and to his remark to a visitor, "I can not promise you anything here of interest but beautiful natural scenery."[125]

In 1855, with his financial claim to the telegraph assured (by ruling of the U.S. Supreme Court), Morse purchased a house in New York City as his winter residence. After this, the family spent spring through autumn at Locust Grove, with gaps for trips to Europe. In 1859, after an extended stay abroad, a greenhouse was erected north of the house, seen in later photographs. There was also a separate greenhouse, called a "grapery," specifically designed for grape production.

In June 1866 the Morse family went again to Europe and remained there for two years, returning in June 1868. Morse wrote: "the farm looks splendid. Never did the Grove look more charming. Its general features the same, but the growth of trees and shrubbery greatly increased."[126] Thus began Morse's last years at Locust Grove. Despite the inevitable need to manage the rampant vegetation, it is not likely that extensive landscape alterations were made after 1868. None are recorded. Morse spent his last summer at the property in 1871 and died in New York City on April 2, 1872, just short of his eighty-first birthday. Locust Grove became a sporadic home to family members until it was sold out of the Morse family in 1900. By then, Morse's designed landscape, a singular creation, was overgrown, its former farm fields abandoned, so that by the 1970s the riverfront was deemed most valuable as a wildlife sanctuary.

CHAPTER 11

HIGHLAND GARDENS

In the late 1840s, as Samuel F. B. Morse began his landscape gardening at Locust Grove, Andrew Jackson Downing was reaching the apex of his career, having followed the publication of *Landscape Gardening* (1841) and *Cottage Residences* (1842) with the expanded 2nd edition of *Landscape Gardening* (1844) and *Fruits and Fruit Trees of America* (1845). In July 1846 he became the editor of the popular magazine *The Horticulturist*. This lifetime of achievements took less than a decade, with Downing's most elaborate book, *The Architecture of Country Houses*, published in July 1850.

In that very same month Downing journeyed briefly to England. While there, he met and recruited a young architect, Calvert Vaux (1824–1895), who returned with him in September 1850. For about two years Vaux served as an assistant in Downing's expanding architectural practice. While he was not an architect, Downing's writings had established his reputation as a designer and he was increasingly commissioned by private and public clients. Downing's blossoming professional life was cut short by his tragic death in a steamboat accident on the Hudson River only two years after meeting Calvert Vaux. Vaux was left to carry on Downing's legacy (see Chapter 13).

Downing's residential landscape gardening reveals some interesting comparisons vis-à-vis the

Figure 101. Photograph Portrait of Calvert Vaux, no date. Calvert Vaux emigrated from England when he was in his mid-twenties. Less than two years later, his partner, Andrew Jackson Downing, died. Thereafter, Vaux had an accomplished career as an architect and as a "landscape architect," a professional title he coined in about 1863. Courtesy of the National Park Service, Frederick Law Olmsted National Historic Site.

Figure 102. *View from the Lawn* at Highland Gardens, engraving from *The Horticulturist*, January 1853. Highland Gardens was situated less than a quarter mile from the Hudson on an elevated hillside. Views from the grounds were varied, framed by Downing's judicious planting and pruning of the foreground vegetation. Here, the Beacon Hills are seen, looking east.

contemporary work witnessed at Sunnyside, Knoll, Locust Grove and other sophisticated landscapes then being assembled in the Hudson River Valley. Still, Downing's career was founded on horticulture and the intricacies of plant materials; his actual design work in residential landscape gardening seems to have been modest. His advice was often given informally. He rarely guided the development of a house site from its outset. More typically he consulted, usually for a brief period, on portions of already established properties. In fact, only two complete residential landscapes can be definitively attributed to Downing. Appropriately, both are located in his native Hudson River Valley.

A. J. Downing's Hudsonian life story is nearly legendary. A few years before Andrew's birth, his father, Samuel Downing, started a nursery business, selling plants from a small cottage and a twelve-acre property north of Broad Street in the burgeoning village of Newburgh-on-Hudson. The site commanded a magnificent vista to the south, with the wide expanse of the Hudson River backed by the majestic Highlands. Appropriately, the Downing Nursery was eventually christened "Highland Gardens" (Figure 102).

In 1822, Samuel Downing died and his older son, Charles, stepped in to manage the nursery. This allowed Andrew to continue his schooling for ten years, until age seventeen, when he joined the business. Seven years later, in 1839, the Downing brothers divided their holdings. The original cottage, a greenhouse, nursery office and adjoining outbuildings, and about 4 ½ acres, became A. J. Downing's sole possession. At age twenty-four, Downing was now married. His wife Caroline was charming and intelligent. One observer called her "equal to her husband." For their home Downing began construction of a Tudor-

Figure 103. *Garden Front of Mr. Downing's Residence* at Highland Gardens, from the *Magazine of Horticulture*, November 1841. For Downing, the house was "Tudor" in style, which was his early favorite among the various modes of the Gothic Revival. It was largely copied from an English pattern book. The Old World character is replete with oriel window, intricate tracery, chimney pots, and twin decorative towers. The lawn area shown includes several exotics set out in pots, which would have been in the protective greenhouse during the winter. The rustic basket with flowers, far right, was another fanciful lawn ornament.

style, picturesque house adapted from English design sources. It was located in an open landscape a few hundred feet north of his father's workaday cottage and adjacent nursery yards. These facilities remained, serving as infrastructure for the elegant new residence (Figure 103).

Our knowledge of A. J. Downing's early development of Highland Gardens comes primarily from an article by Charles M. Hovey published in November 1841.[127] Hovey knew Downing well, and his background in horticulture produced a creditable and informative description. The narrative included a helpful plan of the site and an illustration (Figure 104). Hovey reported that, while the basic design of the landscape was settled with house construction, the "garden," as the grounds were referred to, was unfinished at this early date.

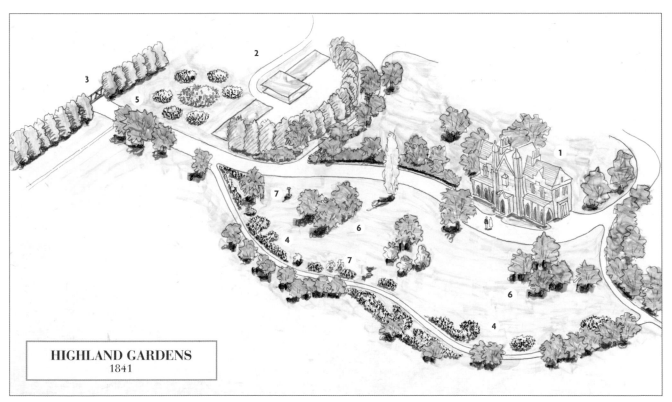

HIGHLAND GARDENS
1841

Figure 104. Bird's-Eye View of Highland Gardens (1841), by R. M. Toole. This aerial view is based primarily on a plan published in 1841. North is to the right. The sketch shows the house set off from the former nursery yards and greenhouse, and the ornamental front lawn that was Downing's earliest efforts at landscaping after house construction two years earlier. Note the many flower beds cut into the lawns. The number keys are as follows: (1) house; (2) nursery (site of gardener's cottage, greenhouses and sheds); (3) carriage entrance onto Broad Street; (4) flower beds cut into the lawn; (5) circular flower beds at entrance; (6) specimen trees; (7) lawn features (sundial, urn, potted plants, etc.).

Figure 105. *Sundial* at Highland Gardens, engraving from *The Horticulturist*, January 1853. The sundial, another of the features set out on the front lawn, was inscribed: "*Horas non nomero nisi serenas*" ("I number none but sunny hours").

Despite this, Downing appears to have had a clear aesthetic in mind for the landscape, and his approach can be shown to have had decidedly "Beautiful" design effects, influenced by the latest English fashion.

The new house stood in a portion of the former nursery grounds. Only a few remnant plantings were preserved as part of the new scheme. Access to the house was provided at an older gateway and carriage entrance on Broad Street. After house construction, Downing replaced the older gates with a design that complemented the Tudor house architecture, a testimony to his intention in creating a unified sense of place. Highland Gardens, the humble nursery operation, was to be skillfully adapted to become Highland Gardens, a stylish country seat. Downing built the house so that an existing evergreen hedge, originally intended as a nursery windbreak, screened the service buildings and yards. The entrance drive bypassed these areas and curved from the new gateway to the front door, approaching from the left—showing the house in the preferred oblique orientation—before circling north

and west to the service areas, where there was a separate gateway (formerly the nursery entrance). The house front faced directly east toward the Hudson River, with a narrow, sloping lawn in the foreground. It was an ideal arrangement on only about two acres.

Beyond the basic layout, Downing's early efforts on the grounds focused on the quarter-acre "embellished" front lawn east of the house. This lawn dropped down a moderate slope to a planted hedgerow of shrubs and trees that separated the new residence from an active agricultural field (soon planted as a vineyard—see Figure 107). From the house, the hedgerow was a natural-appearing bottom frame to the river panorama. Located only ten feet below the elevation of the house, the trees and larger shrubs that made up the hedgerow required thinning and topping to maintain the desired views. One visitor said the hedgerow was "dexterously trimmed" by Downing as it matured.[128]

The treatment of the front lawn was of great interest to Downing. In 1841 it was highly ornamental with multiple features, notably the exotic display of at least fifteen different trees, each set off as a specimen. There was a collection of four different magnolias, and two groups of such widely varied trees as weeping cherry and the Japanese pagoda tree (*Sophora japonica*), besides several mundane natives such as box elder (*Acer negundo*) and arborvitae (*Thuja occidentalis*). As described earlier, this arboretum-like exhibit was a central theme of J. C. Loudon's Gardenesque style, where worthy trees were to be displayed in a way that allowed each to develop its natural form unencumbered by other plants. At Highland Gardens some of these trees may have been holdovers from the nursery grounds, but others were newly planted as part of Downing's residential development.

Even more visually striking than the trees were the lawn's many flower beds (Figure 104). These were cut into the grass as circles, ovals and free-form (so-called "arabesque beds"), planted, said Charles Hovey, with "choice flowers, such as roses, geraniums, fuchias, Salvia patens, fulgens, and cardinalis, etc. ... turned out of pots in the summer season after being wintered in greenhouses or frames." Other beds were composed of "petunias, verbenas ... Phlox Drummondii, nemophilas, nolanas, dwarf morning-glory, etc." Calling this bedding-out approach "modern," Downing later praised it in his writings by saying that "as the object in a flower garden is gayety, this bedding or massing of flowers is certainly the most complete and beautiful mode of attaining it."[129]

"Gayety" ran riot on Downing's front lawn. Together, there were nine separate flower beds with a total bed area of perhaps 3,000 square feet. To this must be added a large formal layout of six circular beds grouped around a center circle in the gravel forecourt of the adjacent greenhouse, clearly on display as a visitor entered the property. In Downing's writings he described this circular layout as an "architectural flower garden" and he contrasted it unfavorably with the turf-cut circular and arabesque beds, which he thought a prettier technique, especially on smaller properties. Charles Hovey called the greenhouse plantings the "flower garden," and it added at least 1,000 square feet of flower beds to those on the front lawn. In 1840 America, Downing's extensive and complex use of bedded-out annuals was atypical. The ideas were imported from English sources, but few indulged themselves with so extensive a display. The botanic embellishments, the varied trees, shrubs and floral presentations, distinguished Highland Gardens as Downing's showplace, the living embodiment of his career. It must also be true that Downing found it handy to have numerous

and skilled nursery laborers available for the installation and maintenance of these flower beds.

Gilding the lily, Downing presented ornamental features on the front lawn, including a fine urn (a copy of the "Warwick Vase" from England), a sundial (which included a "timely" inscription, Figure 105), and a rustic basket planted with flowers, for which Charles Hovey gave construction hints. There were also potted palms set out on the lawn in summer (Figure 103). Under the trees were rustic seats, again built to designs illustrated in Downing's writings.

Varied and flamboyant, Downing's front lawn was as good an example of his Beautiful design mode as can be documented in this period. In truth, it was an early Victorian prototype, inspired by the best of the "fancy" English Regency-period gardens. This elegant fashion of the 1810s and 1820s was a well-established style by 1840 and was "modern," as Downing described it, soon to go to excess with the reign of Queen Victoria.

Of course, Victorian taste came well after the eighteenth-century evolution of English landscape gardening. Downing knew and appreciated the long tradition of landscape gardening and its adherence to the "genius of the place," but he was also drawn to current fashion, gleaned from a wide variety of contemporary, primarily English, source material. Downing's reading of J. C. Loudon's encyclopedic writings could alone have influenced many of his ideas. According to Charles Hovey, "a complete set of Loudon's work" was in Downing's library at Highland Gardens.

At the time of Downing's death in 1852, less than twelve years after Hovey's report, the residential grounds at Highland Gardens were again the subject of an expert description. In this instance the commentary was by Clarence C. Cook, a noted art critic who was a friend of Downing's. Cook's article appeared in *The Horticulturist* in January 1853.[130] Cook was not a horticulturist, but his interest in the site as an example of landscape gardening addressed its design in great detail. Cook had visited Highland Gardens in 1852, just prior to Downing's death. His recitation of Downing's intentions can be relied on.

Figure 106. *Office Porch* at Highland Gardens, engraving from *The Horticulturist,* January 1853. After Calvert Vaux was hired, Downing built an office addition west of the house. This vignette from Clarence Cook's 1853 article shows the entrance porch of what Downing called the "Bureau of Architecture."

The chronology of landscape changes from 1841 to 1852 is not recorded in all its specifics, but surely the most significant event in the late 1840s was Downing's retirement from the nursery business after it was sold in 1847. From this date, Downing concentrated on his writings and design practice. By February 1852, Downing had built an office addition to his house, calling it the "Bureau of Architecture ... full of commissions, and young architects, and planning for all parts of the country" (Figure 106).[131] With his career changing, Highland Gardens lost all trace of its former commercial use. The property was purely residential at the time of Downing's death.

In the dozen years from 1841 to 1852, the landscape had evolved (Figure 107). The original front lawn had to some extent been naturalized, hinting, perhaps, at Downing's growing maturity and sophistication. He seems to have been searching for the *genius loci* at Highland Gardens and increasingly finding it in the Picturesque design mode. For example, the extensive floral displays had nearly disappeared by 1852, possibly along with the nursery workers. Downing had continued to maintain flower beds, but their visual impact had been much reduced from the showy earlier scheme, with only four circular beds, perhaps 400 square feet, remaining. Only two small circles seem to have been located on the front lawn.

Importantly, the grounds at Highland Gardens had been expanded into areas not discussed by Charles Hovey in 1841. A gravel footpath that traced the bottom of the front lawn was lengthened to loop north into a new lawn area. This northern lawn constituted a separate outdoor room, isolated from the house and the older front lawn by a dense planting of shrubs and trees. Over time the plantings Downing relied on to provide screening were maturing, becoming more substantial and more effective in creating a separate sense

Figure 107. Bird's-Eye View of Highland Gardens (1852), by R. M. Toole. This view is based primarily on a plan prepared by Frederick Clarke Withers, an architect working for Downing. It shows the site's development since 1841 (compare with Figure 104). Telltale is the emergence of a picturesque sensitivity to the aesthetics of landscape gardening. Note the reduced floral displays and new features such as the "Rock Garden" and "Hermitage," set in natural-appearing wooded areas. The number keys are as follows: (1) house, with office wing at southwest corner; (2) former nursery, site of greenhouse, cottage, barn and yards (service area); (3) carriage entrance onto Broad Street; (4) Liberty Street; (5) Grand Street; (6) the lawn; (7) single flower bed, with evergreen tree at center; (8) hedgerow; (9) vineyard; (10) north lawn; (11) kitchen garden; (12) hermitage (summerhouse); (13) rustic arbor (seat); (14) rock garden.

Figure 108. *Arbor* at Highland Gardens, engraving
from *The Horticulturist*,
January 1853. This illustration, which was included in
an article about Highland
Gardens published in 1853
just after Downing's death,
depicted a small, rustic, garden shelter. Vines are shown
climbing amid the filigree
of branches. Natural bark
is suggested as the roofing
material.

of place. This came from their enhanced growth, but also from their carefully mingled layout as wooded areas where individual trees were less important than the overall visual effect of a mixed thicket, a decidedly Picturesque landscape planting. One commentator claimed "the thicket, ... was ... trimmed as to reveal the loveliest glimpses of the river, each a picture in its frame of foliage, but which was not cut low enough to betray the presence of road or town."[132]

The new north lawn was ornamented with additional features, although not to the highly embellished effect seen earlier on Downing's front lawn. There was a bronze vase, a reproduction of the "Borghese Vase" of Florence, and a few specimen trees, but no flower beds are thought to have been maintained. Along the north lawn's well-defined edges were two rustic structures—an open-roofed, vine-embowered seat that Downing called the "Arbor;" and a more enclosed summerhouse, called the "Hermitage" (Figures 108 and 109). These seem to have been built in the late 1840s. The Hermitage was described as a "cool retreat" in warm weather and featured a shelf of beehives along one side, a decidedly pastoral and vernacular touch.

Close to his rustic structures, Downing developed two floral areas, not as formal bedded-out displays, but as naturalized rock gardens set against wooded backdrops. These informal flower beds combined with the nearby rustic structures to create a Picturesque design ensemble not discernable at Highland Gardens in 1841. The hedgerow of trees and shrubs that screened the former nursery grounds from the house was, by 1852, extended around the northern and western sides of the grounds, screening out a kitchen garden (farther north) and a narrow orchard (to the west). With its reduction of features and its unifying plantings, the entire site formed a harmonious, naturalized whole that melded easily with the wider Hudson River Valley setting.

In 1852, Highland Gardens continued to present elements of the Beautiful design mode, but the evolution of the garden's aesthetic was clear. As Downing tempered his interest in imported themes inspired by England's Regency-period fashion, he emphasized the "leading expression" (as he called it) of the Picturesque. This evolution is important, tied as it was to Downing's growing maturity from youthful enthusiasm for the latest English trends to increased reliance on indigenous themes and concern for an expression

Figure 109. *The Hermitage* at Highland Gardens, engraving from *The Horticulturist*, January 1853. Another garden structure illustrated in the 1853 article was this tiny cottage of considerable rusticity. Whole logs were used for the posts and rafters, and upright rough-sawn boards formed the walls. Slabs of bark seem to have provided the roofing. A beehive occupied an outside shelf.

of the Hudson Valley's *genius loci*. Downing appreciated the native appropriateness of Picturesque design, but he continued to find it in elegant and well-composed design work, rather than an approach where art might appear absent. This approach will be apparent in the next chapter when visiting Downing's only surviving garden commission, Matthew Vassar's Springside, in Poughkeepsie, upriver twenty miles from Highland Gardens.

The fate of Highland Gardens was sealed swiftly after Downing's death. Within two months the property was auctioned. Childless, Caroline Downing quickly remarried. By 1900 only the immediate house grounds, minus all the ornamental lawns, features and plantings, remained intact. The house was later demolished. Today, Highland Gardens is a residential neighborhood of multiple dwellings and small backyards. ●

CHAPTER 12

SPRINGSIDE

The Springside landscape garden is one of the most historically significant gardens in North America because of its unique attribution and status as Andrew Jackson Downing's only surviving landscape design. Today it is open to the public, maintained and operated by the nonprofit Springside Landscape Restoration, Inc.

A. J. Downing consulted on the layout of Springside from autumn 1850, immediately after he returned from recruiting architect Calvert Vaux in England. Less than two years later, in the summer of 1852, Springside was a finely crafted example of Downing's landscape design themes. All other sites attributed to Downing are either unsubstantiated or changed beyond recognition. Springside represents the only remaining documented and generally unaltered example of Downing's work as a landscape gardener and as an architect.

Downing became involved in the Springside development on the initiative of Matthew Vassar (1792–1868), a wealthy Poughkeepsie businessman and later the founder of Vassar College (1861) (Figure 110). Vassar eventually lived at Springside, but in 1850 he was involved with the community's search for expanded cemetery space, a public endeavor that led to the initial development of the property.

Cemetery development was an important facet of landscape gardening in America's pre–Civil War decades. "Rural cemeteries," as they were called, were innovative, reacting to the unhealthy, unattractive and overcrowded conditions of older churchyard burial plots inherited from the colonial period. The new cemeteries, beginning with Mount Auburn Cemetery outside Boston (1831), were designed as expansive landscape gardens, dedicated to the dead but appreciated by the living for their artistic landscape design qualities. It was the need for a public cemetery that prompted the Springside work.[133]

Vassar took the lead in this public campaign as the chairman of the cemetery committee, which began its work by acquiring a site. Vassar quickly commissioned A. J. Downing to provide design services. Downing had previous experience with cemetery design and had written on the topic.[134] At Springside, Downing's involvement extended from the basic layout to the important architectural elements, other garden features, and technical aspects of the work, all achieved before his death in July 1852.

Figure 110. *Portrait of Matthew Vassar*, by James Henry Wright, 1861. This portrait was painted in the same year Matthew Vassar founded Vassar College. Springside, developed from 1850, had by this date become Vassar's home. The Porter's Lodge (gatehouse) and entrance off Academy Street are shown in the background of this painting. Courtesy of the Frances Lehman Loeb Art Center, Vassar College.

Figure 111. Springside's Porter's Lodge (Gatehouse), photograph by Holly Wahlberg. This is the sole survivor of A. J. Downing's work as an architect, at the entrance to Springside, which is itself especially unique as Downing's only extant landscape design. Courtesy of Springside Landscape Restoration.

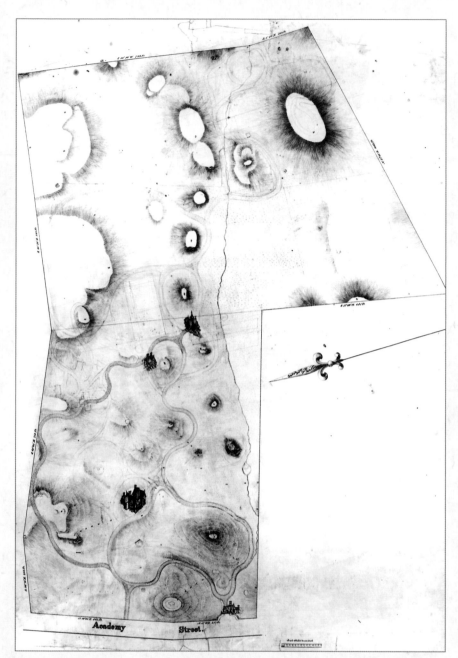

Figure 112. Plan of Springside, by W. D. Jones, engineer, c. 1850. This is the earliest surviving plan of Springside (north is to the left). The original landscape garden, and today's National Historic Landmark, occupied the western (bottom) portion of the site fronting Academy Street. Study of the original document shows early proposals, including sketches of buildings by A. J. Downing, and subsequent changes. Courtesy of Special Collections, Vassar College Libraries.

In the winter of 1850, a newspaper suggested that the cemetery committee's initial task was "to fix upon a desirable location, one that nature has endowed with beauties which art never could accomplish."[135] The property selected by Vassar's cemetery committee was subdivided from an old farm located off Academy Street south of the village. Of the total forty-four acres, about half was to be burial grounds. It is this core area that was the garden site (about twenty acres) designed by Downing. The former farm was conducive to cemetery use, being of ample acreage and generally undulating, open terrain. The site's secluded valley formation fostered a strong sense of enclosure, which was important to its contemplative sense of place. An east-to-west-flowing brook formed the south property line, with the land sloping up toward the north forming a south-facing slope for the grounds, a desirable orientation. The otherwise gentle topography was punctuated by small hillocks formed around exposed bedrock. These geological formations were unusual in their setting, but would have been hidden in dense woods had not agricultural use cleared much of the surrounding ground by 1850 and revealed them as features. Each of these hillocks was accentuated by groves of trees that had been left on the steep rocky slopes. Downing used the mounds in the landscape garden scheme as important structural and focal elements, responding to the genius of the place.

Figure 113. Painting Showing Cottage at Springside, by Henry Gritten, 1852. This view, looking east along the approach drive toward the wooded "Knitting Knoll," shows the cottage on the left and the coach house/stable on the right. Courtesy of the Frances Lehman Loeb Art Center, Vassar College.

As attested in the cemetery committee's report, substantial site improvements were considered essential to promoting the cemetery scheme. Success depended on signing up subscribers who would invest in the venture. While the newspaper accounts gave the issue considerable coverage, no actual construction was reported during the summer of 1850 while Downing was abroad. He returned in September, and site improvements got underway shortly thereafter, suggesting his close involvement. Two months later, on November 25, 1850, Vassar's nephew recorded his uncle "exhibiting plans for his Farm and Villa below town."[136] This marked the first reference to Matthew Vassar's option to use the site as a private residence if cemetery use did not materialize. This was confirmed by a December 1850 newspaper account that described Vassar as keeping the cemetery use firmly in mind as "that object in his disbursements and plans as far as would be compatible with its improvements as a private residence."[137]

Vassar's initial work on the site was the construction of a coach house/stable and a cottage (intended for the cemetery superintendent). These, combined with a kitchen garden and barn complex, formed an impressive architectural ensemble. Downing's architectural plans were described by him in *The Horticulturist* in February 1851. Downing called Vassar's property an "establishment, [that] will be remarkable for the completeness, convenience, and good effect of the various buildings, joined to much natural beauty of features of the locality in

which they are placed."[138] In the spring of 1851, work commenced on the road and path arrangements. While the buildings were under construction, selected trees were removed and new trees were planted. The site design was intended as a cemetery garden, but a house site was a compatible use, and Vassar felt the grounds could be adapted as a residence without great difficulty if the cemetery promotion failed.

Documents guiding the 1851 construction included a map prepared by William D. Jones, an engineer, which showed the boundary lines and topography of the site and the road work that had been completed the previous December (Figure 112). Older farm roads are also shown. Some were incorporated into the new scheme; other sections were abandoned. Jones's map was displayed publicly in April 1851 to promote the cemetery scheme. Also exhibited at this time, as reported in the press, was a "draught of a gate or keepers lodge ... executed by A. J. Downing."[139] Downing's design was an imposing stone portal with attached stone gatehouse. It was never constructed. The design, a drawing of which survives, was elaborate. It was appropriate for a cemetery entrance, but out-of-character for a residence in this period. The stone gatehouse design was probably prepared as a sketch simply to advertise the cemetery venture.

Fortified with Jones's map, Downing's architectural schemes and, more intangibly and critically, Downing's trained and experienced eye as a landscape gardener, the 1851 season saw major construction at Springside. In the next eight months the grounds evolved to the point of a roughed-out, but essentially complete, arrangement. The possible cemetery use remained an option. At one point in the summer of 1851, the press reported that "the prospect is now good [that the cemetery use would go forward]." Again, the improvements were called "suited to a Cemetery." The eventual failure of the cemetery was never clearly explained. As the landscape garden design was realized, however, Matthew Vassar became more and more personally associated with the property that he would, by the spring of 1852, call Springside and where he would live, at the intended superintendent's cottage, for the rest of his life. After Downing's death in July 1852, Vassar commissioned an English-born landscape painter, Henry C. Gritten (1818–1873), to undertake a series of oil paintings showing the landscape garden at Springside. Executed in a realistic manner in the autumn of 1852, the paintings provide a nearly comprehensive overview of the property as Andrew Jackson Downing last saw it (Figures 113 and 114).

Downing intended that the Springside design be directed towards achieving an internalized composition with a strong, inherent, sense of place. Outward views from within the grounds were possible from a few exposed high points, but these were less indicative than the inward orientation, which resulted in the scheme being described from an early date as an "enclosure." The garden's effective boundaries were crucial, because this condition allowed Springside to be perceived as a separate, private place. On the north side

Figure 114. Painting Showing Center Circle at Springside, by Henry Gritten, 1852. The view takes in most of the landscape garden. On the right (west), the Porter's Lodge (gatehouse) and south entrance are seen next to an open hill, site of a future summerhouse. On the left (east), a conservatory is seen ornamenting Center Circle. Evergreen Park and Jet Vale are illustrated in the center of the scene. Numerous newly planted evergreens are shown, and the turf is closely cropped by grazing sheep. Courtesy of the Frances Lehman Loeb Art Center, Vassar College.

were an old stone wall and hedgerow. The south line was the wooded stream. On the west was Academy Street, set off by a stone wall. The eastern limits of the landscape garden were ingeniously defined by Downing's arrangement of farm structures and a long picket fence crossing behind the cottage grounds. Together these alignments amounted to a 500-foot-long boundary on the east side of the garden (Figure 115).

Within these insular borders the Springside landscape garden was sculpted into a free-form design, where a meandering road layout combined with the natural topography to achieve garden variety within a unified, stylized whole. The road system was a series of looping alignments, providing the broad access suited to a cemetery. The rural cemetery was to be a park, and definition of space was integral to the design, which sought to subdivide the landscape to form areas that were small in scale, suited to meditation and reflective thought. Responding to the site and the cemetery use, Downing was not concerned with the placement of individual monuments and graves, or even family plots, but he was consciously creating several individual garden settings within the strongly unified, twenty-acre scheme. The result was a complex landscape garden of unusual intimacy with separately defined subareas, each focused on a decorative feature.

Downing's design intent at Springside seems to have favored the Beautiful design mode, although its use was restrained. There seem to have been good reasons to use the Beautiful mode, beginning with the property's natural attributes. Insular, the landscape had little of the sublime prospects or stunning assets that constituted picturesque scenery elsewhere in the Hudson River Valley. The site was pleasant and physically suited to its intended use and could, as one newspaper boasted, "be rendered as romantic and

Figure 115. Photograph Showing Archway/Dovecote at Springside, early 1900s. The archway is a carefully proportioned feature providing access from the farmyard beyond to the landscape garden, seen here in the foreground. A dovecote provided an ornamental use for the attic space. Courtesy of Special Collections, Vassar College Libraries.

KEY TO SPRINGSIDE PLAN

BUILDINGS:

A. Porter's Lodge
B. Cottage (Vassar Residence)
C. Cottage Annex
D. Coach House/Stable
E. Dairy/Ice House
F. Archway/Dovecote
G. "Auxillary Building"
H. Sheds
I. Granary (?)
J. "Glass House"

LANDSCAPE COMPONENTS

1. South Entrance Gate
2. Entrance Road
3. "Summer House Hill"
4. North Entrance Gate
5. Willow Spring
6. Walnut Grove
7. Jet Vale Fountain
8. Evergreen Park
9. Center Circle
10. "Gold Fish Pond"
11. "Stone Feature" (?)
12. "Deer Park"
13. Group Gap
14. Little Belt
15. Rock Roost
16. "Gentler Knoll"
17. Stonehenge Knoll
18. "Shady Knoll"
19. Knitting Knoll
20. Cottage Avenue Gate
21. "Farm Entrance"
22. Farmyard
23. "Lack Lawn"
24. Kitchen Garden
25. North Orchard
26. Lawn Terrace
27. Villa Site
28. Maple Hill
29. Brook
30. Scraggy Knoll

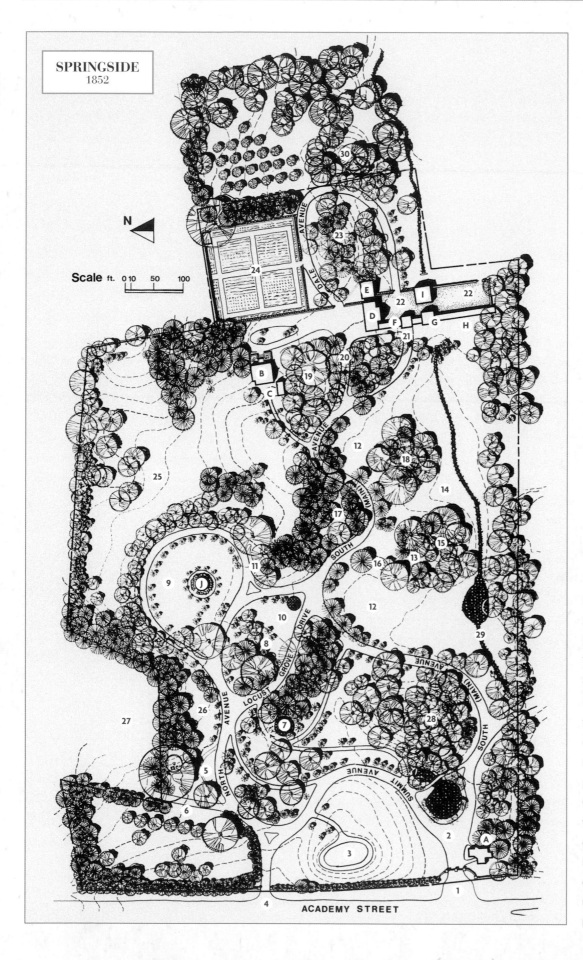

SPRINGSIDE
1852

N

Scale ft. 0 10 50 100

Figure 116. Plan of Springside (1852), by R. M. Toole. This plan is based on modern survey information, historic written and cartographic documentation, and four paintings by Henry Gritten. It shows the landscape garden at the time of Downing's death, overlaid on the modern vegetation pattern.

beautiful as any public burial ground in the State," but it could not be called remarkably picturesque.[140] An even more important motivation for the design approach was the derelict character of the property when first purchased by the cemetery committee. In the local press, Vassar's improvements were repeatedly contrasted as embellishing the "rude forms" and "barren state" of the old farm that preceded it. One report addressed the predevelopment site in foreboding terms, asserting that "Wings of wildness and desolation brooded darkly over thy scenes. Hoarse voices at nightfall were heard chanting dismally from thy swamps and the noisome reptile held its course unchecked."[141]

This was not the sort of landscape likely to gain wide support as a public cemetery, and it must have been obvious to Downing and Vassar that a striking change of appearance was needed. The cemetery project remained a public focus at least through the summer of 1851. Springside was initially a public-betterment project, leading to a design of elegance and polish. A personalized experience with picturesque nature was ill-suited to the need for public acceptance of the cemetery project, while the Beautiful design mode, as defined by Downing himself, provided tasteful refinement.

The use of landscape features at Springside was, by and large, formal in aspect and positioning. A striking Gothic-styled conservatory formed an elaborate embellishment in Center Circle, a carriage roundabout located near the center of the site. Likewise, an area called Jet Vale focused its aesthetic effect on a so-called "Swain Fountain" and its geometric, circular basin. Elsewhere, a "Gold Fish Pond" was an exacting circular pool, providing the focus around which separate drives converged at an intersection. The rocky hillocks were given fanciful names like "Rock Roost," "Shady Knoll," and "Knitting Knoll." However, these were not experienced as culminating a picturesque scene, but rather as statuesque oddities, islands of rock and old trees dotted across an otherwise open landscape. This sort of aesthetic manipulation in a landscape garden, with other focal elements, suggested an artful effect reflective of the Beautiful design mode. Out on the lawns, the 1852 Henry Gritten paintings show sheep (and some cattle) grazing the site's extensive open turf. Sheep provided a uniform, closely cropped Beautiful effect. This surface treatment tended to unify the garden as a distinct ornamental place and enhance the display of features (Figure 114).

The architecture at Springside was a focus of the garden experience. The Springside buildings were inspired by the Gothic Revival style and, except for the conservatory (or glass house) in Center Circle, were wood structures. The style had

been initiated by A. J. Davis's cottage at Blithewood fifteen years earlier. Downing had published an example of the style in 1842 and said it was "especially [for] our farm and country houses, when wood is the material employed in their construction." Eventually Downing concluded that these types of modest but artful buildings were seen by Americans as indigenous, having "a distinct shape and meaning in the hands of our countrymen." The Springside buildings constitute a remarkable collection, and the fact that they can be so closely associated with Downing is fortunate given the general scarcity of Downing documentation and his historical importance as an arbiter of architectural design in antebellum America. Most importantly, Downing would have been responsible for placing the garden architecture as individual features and as ensembles within the Springside landscape garden. This is an aspect of the design that is a hallmark at Springside. Calvert Vaux, who had just begun his employment with Downing as the Springside work began, can be assumed to have influenced the architecture, later relating that "each [building] … [had] been studied with some reference to its position and artistic importance in the landscape, as well as its more immediately useful purpose."[142] As always in this era, architecture was visually subservient to the landscape composition. Downing's Springside work is an excellent example of this discerning harmony of architecture and site that so distinguished landscape design in the Romantic period.

In the spring of 1852, the local newspaper called Springside an "establishment," noting that the site was being embellished with the plantings of "more than a thousand forest trees." The report concluded that Springside was "A Paradise."[143] The transformation of the site inspired in a Poughkeepsie newspaper a front-page poem—"Ode to Springside"—which hailed, in appropriate romantic verse, "the newer charms" and "fresh beauties" of the design.[144] Throughout the summer of 1852, there appeared several accounts that praised the site's design quality. In July, for example, the site was called the "realization of a painter's dream, the embodiment of the poet's glowing thought."[145] Springside was maintained as a showplace. The garden exhibited its varied features in a refined, polished composition, carefully using themes and expressions of the Beautiful design mode and avoiding over-embellishments and a scattered appearance. Wrote the *Poughkeepsie Eagle* in June 1852: "[Springside] is a charming spot [with] park-like and pastoral landscape … meadows, woodlands, water courses, jets and fountains, elevated summits gently sloping into valleys, forming the natural openings for the roads to girdle the hills and knolls."[146] As these accolades were received, on July 28, 1852, Andrew Jackson Downing drowned with the fiery sinking of the steamboat *Henry Clay* on his beloved Hudson River.

Sixteen years later, in 1868, Matthew Vassar died. The Springside property was sold to a neighbor. It was eventually purchased by an owner who built a substantial house close to, but not on, the garden.

Figure 117. Photograph of Willow Spring at Springside, 2009, by Steve Benson. Preserved, Springside remains the Hudson Valley's most significant artifact of landscape gardening, being A. J. Downing's only garden design to have survived. Modern interpretive panels (lower right) use nineteenth-century engravings to recreate the historic scene. The old sycamore tree is still standing to the left of the Willow Spring.

For a hundred years thereafter, Springside remained a residential property, and the landscape garden, if haphazardly maintained, survived. Then, beginning in 1966, proposals to develop the site for commercial use spawned efforts to record the historic importance of the property and prompted its designation as a National Historic Landmark in 1969. In 1970 the site was again seriously threatened by development that would have obliterated the garden. These plans were not executed, but the site was neglected for twenty years. Vandalism and fire led to the destruction of the cottage, coach house/stable and other farm buildings, and most of the landscape features. New preservation and environmental objections led to litigation that resulted in a settlement that saved the property, and a local preservation group was established to oversee the site in the late 1980s. Efforts to restore and maintain Springside continue. At times the site is interpreted to its conditions after Downing's death, when Mathew Vassar made embellishments to the landscape that were never intended in Downing's original scheme. As such, even while celebrating Springside as A. J. Downing's masterwork, current stewardship encompasses a landscape not designed by him.

In 1852, unlike in subsequent years, Springside was a unified landscape garden composition. Its design had been exceptionally well-handled and was characteristic of A. J. Downing's themes, as recorded in his numerous writings, at the apex of his career. Because of the maturity of its magnificent specimen trees, the garden's loveliness is in some respects more evident today than during Downing's lifetime. Design quality and the site's basic preservation enhance Springside's potential as an historic garden of national importance and international interest.

CHAPTER 13

Idlewild, The Point and Wilderstein

Andrew J. Downing's design at Springside was a shining moment in the history of landscape gardening on the Hudson, but it was also somewhat atypical as a residential landscape, given the design's conception as a cemetery. In fact, Downing's professional focus on residential work was shifting in the final years of his brief career. In his mid-thirties Downing was attracting national attention. He provided plans for the National Mall in Washington, D.C., in the same year that he was working at Springside. It is likely that Downing would have been increasingly involved in larger public projects had he lived.

There were, of course, other examples of residential landscape gardening along the Hudson that caught Downing's attention. Some of these could be beneficially discussed, but they are "lost landscapes" much altered from their historic conditions. These properties are not routinely open to the public, and research into their nineteenth-century designs has been rudimentary. Still, in one neighborhood alone, near Rhinebeck in Dutchess County, three properties—Wittmount, Ellerslie and Linwood—mentioned by Downing in *Landscape Gardening* (1844)

can be cited as typical of the scores of others that lined the river (see Figure 9).

The first, at Staatsburg, had been a colonial-period farm before being purchased in 1835 by a wealthy New Yorker, William Emmet, who erected an early castellated Gothic house and employed an Irish landscape gardener named James Downing to enhance the property. Emmet called it "Wittmount" in romantic tribute to the land's first farmer, colonist Petrus DeWitt. A. J. Downing visited Emmet and found his designed landscape "pleasing ... on the margin of the river." This property remains in private ownership, now called The Locusts, named for the huge specimens of black locust trees that still border the old road alignment from the river landing.

Close by was Ellerslie, a property of about 500 acres whose owner, William Kelly, was especially praised by Downing for his landscape gardening. Downing recognized Ellerslie as "One of our finest examples of high keeping and good management, both in an ornamental and an agricultural point of view. ... This is one of the most celebrated places on the Hudson, and there are few that so well pay the lover of improved landscape for a visit." Some considered the view from Ellerslie equal to Hyde Park's—high praise indeed. Today, Ellerslie remains, but the landscape accommodates a large, unused institution, not a private home, and the grounds have many modern buildings and a fully reconfigured landscape featuring parking lots. This has been the fate of several of the old estates along the Hudson.

Two miles south of Ellerslie is Linwood, originally developed in the 1790s by another of Chancellor Robert R. Livingston's siblings, Margaret Livingston, and her husband, Thomas Tillotson. After their deaths it was purchased in 1836 by John Barber James, who was an acquaintance of A. J. Downing and an uncle of author Henry James (1843–1916), who visited as a child and remembered "the great bluff of the Hudson on which it stood. ... This ground, the house and precincts of Linwood ... bristle with great views and other glories, with gardens and graperies." James remembered "creeping off to the edge of the eminence above the Hudson," where he "felt the great bright harmonies of air and space becoming one."[147] Linwood is today a nunnery.

Downing's fleeting connections with these landscaped properties and his work at Springside in the summer of 1852 marked the end of his personal connection with landscape gardening in the Hudson River Valley. But there are three properties closely related to A. J. Downing that partially survive and can be explored—Idlewild, The Point, and Wilderstein. These three were never discussed by Downing, having been developed only in the early 1850s, but they show that his principles for landscape gardening were actively engaged by a new generation of amateur and professional designers. All three properties have a strong link to Downing because of their association with the architect Calvert Vaux. Vaux had been brought to America by Downing in 1850 and was his artistic heir apparent after Downing's death in the summer of 1852. In 1856, Vaux moved to New York City and, in 1858, went on to team up with Frederick Law Olmsted in the glorious design of New York City's Central Park—a crescendo of American land-

scape gardening—representing the birth of American landscape architecture. As well as any other period designer, equaled only by A. J. Davis, Calvert Vaux fulfilled the ideal of joining architecture and landscape gardening to celebrate the distinct genius of place in the Hudson Valley.

Today, it is unfortunate that famed Idlewild, with its celebrity owner and well-documented history, is much altered, and disheartening that The Point continues to deteriorate even in public ownership. Happily, Wilderstein is preserved as one of the Hudson Valley's historic landscape gems, still intact and accessible.

IDLEWILD

Five miles south of Downing's Highland Gardens at Newburgh was Idlewild at Cornwall-on-Hudson. In the pre–Civil War decades, Idlewild was perhaps the most celebrated and best-known example of landscape gardening in the Hudson Valley. From 1851 it was the home of author Nathaniel Parker Willis (1806–1867), one of the Romantic period's most popular writers (Figure 118). Our understanding of the Romantic period and of Idlewild is aided immeasurably by Willis's book *Outdoors at Idlewild, or The Shaping of a Home on the Banks of the Hudson* (1855), which documented not only the chronology and composition of the designed landscape at Idlewild, but also Willis's design intentions and motivations in creating it.[148] Sophisticated domestic life in antebellum America is exposed in Willis's prose.

Nathaniel Parker Willis brought artistry and impressive credentials to his landscape gardening at Idlewild. At age twenty-five he began an association with noted New York City publisher George Pope Morris. In his writing career Willis traveled widely overseas and immersed himself in the genius of the place wherever he went. Each new destination was a distinct melding of nature and man. Willis evoked these observations in his writings. As one critic said, Willis "had a pencil quality in his pen, and could put life and picturesqueness into worn paths and dull statistics."[149]

Returning to America in 1836, Willis visited the Susquehanna River Valley while working on his book *American Scenery Illustrated* (1840). He purchased a 200-

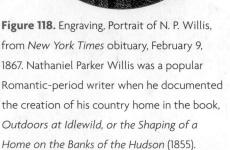

Figure 118. Engraving, Portrait of N. P. Willis, from *New York Times* obituary, February 9, 1867. Nathaniel Parker Willis was a popular Romantic-period writer when he documented the creation of his country home in the book, *Outdoors at Idlewild, or the Shaping of a Home on the Banks of the Hudson* (1855).

acre farm near Owego, in Tioga County, New York. He called the property "Glenmary," for his wife, and chronicled the experience in "Letters from under a Bridge," collected in the book *A l'Abri or, The Tent Pitch'd* (1839). These narratives show the author as a sensitive romantic, attuned to the artistic implications of residential life and landscape gardening amid the primeval forests of America. Sadly for Willis, financial setbacks necessitated his giving up Glenmary and returning to New York City. In 1845 his wife died in childbirth. Willis eventually remarried, and he again teamed up with George Pope Morris, starting a daily newspaper, the *Evening New York Mirror*. A year later, Morris and Willis sold that paper and started a literary weekly called the *National Press*. In 1847 the name was changed to the *Home Journal*, soon to be one of the era's most popular periodicals, thriving until 1864 when the Civil War and Morris's death brought it to a close. It was in the *Home Journal* in the early 1850s that Willis published his numerous "Letters" concerning Idlewild, eventually collected into *Outdoors at Idlewild*. The quotations below are from this unique record.

As Willis entered his mid-forties, his family began to spend their summers in Cornwall-on-Hudson amid the mountain setting of the Hudson Highlands. Willis's new wife brought financial security to the family's unsettled past, and Willis's health improved with summers spent out of town. Later he would write about the Cornwall area in glowing terms, naming it the "Highland Terrace":

> ... a complex wilderness, of romantic picturesqueness. ... The entire area of the Terrace contains several villages, and is divided up into cultivated farms, the walls and fences in good condition, the roads lined with trees, the orchards full, the houses and barns sufficiently hidden with foliage to be picturesque.

With this sort of praise, Willis was largely responsible for making the Highland Terrace a popular summer destination. The author made over the area, much as his friend Washington Irving had done downriver in the earlier Knickerbocker period. In this way Willis renamed nearby Butter Hill, "Storm King," for its dramatic implications, and changed the unpleasant-sounding Murderer's Creek to "Moodna Creek," to honor a local Native American. The names, and their romantic imagery, stuck.

The mix of dramatic topography, the noble river, and the healthful air reinvigorated Willis. He responded in his writings with a romantic fervor seldom experienced in the literature of this period. Willis boldly recommended an alternative to Sunday worship, preferring to "spend its 'service time' with Nature," and observing that in the Hudson Highlands, a church:

> ... is but a chapel within a vast cathedral—the Hudson a broad aisle, the Highlands a thunder-choir and gallery, Black Rock a pulpit, and a blue dome over all—and lo!—Nature, in her surplice of summer, ready to preach the sermon! Why not do my worshipping out of doors?

As was common for an artistic man of his era, Willis found landscape gardening, as he said, "a pleasant subject to expand upon." His background was no doubt forged by his many years of travel, especially in England. Also, he had direct involvement in landscape gardening at his earlier residence at Glenmary. Willis's writings were peppered with references to landscape design, and he devoted one of his essays to providing good-natured advice to a homeowner "with fifty acres and a spare hour in the evening."

For Willis, nature and landscape design were closely allied. His earliest biographer concluded that he viewed nature "more as a landscape gardener than as a naturalist,"[150] and, from his achievement at Idlewild, he must be recognized as an accomplished and practical amateur landscape designer, ever intent on the optimum visual effects. In his writings Willis's advice and commentary were decidedly artistic in tone:

> Separate a rural spot from the rest of the world, either by poetry or property—only putting around it the fairy ring of a thought-haunt, where your love and sadness are at home—and it is curious how you are made gradually conscious that there is a *genius loci*, a spirit, inhabiting just what you have fenced in with thoughts and rails.

Willis found guidance in the basics of land and topography, which he felt needed not only a good climate and good soil, but also "shade, water and inequality of surface," all attributes that were in abundance at Idlewild.

In all his notions regarding landscape gardening, Willis espoused the Picturesque design approach as defined by A. J. Downing, where art is hidden so that a fully natural and vernacular expression could prevail. For Willis the authenticity of nature overwhelmed whatever attempt might be made at what he called landscape design "improvements." He also valued practicality: "The only rule of perfect independence in the country is to make no [landscape] improvement which requires more attention than the making." For Willis the "choosing and arranging of a home is an out-door matter." Contemplating a residential development, the landscape gardener's task was clear—"tell all its capabilities, foresee all its difficulties, direct its location of buildings and garden, and planting of trees and orchards, and, in short, give the wisdom beforehand." The landscape gardener is ideally one who:

… has passed a life of rural industry and economy, is a most successful raiser of fruit, and a skillful gardener, knows everything about buildings and farms, and their wants and conveniences; and, to the very best of practical good sense, he adds a taste and a knowledge, and a love of scenery that is quite above his condition in life.

These comments are an apt description of the career of Andrew Jackson Downing. Despite their proximity, it is not known if N. P. Willis ever met A. J. Downing. Willis's decision to build in the area and to purchase land in the spring of 1851

Figure 119. Engraving Showing Idlewild House from The Glen, from *The Hudson: from the Wilderness to the Sea* by Benson J. Lossing (1860). This view from the north shows Idlewild Brook flowing through the lower meadow. This was the view along the approach drive from the so-called Pig-Tight Gate. From this location the drive crossed the glen and climbed the far hillside to the house.

Figure 120. Engraving Showing The Glen, from *The Hudson: from the Wilderness to the Sea* by Benson J. Lossing (1860). N. P. Willis developed his Picturesque landscape garden at a spectacular setting overlooking the Hudson River. Two deep ravines isolated the perch-like house site. The ravines were heavily wooded, with small clearings that Willis developed as landscape features. Rustic footbridges crossed at several locations.

predated Downing's death by over a year. Also, Willis apparently commissioned Downing's partner, architect Calvert Vaux, before Downing's death. Still, no record of an actual meeting between the two has been found, nor did Willis later claim, or imply, that they had direct contact. Willis did comment often on Downing, calling him "one of our most eminent horticulturists" and championing Downing's "elegant and tempting book" on landscape gardening. Willis argued that Americans lacked a "common currency," an inherent sense for "the creation of beauty in the landscape." He then asserted that:

Downing's genius was our country's one solitary promise of a supply for this lack of common currency—this scarcity of beauty coin in our every-day pockets. He was the one person who could be sent for—by a gentleman who had purchased land for a country-seat, and who had not given up his attention to the development of natural beauty—to look at fields and woods, and tell what could be made out

of them. It takes a habit of looking at such things—at Nature wild in contrast with Nature improved—to know how to lay out paths and clump woods, plant avenues and inlay brooks among greensward and foliage. It takes a poet.

Willis's home, so aptly named Idlewild, was initiated in April 1851 with the purchase of a fifty-two-acre property in the family's beloved Highland Terrace at Cornwall. The land offered dramatic contrasts. On the south was a nearly level, raised plateau (the "Terrace"). It sloped gradually toward the north, down to the Hudson River. West of this open ground was a steep, wooded ravine. Willis related that when he first looked at the ravine portion of the property and asked its price, he was met with "the disparaging remark that it was of little value—only an idle wild of which nothing could ever be made." The "glen," as it was called, was to be the soul of Idlewild, with Willis ecstatic that "nothing could well be wilder or more lawlessly picturesque" (Figures 119 and 120).

Shortly after his purchase, Willis commissioned Calvert Vaux to design a house. Throughout this period Vaux was associated with A. J. Downing at their "Bureau of Architecture," until Downing's death in July 1852. Five years later Vaux described Idlewild in his book *Villas and Cottages* (1857), titling it "Design No. 23, A Simple Picturesque Country House." The design was Gothic-inspired, but modified to a more regional motif. By 1857 this style of house was considered a quintessential response to the Hudson Valley's picturesque landscape.

In his book, Calvert Vaux confirmed Willis's direct involvement in the creation of Idlewild's designed landscape, saying he took "great interest in accommodating the house to the fancies of the genius of the place." Idlewild's dramatic setting allowed "picturesque and artistic beauty [to] belong to whoever can realize them," claimed Vaux, who clearly felt Willis had the needed "poetic spirit" to develop the landscape in harmony with nature. Willis was directly involved in positioning and orienting the house, carefully considering the views from each window and insuring that service areas were screened by evergreen trees.

In the landscape, Willis developed two entry gates. The first, more practical, was an existing lane on the south that provided access to Cornwall Landing (Figure 121). The lane was dramatically perched on the raised plateau above the Idlewild ravine. The edge was lined with mature hemlock trees, and the drive followed along the boundary of a large kitchen and flower garden set off within a walled enclosure. Willis built an extensive service area off this entry, including stables hidden in trees south of the service side of the house. The lane swung around this service area, looping out into the open ground east of the house. This area was kept as a park and featured specimen trees and varied river views. A large rustic shelter was built there, and the area was an attractive foreground for viewing the house from varied angles along the drives and footpaths.

In addition to the rustic shelter, there were several features in the house grounds, but none can be termed traditional let alone classical. For example, Willis kept a "marvelous old stump," which he named "the Czar, or Russian Bear," mounted on the lawn as an ornament. Other features were equally quaint. Some were dedicated to individuals, such as a seat that Willis called "the Judge's Bench," being a stone around which a tree had grown, so that the stone was supported at a height of two feet off the ground and formed a natural seat where, on one occasion, a "Judge Daly" sat. Willis had the bench formally christened, and intended to plant

mountain laurel shrubs around it because he found the setting "barren."

In addition to developing his house grounds and the approach road from the south, Willis built a new approach road from the river road that led north towards Newburgh. Such a road access already existed on the old farm, but Willis altered it to optimize visual drama. The new gateway was built at an angle to the public road, a decidedly Picturesque arrangement. The entrance was located in a mature grove of hemlock trees so that, as Willis explained, "the main gate on the river would be thus set in a picturesque frame." The gate itself was first designed by Willis, but when his workers told him that the design "isn't pig tight," he had Calvert Vaux draw an alternative—"The Pig-Tight Gate"—mentioned often and made famous in Willis's writings.

From this entrance a "shelf-road" was cut into the hillside as it circled around the low-lying wet meadow where Idlewild Brook entered the Hudson. The new drive was designed to cross a series of bridges built across the meandering water courses, which included a secondary stream, called "Funnychild Brook," flowing from an adjacent glen that Willis named "Home-shut." Willis enthused about "the two streams [Idlewild and Funnychild], from their two separate glens, meeting in the meadow with a hemlock-sheltered lawn between such as fairies would choose to dance upon." He constructed natural-appearing dams to form pools, and perfected a waterfall between them. Willis described one pool as "where four of five noble young hemlocks guarded a spring." After crossing the watery low ground, the new entrance road turned up the slope on the ravine's east side, where it may have followed an existing farm road for the final dramatic ascent to the new house. One reporter, T. Addison Richards, described this approach:

> The meadow and its bridges crossed, there comes the winding ascent of the steep hill-side, with its diverging paths, ever tempting you down into the unknown depths of the dark ravine. Up, up, and still up, and at last we rest upon the lofty terrace-lawn, with all the world at our conquering feet.[151]

Starting in the spring of 1853, Willis built a footpath system in Idlewild Glen. At the top he constructed a "passable bridge," which he described as a "rude foot-bridge" constructed of tree trunks and rough boards. Higher up, the path led to an old mill, located at the south boundary of Idlewild where the public road

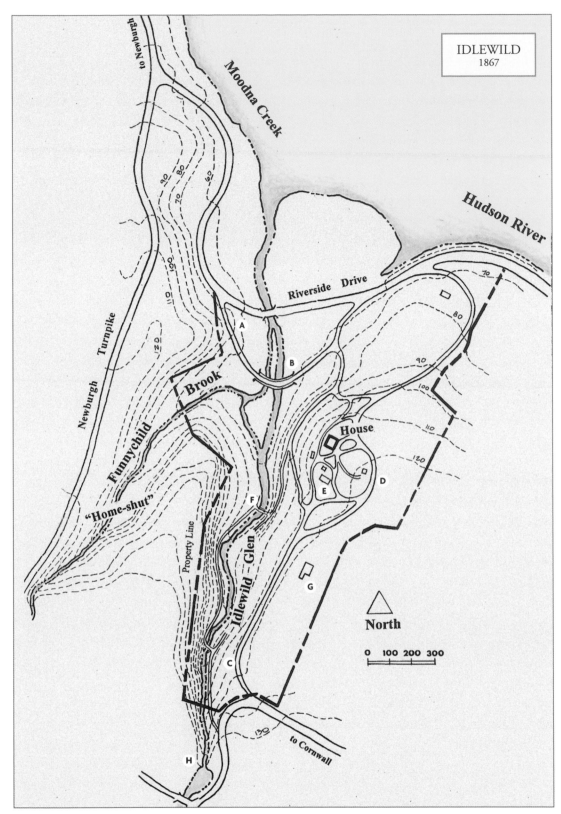

Figure 121. Plan of Idlewild (1867), by R. M. Toole. This period plan is based on a map of Cornwall that shows Idlewild six years after N. P. Willis's death, when the property is not thought to have been altered from its originally layout. The letter keys are as follows: (A) The Pig-Tight Gate; (B) The Lower Approach Road; (C) The Lane (upper approach road); (D) Loop Approach Road and Lawn; (E) Service/Stable; (F) Footpaths to Zigzag Bridge, Drip Rock and Chapel Rock, etc.; (G) Kitchen/Flower Garden; (H) Old Mill.

bridge crossed Idlewild Brook. Willis connected the path system to the new house "by dint of pick-axe-ing ... ridged a pathway, aslant down the face of the rock." Along his glen paths Willis built "rock-seats" and "rustic seats." The path made the glen "promenade-able," as Willis put it. Farther down was another bridge, called the "Zigzag Bridge" because of the intricate rustic work that adorned its railings. Here was the glen's "most beautiful feature ... at the farthest depth between precipices, hidden and romantically wild, lies a sanctuary of rock and water ... [a] drip-rock parlor, with its overhanging eaves and cool floor, its lofty shading of trees and its deep-down basin." This "Drip Rock" was close to another feature, "Chapel Rock," which was described by reporter T. Addison Richards in spiritual terms:

> In the dim religious light ... worshipers may kneel when they have dipped their fingers in the holy water of the pure spring with which the spot is blessed. ... This rugged passage [the Idlewild ravine] is a grand gallery of wonderful pictures, which Mr. Willis's magic art—his vistas, his bridges, and his wood-paths—has restored, and framed, and hung up for the delight of the public eye.[152]

In the ravine, Willis was literally landscape gardening on a cliff face where, as Richards put it, with "spade and pick on the sides of the precipices, he is every day providing new gems for his walls."

In 1853, Willis summarized for his readers his landscape gardening achievements:

> You see [Idlewild's] front porch from the thronged thoroughfares of the Hudson; but the grove behind it overhangs a deep-down glen, tracked but by my own tangled paths and the wild torrent which they by turns avoid and follow. ... Idlewild ... its dark glen of rocks and woods, and the thunder or murmur of its Brook—is but this every man's inner life illustrated and set to music.

Almost from the first, Idlewild was favorably received. Willis himself quoted a "Mr. Allison," editor of the *Newburgh Gazette*, who in July 1853 described the "wildness of its solitudes ... its solitary walks—its serpentine streams—its wild waterfalls ... A beautiful variety of trees, judiciously improved by the hand of Art."

After 1855 less detailed information regarding Idlewild emerges from Willis's writings. Improvements can be presumed to have continued, although at a less active pace. Numerous notables arrived on visits, and Idlewild became an icon of a celebrity's home in the pre–Civil War period. During the summer of 1854, Washington Irving visited Willis at "his poetical retreat." Irving's comments praised the landscape:

> It is really a beautiful place. The site well chosen, commanding noble and romantic scenery; the house commodious and picturesque and furnished with much taste. In a word it is just such a retreat as a poet would desire.[153]

An important article about Idlewild appeared in *Harper's Magazine* in January 1858. Its author, T. Addison Richards, provided a detailed account, gushing over "that sweet idyl of Art—embellished and Fancy-veiled landscape—Idlewild. ... the merry waters, the shady glen, and the sunny hill-sides, have each its pleasant tale of poetic tradition and historic association." For Richards, Willis was "a magician ... so ready, indeed, and so sure is his perception of the picturesque in Nature."

Unfortunately, after Nathaniel Parker Willis died in 1867, his family quickly sold Idlewild. Several owners followed until, in the 1950s, the property was developed and subdivided. Calvert Vaux's house was subjected to a bizarre remodeling, with its upper floors removed and the ground floor altered to a ranch house with a flat roof. A score of suburban houses now occupy the raised terrace, site of the lawns, orchards and gardens that earlier surrounded the house. Only the inaccessible glen remains, abandoned except by Idlewild and Funnychild brooks, where the springtime roar from their flow stirs remembrances of Willis's sensibilities and his rustic approach to landscape gardening.

❧ THE POINT

In the summer of 1852—the summer of A. J. Downing's death—his architectural associate, Calvert Vaux, was commissioned to design a house at Staatsburg-on-Hudson a few miles south of Rhinebeck on a 100-acre riverfront property called The Point. While overgrown and decaying today, The Point is part of the Mills-Norrie State Park and can be visited (Figure 122).

The Point property was adjacent to the old Staatsburgh estate, originally developed in 1792. Staatsburgh was a Livingston family farm and, in 1852, the home of Maturin and Margaret Livingston. It was their daughter, Geraldine, and her husband, Lydig Hoyt, who initiated acquisition of the adjacent property, apparently to be close to her parents. The Hoyts and Calvert Vaux went on to create one of the most perfect artistic marriages of house and landscape to survive intact from the Romantic period.

Figure 122. Photograph Showing Entrance at The Point, 2009, by Steve Benson. The Point has been mismanaged by New York State since it was taken from the original family in the early 1960s. The property was a quintessential Picturesque landscape scheme, a worthy setting for a fine Calvert Vaux house. It is now a near-ruin. The land is essentially preserved, albeit overgrown and abandoned beyond recognition.

Figure 123. Engraving Showing the House at The Point, from *Villas and Cottages* by Calvert Vaux (1857). The house was built by Lydig and Geraldine Hoyt. The design, by Calvert Vaux, was an exceptional example of the Hudson River vernacular style. The east entrance porch was flanked by a wraparound veranda to the south and west, offering a broad panorama over the river.

In size and configuration, Vaux's house design for the Hoyts closely resembled Willis's house at Idlewild, suggesting Vaux may have been pursuing a regional motif suited to the genius of the place (Figure 123). As at Idlewild, Vaux published the design in *Villas and Cottages* (1857), with a title similar to that used for Idlewild. Here, the house was "Design No. 31: Picturesque Stone Country House." The building site was dramatic, a true point that thrust itself into the Hudson's flow. Magnificent views opened to the north across four miles of open water, with the overlapping silhouettes of the Catskill peaks backing a delightful panorama. The Esopus lighthouse was a mid-river feature. On their property the Hoyts created an idealized farm, a *ferme ornée*, firmly in the Picturesque design mode. Here the spectacle of the natural world was joined with a modest, vernacular presence. There was not so much as a straight line or formal accessory to spoil the pastoral splendor.

Calvert Vaux was involved in the landscape design at The Point, siting the house, and he can be presumed to have consulted with the Hoyts on landscape gardening. In fact, before finalizing the house design, Vaux lobbied successfully for the acquisition of more land on the riverfront. As at Idlewild, special care was given to orient the house to maximize the varied prospects. Vaux indicated that owner and architect collaborated on the use of a Picturesque design approach, even close to the house, because "the ground was so irregular and broken ... that it seemed judicious to aim at a varied outline and picturesque effect in the immediate vicinity of the house, rather than to attempt smooth extents of lawn on a level."

With all this artistic history, it was unfortunate that New York State acquired the property (then still the Hoyt family home) in 1963 by the threatened use of eminent domain, with the intent of razing the house and outbuildings and then using the site for an Olympic-sized swimming pool. Those misguided plans were later abandoned, as was The Point. Today, the intact property and the Vaux-designed house are increasingly seen as no less historic than the adjacent, Gilded Age Staatsburgh mansion and its stiffly elegant grounds. The Point is a quintessential example of the Hudson's golden age in the Romantic period. The

State's ineffectual attempts to reuse, restore, or even stabilize the endangered Hoyt house have led only to further decay and an ever more forlorn property. At present a friends' group, the Calvert Vaux Preservation Alliance, has been formed to lobby for its revival.

A quick historic tour is described below, highlighting the landscape's fully organic, naturalized arrangements (Figure 124). With a basic understanding, a visit to the site can be a rewarding, if challenging, exercise in imagining the historic landscape amid the architectural remnants and the site's rampant growth of vegetation that obscures the once open fields and views (go in late autumn or early spring). For access, travel just north of the hamlet of Staatsburg along the Old Post Road to a modest set of brown stone piers marking the gateway to the Hoyts' country seat (Figure 122). After entering (on foot), the carriage drive quickly crosses the railroad tracks, which in this area followed an inland route—a happy situation for the Hoyts' privacy and The Point's unspoiled river frontage.

From the railroad, the Hoyts' entrance drive entered a varied natural scene that sheltered the privacy of their farmstead and house grounds farther west. This separation was enhanced by a rocky ridge that cut north-south across the site, forming a physical barrier to the outside. Rather than cutting through this formation, the entry drive was extended around its northern end, through a narrow passage that required a boundary alteration along the north property line (see Figure 124). Passing this prominent ridge, the carriage drive turned south into a more domesticated and open landscape as it followed a broad curve along the eastern and southern edge of an expansive sloping meadow drained by a small spring. With a backdrop of dense woods, views were oriented west and northwest across the meadow and up to the farmstead complex. In the nineteenth century these views introduced a richly detailed pastoral scene. Farm operations at The Point were limited by the acreage, but still amounted to a complete gentleman's farm. Lydig Hoyt was apparently actively involved, listing his occupation as "farmer" in the 1860 census. In that year the property produced several "meat" cattle, the milk from five "butter" cows, pigs and poultry, together with the cultivation of winter wheat, oats and potatoes grown on twenty-five acres of arable land. There were also twenty-five acres of meadow, and forty orchard trees of varied

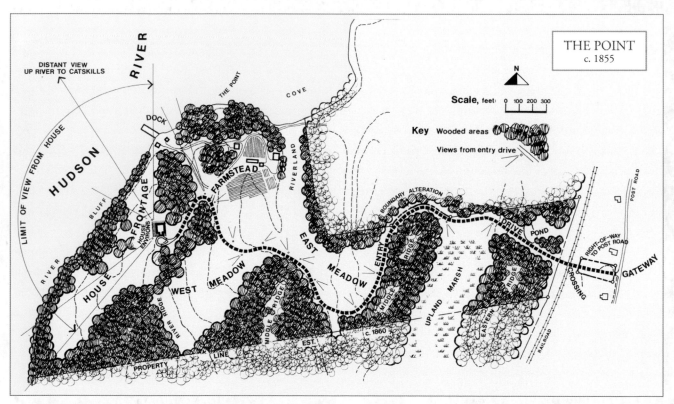

Figure 124. Plan of The Point (c. 1855), by R. M. Toole. The house site was unsurpassed, with long views both up and down the river. The approach drive took a sinuous route from the gateway on the public road, crossing the railroad tracks (which were fortuitously located away from the river edge in this area), and passing around a ridge line before overlooking the farm. From there, the drive climbed to the raised house grounds.

Figure 125. Engraving Showing the Farm Cottage at The Point, from *Villas and Cottages* by Calvert Vaux (1857). The farmer's cottage, with its chimney pots and bargeboard trim, closely related to the main house, indicative of the Hoyts' unified design approach at The Point.

fruits were documented. A cottage, cow barn, stable/carriage house, garden shed and greenhouse, and various small auxiliary buildings adjoined the cultivated fields. The farmer's cottage, designed by Calvert Vaux, was sited as a feature, as he described it, "in full view from the principal drive ... an accessory in the landscape" (Figure 125).

Continuing to the house, with the farm left behind, the driveway turned sharply south and uphill to the riverfront. The house and its broad views of the Hudson, hidden until the final moment of arrival, were now revealed. Set back from the edge of the river bluff, the house, built of stone quarried on the premises (the romantic ideal), was a quiet beacon in a splendid setting. Public rooms on the first floor opened to a wide veranda, a covered porch that extended around three sides of the house. A discreet basement kitchen and lower-level service area were accessible from the north, screened by a mature wooded area retained on that side of the house. Varying views from the interior rooms took in a nearly 180-degree sweep of the river. Open parkland, studded with numerous mature white oak and maple trees, surrounded the house on the east and south. The house design and its construction were carefully undertaken to preserve these trees, some of which still survive. A few floral plantings enlivened the scene. Ornamental trumpet vine and wisteria cloaked the veranda. As Vaux explained, areas of lawn were limited by steep grades and a desire for an unpolished, rustic look.

The Hoyt family enjoyed this rural paradise for over a hundred years, and then New York State knocked on the door.

WILDERSTEIN

The year A. J. Downing died, in the same year that the Hoyts began the development of The Point, a close-by country seat was being established on an equally spectacular property that in this instance oriented down the Hudson River with superior views to the south. This landscape was initially part of a larger Livingston family estate called Wildercliff, dating to the 1790s. In 1852 another Livingston descendant, Thomas Suckley (1810–1888), purchased a riverfront portion of Wildercliff from his cousin, Mary Garrettson, in order to develop a new residence. About thirty-two acres were initially included, and the property was enlarged from that beginning to an estate of over one hundred acres. Thomas Suckley and his wife Catharine built a simple Italianate-style house and gave the mini-estate an appropriate name, The Cedars. Later this was changed to the more evocative Wilderstein, loosely translated as "Wild Man's Stone," a reference to a petroglyph of uncertain origins discovered below the house at the river.

In the next thirty years Thomas Suckley presided over a modest gentleman's farm at Wilderstein. He was especially interested in his orchards and planted a varied mix of fruit trees along the slopes south and east of the new house. As with all such properties, there was an extensive kitchen garden and several farm buildings. Suckley was also known to have planted ornamental trees close to the house, although the specifics of the early ornamental landscape have not been studied in detail. A straight entrance drive came directly from the public road, ending at a circle fronting the house, no doubt Suckley's gesture to the landscape formality commonly associated with the Italianate style.

Later, with the ownership of Thomas Suckley's son, Robert Suckley (1856–1921), his wife Elizabeth (Bessie) and their large family, Wilderstein evolved to its full complement. Many outbuildings were added, including a large and intricate stable/carriage house, a handsome greenhouse/potting shed, a gatehouse/lodge, and several garden structures. Most significantly, the story of landscape gardening on the Hudson reached its last chapter at Wilderstein, in 1890 after the house had been enlarged and remodeled to the then-fashionable Queen Anne style (Figure 126). For a revamped landscape, Robert Suckley commissioned Calvert Vaux to rearrange and develop the grounds (Figure 127).

Calvert Vaux was then in his mid-sixties, close to retirement and only five years from his death in 1895. Much of the work at Wilderstein is attributed to his son, landscape architect Downing Vaux (1856–1926)—named for his father's former mentor, A. J. Downing—who now worked with his father and authored much of the correspondence with Robert Suckley over the ensuing three years. Also associated with the Wilderstein commission was landscape architect Samuel Parsons, Jr., known especially as a plantsman, and George K. Radford, an architect. Given this collaboration, it is appropriate to call Suckley's landscape design consultants the "Vaux Office."

On stylistic grounds, as Calvert Vaux and his generation approached the end of the nineteenth century, Picturesque landscape design had lost popularity, even along the Hudson where its use had persisted throughout the post–Civil War era. On the other hand, in 1890 the resurgence of classical, Italianate-style landscape design, to be championed by Edith Wharton, among others, was still a few years away when Robert Suckley ordered up his improvements at Wilderstein. In consequence, this was a transitional moment, without the fervor of the romantic heyday and, in turn, enamored of horticultural display that is seen as

Figure 126. The House at Wilderstein. In 1889 the older, sedate, Italianate-style house (1852) was radically remodeled to a polychromatic Queen Anne, now well-restored. Courtesy of Wilderstein.

epitomizing Victorian taste. It was a taste that could be an awkward mesh with Picturesque landscape gardening. The resulting design work at Wilderstein took on that challenge.

The traditions of the Picturesque were exhibited in Vaux's proposed roads and footpaths. Thomas Suckley's straight formal entrance drive was replaced by a much longer, curving driveway set off at the public road on an angular alignment, indicative of the Picturesque mode. Within the grounds an extensive walk system was developed, gravel-surfaced from a mechanical crusher and an onsite quarry. Paths curved along the steep hillside between the house and the river, and there was also a circuit drive laid out around the northern edges of the ornamental grounds, providing a long way around between the garden and greenhouse on the east and the river landing on the west. Several garden buildings and seats were planned along the path system, including shelters (called here "gazebos") and a rustic "umbrella seat," whose thatched roof supported by a single post resembled an umbrella, located on a prominent knoll directly south of the house.

While the Vaux design work at Wilderstein retained Picturesque themes, the new plantings were decidedly Gardenesque as compared with the simpler, more natural planting scheme thought to have been maintained by Thomas Suckley. In contrast, the new plantings were arranged in eye-popping, monolithic groupings. For example, five shrub beds were planted along a footpath leading from the umbrella seat to the kitchen garden (see Figure 127). Each bed was dedicated to a single shrub type. So, around the otherwise rustic umbrella seat were about twenty-five winter honeysuckle shrubs (*Lonicera fragrantissima*), and nothing else. Farther down the path another bed was reserved exclusively for golden bells (*Forsythia viridissima*), while another was

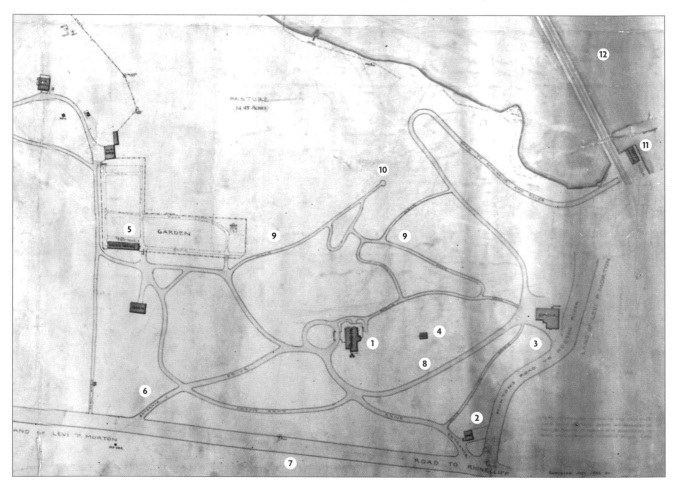

Figure 127. Plan of Wilderstein, 1892. Prepared by the Vaux office, the plan shows changes developed after 1891. Key numbers are as follows: (1) house; (2) gatehouse; (3) stable; (4) icehouse; (5) kitchen garden/greenhouse; (6) entrance drive; (7) public road; (8) circuit drive; (9) footpaths; (10) umbrella seat; (11) dock and railroad; (12) Hudson River. Courtesy of Wilderstein.

Figure 128. Photograph Showing Fields and Stable at Wilderstein, 1890s. This photograph may have been taken before the ornamental landscape improvements that are represented in the Vaux planting scheme. The photograph shows a roughly mowed meadow between the house and the river. Courtesy of Wilderstein.

given to scentless mock-orange (*Philadelphus grandiflorus*), and another to jetbead (*Rhodotypus*). The fifth of these horticultural set pieces was a grouping of Carolina allspice (*Calycanthus floridus*). Elsewhere were similar massed plantings, with little of the admixture of varied native species that would have promoted a natural appearance. The plant list was extensive, but in some cases 100 or more of a single plant were ordered. There were, for example, 203 *Spiraea opulifolia*, 186 *Ligustrum ovalifolium* (California privet), used to create a conspicuous hedge, and 100 purple barberry (*Berberis vulgaris atropurpurea*). One large plant bed on the west lawn was about fifty feet in diameter and was composed only of purple- and green-leafed barberry.

In total, an average of fifty plants were listed for each of thirty-four named varieties, for a total of about 1,700 shrubs which, combined with over forty trees, made for a sizable order. The plant beds were set along the drives and paths south and west of the house, and along the public road, presumably to enhance screening, close off the old driveway and set off the new entrances. Once installed, the new shrub beds would have produced a highly ornamental and artificial composition, a decidedly Victorian conceit.

After a few seasons nurturing his new shrubberies, Robert Suckley had financial difficulties. He left Wilderstein in the

hands of his estate manager and moved his family to Europe, where daily life was less expensive. The family stayed abroad until 1907. When the Suckleys returned to Wilderstein, the Vaux plantings had nearly disappeared, leaving the road and footpath system without the Victorian embellishments. Typical of this period, active recreation was quickly addressed with the addition of a tennis court, sited assertively on the front lawn. The Suckley family remained on the property until the last family member, Margaret "Daisy" Suckley (1891–1991) (Figure 129). Daisy left the property as a house museum.

Figure 129. Photograph of Margaret (Daisy) Suckley, 1957. Daisy Suckley was the last family member to live at Wilderstein. She was instrumental in preserving the property, which is now a privately operated house museum. Courtesy of Wilderstein.

Daisy Suckley provided a footnote to the story of landscape gardening on the Hudson as a distant cousin but close confidante of Franklin Delano Roosevelt. When the long-term American president came to his Hyde Park home, Springwood, he often visited Wilderstein and Daisy Suckley in friendship and camaraderie. As early as 1935, Daisy helped Franklin develop his so-called "Old Hudson River Dutch-style" retreat, Top Cottage, at Hyde Park (Figure 130). Today, Top Cottage is an attraction on the FDR National Historic Site.

When planning Top Cottage, questions of landscape gardening arose. As heirs to the long tradition of family life on country seats in the Hudson River Valley, Franklin and Daisy were in many ways soul mates. The orientations, views and landscaping at Top Cottage were of great interest to them. Once, when Daisy suggested that a flower garden might be included near the future cottage, FDR mildly admonished her:

I can understand the [flower] garden if I translate the flowers in part at least in terms of trees—But, you know, you and I, because we are we, can't quite ever think in terms of a garden only—perhaps it's because of a good many generations in a Big Place—that we like the Hill Top and the distant view—The intimate wood or garden is a part of our bigger whole.[154]

While his comments address the floral design implications at Top Cottage as part of a "bigger whole," this is also direct evidence that FDR's design sensibilities included an intuitive understanding of landscape gardening, an art form that had all but faded to obscurity, but lived on into modern times as a Hudson Valley tradition. ❧

Figure 130. Photograph Showing Franklin D. Roosevelt at Top Cottage, 1941. During his presidency, Top Cottage was FDR's retreat at Hyde Park. Originally conceived as a rustic lean-to, it became a commodious, yet quaint, stone cottage with rustic grounds. When dignitaries came to lunch, tables were set up in the surrounding woods. Courtesy of the Franklin D. Roosevelt Library.

CHAPTER 14

OLANA

In the spring of 1860, David Hosack's landscape gardening at Hyde Park was thirty years in the past. Robert Donaldson had sold Blithewood, and Philip Paulding was living out his last years alone at the Requa farmhouse. Andrew Jackson Downing and Washington Irving were dead. The nation was on the cusp of the Civil War, the beginning of the end of America's fleeting Romantic period. Yet, at this twilight moment, a project began on what is arguably the grandest of all the Hudson Valley's landscape gardens, Frederic Church's Olana. Today, Olana is one of the most popular of the valley's many historic sites.

In truth, the story of Olana can be traced to 1844 and a time when the Hudson Valley was the epicenter of romantic America. In that year artist Frederic Edwin Church (1826–1900) (Figure 132) came to the village of Catskill as an eighteen-year-old to study landscape painting with Thomas Cole (1801–1848). Cole, whose career initiated the Hudson River School was, as Church addressed him, "distinguished," and Church anticipated "the beautiful and romantic scenery about Catskill ... [and] the greatest pleasure to accompany you in your rambles about

the place observing nature in all her various appearances."[155] Church stayed for two years, and during that period first saw the site of his future home.

After leaving Catskill, Church moved to New York City, where he quickly established his reputation. In 1849 he was elected a full member of the National Academy of Design. In the 1840s and 1850s he produced paintings that closely paralleled Thomas Cole's approach to landscape painting, celebrating the genius of the place with such works as *Scene on the Catskill Creek, New York* (1847), *Morning over the Hudson Valley* (1848), *West Rock, New Haven* (1849) and *Mount Katahdin* (1853). In the late 1850s Church completed what are today considered American masterpieces—the large exhibit pictures *Niagara* (1857), *Heart of the Andes* (1859) and *Twilight in the Wilderness* (1860). These works and others, all accomplished before Church was thirty-four years old, assured his fame. Then, in March 1860, Frederic Church returned to a region of fond memories and artistic inspiration when he purchased a 126-acre farm across the Hudson River from Catskill as he prepared for his marriage that summer to Isabel Carnes.

Figure 131. The
House at Olana.
A jewel in a mag-
nificent landscape
setting, the poly-
chromatic scheme
appealed to
Frederic Church's
artistic predilec-
tions. Courtesy
of New York State
Office of Parks,
Recreation and
Historic Preserva-
tion, Olana State
Historic Site,
Taconic Region.

The property had been a modest family farm in the late eighteenth century. After Church's purchase, a salaried farmer was retained to work the fields and occupy the original farmhouse. Church hired Thomas Cole's son, Theodore, to be his caretaker. The Churches built a new, decorative house, called Cosy Cottage, to be their *cottage ornée* at the farm for the next eleven years (Figure 133). One visitor suggested that Cosy Cottage had been positioned by the Churches to catch "the first and last glances of the sun," and its location amid the remodeled farm buildings confirmed the newlyweds' hands-on commitment to a romantically inspired rural lifestyle.[156] After the cottage was occupied, the emphasis was on getting the property's agricultural operations arranged in a way suited to Frederic Church's goals. New buildings were constructed and older structures were improved. Theodore Cole was actively involved managing the farm under Frederic Church's direction, keeping records and notes of the work and rowing a boat across the Hudson River from Catskill on regular visits.

Within a year Theodore reported, "quite a number of trees were set out."[157] From the beginning Church planted trees in large numbers on what had been open farmland. Three years later, in the spring of 1864, the effort was tallied at "several thousand" trees already planted. In addition to orchard trees, there were many ornamental plantings that included native deciduous trees such as maples, oaks and white birch, and native evergreens such as pines, spruce, and especially hemlocks. Most of the deciduous trees were planted in a thirty-acre former cornfield located north and uphill from Cosy Cottage where Church planned a park. He also started work on dredging out a small lake. Together, the future lake and adjacent wooded hillside with its many new plantings extended over the entire western half of the earlier farm. In 1861 the family enjoyed their first full summer season on the property. The Churches' first child, Herbert Edwin, was born in Octo-

Figure 132. Photograph Portrait of Frederic E. Church, c. 1860. Frederic Church was in his mid-thirties when he married and began the development of Olana. He was by that date one of America's most famous landscape artists. Courtesy of New York State Office of Parks, Recreation and Historic Preservation, Olana State Historic Site, Taconic Region.

ber. In the early years some of the Churches' friends seemed a bit startled at the couple's headlong pursuit of farm life. One wondered, "can it be possible that you have abandoned the exquisite field of ideality in which you have reaped so many laurels, for the sure matter-of-fact one of the husbandman?"[158]

In 1864, Frederic Church began a complex series of land purchases that expanded the property to encompass the hill to the north that would be the main house site. Olana was not an ancestral landscape, and Church's varied real estate transactions are fascinating for the care he exhibited in assembling the landscape entity that would constitute Olana. His first purchase was approximately thirty acres of the steeply wooded escarpment lying to the west of the farm. This property fronted on the public road (today's Rt. 9G) that traced the base of the hill, but more importantly it commanded the western views. With its steep topography, the land was not suited to agriculture. But Church knew this lot would be critical to his long-term vision. To his skeptical father (who was financing the purchase), Church argued that the lot was important in "securing fine openings for the views" and as

the site of "a suitable entrance and roadway into my place."[159] With these comments Church revealed his plans, saying the new lot might be sold in the future if another purchase was concluded at the top of the hill, where a permanent house would be constructed.

Before acquiring the hilltop and other land parcels, Church continued to concentrate his efforts on the farm, making further improvements to Cosy Cottage and other outbuildings. He built a driveway to the cottage, the first of Olana's important carriage drives, which would evolve into an intricate seven-mile-long system that largely defined the visual experience of moving through the Olana landscape. Church also planted more orchard trees and hundreds of additional parkland trees. Over several years the success of the tree plantings was evident, with Theodore Cole reporting eight years after Church's initial purchase, "you are occupying the uplands with trees." In addition to planting new trees, areas around the lake were simply allowed to grow up into second-growth vegetation, which was then selectively managed as woodland. Evergreens were planted in selected areas, an activity that seems to have coincided with Church's winter stays on the property, when evergreens became important landscape forms.

Initially, after spending the winter in New York City, Church would visit the farm in the early spring and the family would move there around the first of May. On one April visit he described the scene to his father:

> The grass was fresh and green around the house [Cosy Cottage]. The strawberries had commenced throwing out new leaves. Vines and plants were well started[,] peas have been up some little time—about five hundred trees have been planted and about as many more will be this spring ... I found the air so invigorating there that I think it will be advantageous to take an early start [at moving upriver].[160]

A month later, Church wrote his father again, with this description:

Figure 133. Photograph Showing Cosy Cottage, 1880s. The photograph shows the Churches' *cottage ornée*, their home for eleven years when first developing Olana. Intricate architectural details including a large, mounted birdhouse to the right of the entrance porch, together with the deep shade of surrounding trees, vines on the walls, and a hammock strung between two trees, reflect the intimate rural lifestyle and Picturesque landscape gardening the Churches favored. Courtesy of New York State Office of Parks, Recreation and Historic Preservation, Olana State Historic Site, Taconic Region.

The farm looks better than ever before. ... The peach[,] pear and plum trees are a sight. ... The apple trees are just beginning to come out. ... We have a coop of 15 chickens by the house and he [Church's son, Herbert] feeds them out of his hand—He is fascinated by the horses—I have a pair of pigeons.[161]

The Churches' second child, Emma Frances, was born in October 1864, but the following spring, tragedy struck when both Herbert and Emma died of diphtheria in New York City. Devastated, the Churches spent the summer of 1865 in Jamaica. Cosy Cottage was rented. While away, Church wrote to Theodore Cole, "I cannot think of the farm ... without great longing."[162] The Churches returned in the autumn of 1865 and, perhaps still seeking solitude, spent the winter at the farm for the first time. Church built a large, self-sustaining studio, located in the park-like grounds on the hillside above Cosy Cottage. From this position the Hudson Valley and the Catskill Mountains were visible to the west and southwest in a scene often sketched by Church (Figure 134). After the interlude of mourning, a third child, Frederic Joseph, was born on September 30, 1866. There was a new baby at the cottage, and spirits were much restored.

In 1867, before undertaking a long trip to Europe and the Middle East, Church completed his farm by building a new barn and several other farm outbuildings. The Churches had indeed taken to country life with great enthusiasm. The interest was obvious when Frederic wrote, "Mrs. C. has a digging fit. She flits about with a trowel in one hand and juvenile plants in the other all day." On another occasion he announced, "I superintend my own hot bed this season and if I plant my seed right side up I may expect to see them sprout in a day or two."[163] Despite the self-deprecating tone, the Churches were serious about the farm operations. The farm was repeatedly characterized as "magnificent" and served as an inspiration and subject of Church's art (Figure 135).

Church's plans for a house at the top of the hill moved closer to reality later that year and in 1868, when two lots were acquired that Church concluded would "make my farm perfect."[164] First was the house site, eighteen acres of mature woodland purchased in October 1867. Then, in 1868, a long narrow corridor, about six acres, was acquired that provided access to the north toward the City of Hudson, the region's largest commercial center. Church proclaimed it "all splendid woods" and planned a new main entrance road there.[165] The land was subdivided from the western side of a neighboring farm that was being sold at this time.

In July 1869 the Churches happily returned to the property after nearly a two-year absence while they traveled. Writing to a friend, Church enthused, "Here I am on my own farm—! ... About an hour this side of Albany is the Center of the world—I own it."[166] Shortly after his return, Church added two rooms to Cosy Cottage. He also added rooms to the old farmhouse, repaired other farm buildings, including roofing an "Earth Cellar" (probably a root cellar), and built a new icehouse. He asserted to a friend, "I have not been idle."[167] Despite some subsequent changes in the staff, the farm had settled into a consistent and smooth-running operation. Church confirmed his direct involvement, soberly claiming to one friend that he was "a plain farmer"[168] and to another that he had "a large farm to keep an eye on."[169]

The hardscrabble farm Church had purchased ten years earlier had been profoundly altered. Half the acres had been given over to the ornamental development of the lake, its woodland surroundings, and the parkland north of it, which was hayed but not grazed (in order to protect the many new trees). On the remaining farm acres Church plowed about twenty acres, a small fraction of what had been plowed for subsistence agriculture in the years before Church's purchase. A large drop in grain production accompanied the reduced plowing, but Church could afford to purchase grain. Reflecting the concerns of a landscape gardener, he commented, "[a plowed field] spoils the beauty of the scene somewhat."[170]

Figure 134. *Winter Twilight from Olana*, by Frederic E. Church, c. 1871–72. This was the winter view over the park from the open porch of Church's studio. Inbocht Bay on the Hudson River provides a distant focus. The Catskill Mountains loom to the west. Courtesy of New York State Office of Parks, Recreation and Historic Preservation, Olana State Historic Site, Taconic Region.

While rigorous farming was reduced, Church's agriculture was highly varied. Olana's orchards included multiple varieties of apples, cherries, pears, plums, peaches and grapes, and bush fruits including currants and raspberries, as well as strawberries. Church especially favored peaches. Theodore Cole boasted of "the best peach orchard in this part of the country."[171] After the flurry of improvements following their trip, there is little subsequent evidence of farm development, indicating that the earlier work had largely completed the improvements Church intended to make. Theodore Cole's role was reduced as Frederic Church's attention turned to the new house and a host of related landscape design decisions.

Even before the house was started, construction of what Church called the "North Road" began, laid out in the narrow corridor he had purchased two years earlier. On October 13, 1869, he wrote a friend, "I am constructing a long piece of road to the new house site."[172] Beginning at a distinctive splayed north entrance on the public road, the North Road provided Olana with its primary approach from the City of Hudson. A family friend later said the mile-long North Road had been "invented by Mr. Church to make the place seem as large and remote as possible."[173] Numerous visitors commented on its evocative character, as with this description in 1884:

> The approach to Mr. Church's house on the northern side is along a winding and wooded road, which constitutes a considerable drive in itself. The hill is very precipitous here, and one looks down at times upon this road directly below him in an almost inaccessible gulf. The expenditure of road-building, and in otherwise bringing this huge, wild, steep mass of earth into suitable shape and condition has been immense, and could not have been accomplished by the Bohemian type of artist.[174]

The North Road led to the house which, as planned, was "hardly seen till you are directly upon it."[175] Church's design of Olana's north approach road is certainly one of the most dramatic of this sort of landscape garden component to be found on the Hudson.

Figure 135. *Apple Blossoms at Olana*, by Frederic E. Church, c. 1870. The farm was the subject of several of Frederic Church's pencil sketches and oil studies. This example illustrates the large apple trees that were mature specimens when Church bought the older farm in 1860. Courtesy of New York State Office of Parks, Recreation and Historic Preservation, Olana State Historic Site, Taconic Region.

Figure 136. Photograph Showing Cart and Carriage Drive at Olana, c. 1885. The Churches' daughter, Charlotte, nicknamed "Downie," and Mrs. Church's mother, Emma Carnes, enjoy a ride along Olana's carriage drives. Numerous photographs taken at Olana during Frederic Church's lifetime document the appearance and use of the landscape. Courtesy of New York State Office of Parks, Recreation and Historic Preservation, Olana State Historic Site, Taconic Region.

With the North Road completed, plans for house construction continued. During the winter of 1869–70, Frederic Church engaged Calvert Vaux to help with the house design. Vaux, at this date near the height of his famed career as one of America's foremost residential architects, was well-acquainted with Frederic Church. They collaborated in preparing design drawings for the Olana house. At the time it was said that "Mr. Church designed the house in all its details, consulting with Mr. Vaux, the eminent architect."[176] While Vaux's role was essential, the Persian design style and the role of the house as a primary component in the designed landscape can be rightly attributed to Church. Church was also responsible for the picturesque architectural details, such as the entrance porch, "ombra" (as Church called it, an enclosed porch), piazza (veranda, or open porch), tower, pinnacles and roof projections, and a host of polychromatic decorative elements so important to the house as a landscape feature. More than a year after Vaux's first visit, Church wrote, "I am building a house and am principally my own Architect. I give directions all day and draw plans and working drawings all night."[177] During the summer of 1872, house construction continued and was substantially completed late in the autumn, when the family moved into the second floor. Detailed work on the structure lasted for several more years, as did landscape improvements close to the house, with work there still being reported in 1880.

In siting his house, Church selected a spot off the south summit of the hilltop so that there was higher ground and a wooded backdrop to frame and shelter the dwelling on the north. The house itself, as Church himself declared, was "a curiosity in Architecture."[178] It was exotic—an artist's house—described by one reporter as "a bright open-eyed house, presenting on the landscape side [i.e., south] an almost unbroken expanse of plate glass window. ... It is certainly no rectangle of dead walls."[179] In the context of landscape gardening, to which Frederic Church ascribed, the house was the focal garden feature. Despite its jewel-like presence, the structure melded with nature. Vines grew on its masonry walls.

The immediate house grounds included a pedestal of lawn terraces along the south façade. These terraces graded out to a raised, circular lawn on the east. The western side was a true cliff, and here Church saw his intervention in a clear artistic perspective, commenting, "I am busy Landscape Architecturing. I have nearly completed a cliff about a hundred feet in height," a reference to preparing this area for the studio wing added to the original house beginning in 1887.[180] From the lawn terraces and from the shady sitting spots on the house ombra and piazza, the views south centered on the Hudson River, and to the west, the Catskill escarpment rising sheer from rolling farmland. The panorama was said "to culminate the glories of the Hudson," a fame that endures today.[181] Frederic Church described it as

Figure 137. Photograph Showing the Flower Garden at Olana, 1906. This is the large, mingled flower garden that Frederic Church developed below the retaining wall that circles the final approach to the house. In this position flowers were protected from the wind, and the garden was a Picturesque design feature for those moving along the adjoining carriage drives. Courtesy of New York State Office of Parks, Recreation and Historic Preservation, Olana State Historic Site, Taconic Region.

linking Olana to a wider world "of mountains, rolling and savannah country, villages, forests and clearings. The noble River expands to a width of over two miles forming a lake-like sheet of water which is always dotted with steamers and other craft."[182]

With the main house completed, the Churches were habitually at Olana from spring through Christmas before retiring to New York City for the winter months. Later, winter trips to Mexico were a common occurrence. The Churches were getting older, and the location of the house at the top of the hill sepa-

rated them to some extent from the property's agrarian roots. With farming orderly and routine, landscape gardening continued. A reporter visiting the property in about 1876 stated, "the grounds are not yet finished in all their details," confirming the situation before the active work that would continue into and occupy the 1880s.[183] In these years rheumatism restricted Church's painterly efforts, but his affliction encouraged design in the outdoors. These were active years of landscape gardening at Olana. In 1879 a visitor noted, "The extensive grounds ... are in a constant state of arrangement under the direct supervision of the artist."[184]

Highlighting the landscaping focus was a surge of activity that completed the lake in the spring of 1879. In May, Church

Figure 138. Photograph Showing the Lake, Park and House from the South, c. 1890. The natural-appearing lake was completed in the late 1870s, set in an area Church developed as woods. To the north, open areas of the park contrasted with the heavily planted upper reaches of the hillside. Courtesy of New York State Office of Parks, Recreation and Historic Preservation, Olana State Historic Site, Taconic Region.

declared to a friend, "the lake is overflowing, the birch canoe is ready," and a few days later mused over the nearly twenty-year effort, whimsically estimating the lake excavation as a "great quantity [of muck] not less than 5 million loads"[185] (Figure 138).

In 1880, after experimenting with other ideas, "Olana" was adopted by the Churches as the property's name. It was an appropriate moment for christening; with all the major land pieces in place, the original farm had evolved into a singular and expansive estate. But there was more. In autumn 1884, Church reported, "five men [are] building a road ... I have made about 1 ¾ miles of road this season, opening new and beautiful views."[186] The Ridge Road, a loop to the north end of the hilltop, and a road around the lake, both built in 1884, account for much of this road construction. The Ridge Road became one of Olana's most notable carriage drives. In August 1884, Isabel Church's mother, Emma Carnes, recorded in her diary, "Mr. C. out all a.m. at his new road, north end of the place," and in September, "drove on new road as far as woods, very rough now, but will be beautiful in

views."[187] As part of the construction, animal grazing was eliminated along the immediate edges of the new road, with a barbed wire fence erected out of sight on the slope below the roadway. This restriction on grazing meant that the ground fronting the Ridge Road could be planted and/or selectively returned to second-growth, which could then be managed as parkland, a suitable foreground for the splendid views. In October 1884 it was the Ridge Road that prompted Church's enthusiastic comment on landscape gardening when he wrote to a friend, "I can make more and better landscapes in this way than by tampering with canvas and paint in the Studio."[188]

A year later Church built another ornamental road, this time from the lake to the top of Crown Hill, a hillock in the southeast corner of Olana. In September, Emma Carnes reported, "Drove P.M. over the last new road which was meant for a surprise but has been suspected all along."[189] The road began in the woods east of the lake, then looped around a pocket of wooded wetland before ascending out into open agricultural fields, and

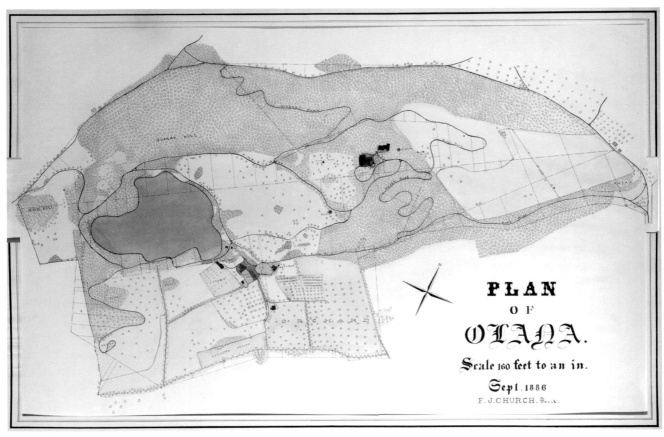

Figure 139. Plan of Olana, by Frederic Joseph Church, 1886. This is the only cartographic depiction of Olana prepared in Frederic Church's lifetime. Despite the notation "Scale 160 feet to an in. [inch]," this is not an accurate survey, but it provides invaluable information concerning buildings, carriage drives, vegetation (woodlands vs. open farm fields), fence lines, and the names of many landscape components. Orchards are indicated by a pattern of circles, while a tan background color indentifies farm areas that were plowed. Courtesy of New York State Office of Parks, Recreation and Historic Preservation, Olana State Historic Site, Taconic Region.

KEY TO OLANA PLAN

1. House
2. Service yards, stable and coachman's quarters
3. Hilltop w/water tank, small kitchen garden and storage
4. Lawns/arrival/carriage turnaround
5. Flower garden
6. Seat (north view)
7. Summerhouse
8. Studio (removed 1888)
9. Cosy Cottage (built 1860)
10. Barn complex w/main barn, stable, wagon house, pump house, sawmill, icehouse, granary, root cellar, tool house, corn crib and barnyard
11. Main kitchen garden
12. Old farmhouse (built 1794)
13. Orchards, bush fruit and vineyards
14. Lake
15. Parkland (not grazed)
16. Farmland (grazed)
17. Main driveways (north and south)
18. Ridge Road
19. Crown Hill Road & Overlook
20. Other carriage drives
21. Red Hill (shale quarry)

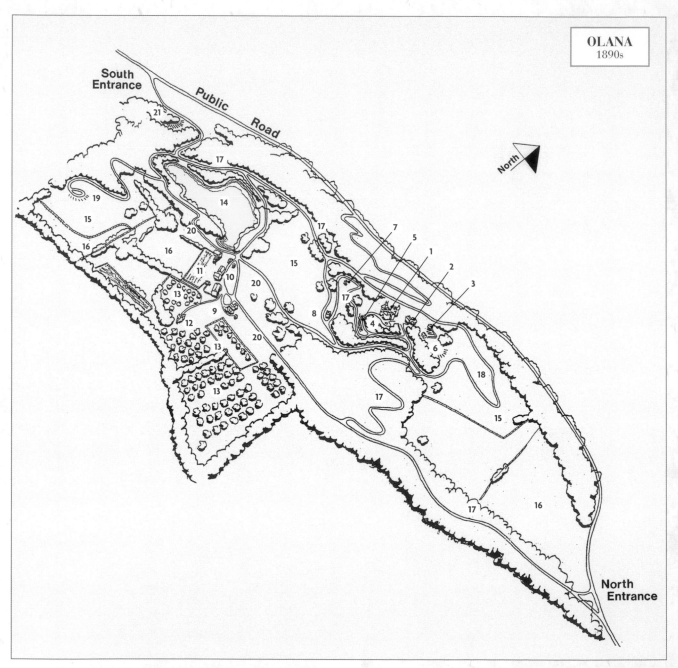

Figure 140. Bird's-Eye View Showing Historic Components (1890s), by R. M. Toole. This aerial view, looking towards the southwest, shows the landscape as it was in the last decade of Frederic Church's life. It is based on historic written and cartographic documentation, modern survey data and the existing site conditions. The number key identifies the components.

then to the summit. On the hilltop, Church built a carriage turnaround. From this modest height the view was panoramic, affording a new prospect of the house seen above the park, and the impressive ensemble of Olana farm buildings fronted by the extensive kitchen garden in the middle distance. Off to the east was rolling farmland backed by the Taconic Hills. As he had done on the Ridge Road, Church constructed a new field fence to restrict grazing, located downslope and out of sight from the summit of Crown Hill. The positioning of this fence meant that about seventeen acres of former agricultural land had been dedicated to parkland fronting the new road. Church treated the area as he had others, allowing it to grow over time into second-growth, which he then selectively thinned to compose the foreground vegetation and complement the more distant views. Other landscape work required selective removal of vegetation, and again Church confirmed his direct involvement, writing to a friend, "I am clearing up underbrush in places and this work requires close supervision."[190] Olana was a work of landscape art in constant need of artistic management.

Church built one other important carriage drive in the mid-1880s. This was a detour off the south approach to the house. It brought carriages through parkland studded with old birch trees he had planted twenty-five years earlier, and led up the slope immediately south of the house. It ended on the old driveway at the same point where the house was first seen when traveling the earlier south road, so that the final arrival at the house was not changed. The new road had the advantage of avoiding close contact with the service areas and stable yards north of the house and, with the many views in the upper reaches of the park, it was a more ornamental and scenic approach.

The new road construction prompted the installation of a new flower garden as a feature seen from the new approach (Figure 137). The garden was planted on sloping ground facing south, sheltered against a curving stone wall. From the original plant lists and period photographs, the garden was a combination of flowering perennials and annuals in a mingled layout meant to be appreciated on foot or from the viewpoint on the nearby drive. Critically, the flower garden could not be seen from

Figure 141. Photograph Showing the Rustic Railing at Olana State Historic Site, 2009, by Steve Benson. Fabricated from the branches of mountain laurel, this unique railing guarded the top of a retaining wall. Long ago dismantled, it was documented from old photographs and restored by New York State in the early 1990s. Olana's creation by a famed landscape artist gives it international interest. It is also one of the most expansive and best-preserved of all the Hudson Valley's landscape garden compositions.

the house, so the bold natural forms and uncluttered setting of the hilltop were uncompromised. A. J. Downing, in *Landscape Gardening*, discussed "the mingled flower-garden," saying:

> The object of this is to dispose the plants in the beds in such a manner, that while there is no predominance of bloom in any one portion of the beds there shall be a general admixture of colors and blossoms throughout the entire garden during the whole season of growth.

With the alterations of the south road and the development of a substantial flower garden, Olana was largely complete (Figure 140). In September 1890, as Frederic Church began to retire from active involvement in the day-to-day management of the property, a long and detailed article about Olana appeared in the *Boston Sunday Herald*. The reporter concluded that "the art of the landscape gardener has been employed, not so much to render Olana beautiful as to make it picturesque," and noted that "the multitude of trees planted under Mr. Church's direction a quarter of a century ago now give convincing evidence of his wise foresight."[191]

Frederic Church approached landscape design at Olana in a way parallel to his painterly art. As with other members of the Hudson River School, Church adhered to a near-literal depiction of nature. Thomas Cole stated this principle succinctly, saying that "imitation is the means through which the essential truths of nature are conveyed."[192] These aesthetic principles echoed the tenets of A. J. Downing's Picturesque design mode, where nature and rural life are celebrated by closely imitating natural and vernacular appearances in landscape gardening. This sense that nature and place—be it on canvas or in the landscape garden—must be approached literally and reverentially was a hallmark of the artists of the Hudson River School and of Picturesque landscape gardening as defined by Downing and his English sources.

Olana's landscape design is, then, an extension of Frederic Church's art into an animated third dimension. It is a design nearly indistinguishable from the Hudson Valley countryside—albeit an idealized countryside—of Church's lifetime. While Pic-

turesque landscape gardening had its English background, its design principles insisted on finding the local genius of the place, thus insuring indigenous design motifs at one with the character of the natural setting. This emphasis on the indigenous is unprecedented in American landscape design history where, later, imported motifs would dominate. At Olana, the indigenous was taken to a grand and exquisite form where landscape garden, pastoral countryside, wild nature, farm fields and the glorious display of an informal flower garden melded imperceptibly through the refined art of America's foremost landscape painter.

Frederic Church's involvement in creating one of the finest surviving examples of Picturesque landscape gardening in America is exceptionally fitting. "I can make more and better landscapes in this way than by tampering with canvas and paint in the Studio," Church had declared. It is a remark that confirms assertions made throughout the history of landscape gardening; early on, in 1734, Alexander Pope asserted that "all gardening is landscape painting." This point was reiterated during the picturesque movement, and finally, a century after Pope, confirmed for America in *Landscape Gardening* by A. J. Downing: "Again and again has it been said, that Landscape Gardening and Painting are allied."

After 1891, Olana's operations were entrusted to the Churches' youngest son, Louis (1870–1943), who eventually inherited the property. Even with Frederic's involvement lessened, he was clearly the arbiter of the landscape's management throughout the 1890s, but very few notable changes seem to have been made. Isabel Church died in 1899, and her husband a year later. His obituary spoke of "his magnificent country home at 'Olana' on the Hudson River, one of the most notable houses in the United States situated in a vast park beautified by the taste of the artist."

Sixty years later, in 1964, the Churches' daughter-in-law, Louis's widow, Sally, died. To settle her estate, the house and contents were to be auctioned. A public campaign led to the preservation of the property and its invaluable collections. New York State took ownership in 1966. Today, with its lands generally intact and with a high level of design integrity remaining, Olana is preserved as a state historic site.

CHAPTER 15

EPILOGUE

In 1900, when Frederic Church died with the nineteenth century, his taste in landscape painting and Picturesque landscape gardening were long out of fashion. The conclusion of the Civil War in the mid-1860s marked the end of the Hudson River Valley's Romantic era. The whimsy of romance had been overshadowed by years of savagery and, in the postwar years, an unprecedented economic boom. The expansionist years that followed the Civil War left America with a taste for imported elegance and lesser interest in bringing nature and romanticized rural life into the garden.

City parks provided continuity for the long tradition of landscape gardening. Frederick Law Olmsted (1822–1903) teamed with Calvert Vaux in the 1858 design of New York City's Central Park, and so initiated an entire generation of urban parks that were both uniquely American and yet perpetuated the older English practice (Figure 142). Olmsted and Vaux became America's earliest and most notable landscape architects, a term Vaux coined in 1862–63. The modern profession of landscape architect was derived from the landscape gardener and amounted to a promotion into the concerns of professional-

ism and public work. Today, landscape architects fill important design positions throughout American life.

While America's urban parks and the profession of landscape architecture were lasting legacies to landscape gardening, there were difficulties in bringing the ephemeral nature of the art form (especially in the Picturesque mode) to newer interests for active recreation and the stultifying limitations of public stewardship. Gone was the single owner, the informed arbiter of taste, now replaced by committees, bureaucracies, and levels of supervision that often denied the artistic factor and led to the scourge of ever more engineering. But that is another story.

In residential landscape design, the post–Civil War period went to excess. As hinted in this treatment of the pre-Victorian era, exhibitionism came to dominate the simplicity and naturalism that was essential to Picturesque landscape gardening and its modest vernacular celebration of the *genius loci*. This trend toward design extravagance can be witnessed at several of the historic sites described as exemplary examples of landscape gardening in the earlier Romantic period. The massed shrub plantings designed by Calvert Vaux and his son Downing Vaux

Figure 142. Engraving Showing Central Park, from *The Hudson: From the Wilderness to the Sea* by Benson J. Lossing (1860). Perhaps the most significant piece of landscape gardening ever achieved in America, New York City's Central Park was designed in 1858 by Calvert Vaux and Frederick Law Olmsted, who then initiated the modern profession of landcsape architecture. As once reported, the park was designed to bring a bit of the Catskill Mountains to the center of the city, an illusion achieved through the art of landscape design on the Hudson.

for Wilderstein are ironic, and George Merritt provided the most extreme example at Knoll (then called Lyndhurst) in Tarrytown, turning the austere elegance of the Pauldings' park-like landscape into a cluttered showplace of horticultural display and Gardenesque flourishes, all before 1873. Remnants of this complex landscape, the antithesis of the original Picturesque design ideal, bedevil preservation, interpretation and restoration efforts to this day.

The naturalism of romantic landscape gardening was also challenged by those who felt formal design was being neglected. This retro-fashion harked back to the rectilinear garden layouts modeled on Italian villas designed in the Renaissance period—the 1500s. In America it was an approach championed for the clients of wealth by an architect, Charles A. Platt, whose book *Italian Gardens* (1894) can be cited as putting a final nail in the coffin of naturalistic landscape gardening in

America. Edith Wharton, with her *Italian Villas and Their Gardens* (1904), popularized the imported fashion. Blithewood, Robert Donaldson's 1830s property, so central to the evolution of Romantic-period landscape gardening, became an Italianate design after its purchase by Andrew C. Zabriskie, who built a large Georgian Revival mansion in 1899 and laid out formal gardens to the west of the house. The grounds were simplified, refined and made more stiffly elegant. The driveways were carefully edged, their gravel surfaces kept uniform and without a weed in sight.

Despite a real shift in design approach, many of the Hudson Valley estates that epitomized the region's romanticism were not substantially altered, at least in their basic layouts. Landscape gardening had been closely linked to the region's sense of itself, and it clung to the region's sensibilities like an old glove, even as national tastes changed. At Hyde Park six years after David Hosack's death, A. J. Downing warned that "the place has lost something of the high keeping which it formerly evinced." This was a reference to the careful maintenance and concern for horticulture that were ignored after Hosack's passing, but the essential landscape layout and spatial character didn't change even into the 1890s when notable landscape architect, Charles Eliot, visited and wrote a subsequent article about the property. Eliot marveled at the "simple, open and stately effect" of the grounds and the "noble age and stature" of the old trees.[193] The ephemeral horticultural displays and the important emblematic features such as the "L'isle des Peupliers" and the classical pavilions had long disappeared. Might Charles Eliot have concluded, wrongly, that this was just a natural occurrence, unaffected by art? Certainly that was a prejudice shared by many of his colleagues up until recent times.[194]

At Montgomery Place, Cora Livingston Barton, the last of the family triumvirate who had rendered the estate a Romantic-period showplace, died in 1873. The property was bequeathed as a life tenancy to Cora's unmarried cousins, Louise and Julia Hunt who, with limited income, lived there for almost fifty years, until 1921. During that period there were no major changes in the designed landscape, except that it slowly dissolved for lack of "keeping," as A. J. Downing would have termed it. The flower garden was neglected and eventually removed, and the elegant conservatory, facing expensive rehabilitation, was demolished. The intricate *fabrique* that dotted the grounds inevitably crumbled.

Rokeby and Steen Valetje experienced similar benign neglect. In 1911, Margaret Chandler Aldrich, a direct descendent of the Armstrongs, commemorated the one-hundred-year anniversary of her great-great-grandparents' founding of La Bergerie by hiring the famous Olmsted Brothers firm of landscape architects to design a revival Romantic-period garden at Rokeby. In his diary, a bemused Frederick Law Olmsted, Jr. related that he was reduced to hastily rereading A. J. Downing's *Landscape Gardening* in order to bone up on his own roots. Despite the common lineage back through A. J. Downing and English landscape gardening, professional practice and aesthetic prerogatives in America had changed utterly.

As at Rokeby, the Livingston properties are well-known for their multigenerational continuity; many stayed in the family until modern times before some became museum properties. In this way Clermont was acquired by New York State in 1962, and Montgomery Place by Historic Hudson Valley in 1986. Properties such as Samuel F. B. Morse's Locust Grove, in Poughkeepsie, were passed down through family members, but eventually were acquired by appreciative modern owners who were instrumental in preserving them as historic sites. Locust Grove's last owner, Annette Young, envisaged in her will a "Samuel F. B. Morse Museum." On her death in 1975, it became a reality.

Sunnyside stayed in Washington Irving's family throughout the nineteenth century, but in 1896–97 a large mansion was constructed that incorporated Washington Irving's diminutive cottage as a hideous appendage. The old Sunnyside pond was modified to an engineered retention basin with an outflow set into a concrete ditch. In 1945, when it was to be sold by the last Irving family owner, famed preservationist John D. Rockefeller, Jr. purchased it as a valuable historic resource. He had the cottage and grounds restored, and opened it to the public in 1948.

Smaller properties close to New York City, like Henry Sheldon's Millbrook and A. J. Downing's Highland Gardens, and such ill-fated landscapes as The Point and Idlewild, were swept aside by changing land use and a vastly altered context of residential expansion and the need for public recreation. Then, too, in numerous examples such as at Kenwood, outside Albany, and Ellerslie at Rhinebeck, institutional use followed the property's residential beginnings. Some important sites barely escaped, as at A. J. Downing's Springside, where preservation was only assured in 1987 after contentious debate, and Frederic Church's Olana, where the death of the last family member in 1964 precipitated an anxious campaign to save what is now recognized as one of the Hudson Valley's premier historic sites.

The naturalism of the Romantic period, so appropriate to the region's sense of place, lived on and still does, but there is considerable work ahead to restore the artful landscapes of today's museum properties. The documentation phase is well advanced, numerous formal studies and reports have been prepared, and some basic restoration themes are apparent. The authentic spatial arrangements of the historic property are fundamental. Most of these old properties, no longer farms, are severely overgrown from their historic situations. At Olana, where the composition of open and wooded areas was manipulated by Frederic Church's scene-making, about fifty acres of once open fields are now dense woods, having grown up when farming was abandoned in the 1940s. At Samuel F. B. Morse's Locust Grove, views to the Hudson River, once a broad panorama, are now reduced to a narrow slit, and similar effects of overgrown vegetation are experienced at Montgomery Place, Knoll (Lyndhurst), Hyde Park, and other sites. Roads and paths are another important restoration need. Most of these sites are experienced today in a way at variance with the historic situation. The historic main entrance at Olana is closed. When Olana was opened to the public, New York State devised a new road approach based on traffic engineering, not historical accuracy or Frederic Church's artistic intentions. At Sunnyside, Locust Grove, Springside, Clermont and others, the historic road routes have also been severely altered or bypassed, often to provide for maximum convenience and the needs of automobiles. Historic appropriateness was not considered.

Historic footpath systems have been largely lost, even if their routes may be well documented. This situation is especially degrading where footpaths were notable, such as at Sunnyside, Montgomery Place and Hyde Park. Plantings have also changed, but here it must be remembered that it was often the pattern of woodland vs. open fields that mattered most. Individual trees and shrubs come and go, and at sites renowned for this element, such as Hyde Park and Knoll, individual plant materials need special consideration. But mixed woods, even if the individual plants have been altered, is still—for the art of landscape gardening—experienced as woods. The same can be said for fields. Whether cultivated open fields, grazing pastures or mown meadows, open ground was a spatial element invaluable to the landscape gardener.

Finally, in this brief review of the current status of the important Hudson Valley landscape gardens, mention may be made of built features that have completely disappeared. There are a few masonry remains of buildings, retaining walls and other features, but the vast majority of this construction was of wood, and it was not designed to last 100-plus years. The sites that were especially noted for their garden structures, such as Montgomery Place, Springside, Locust Grove and even Olana (where more than half the once-standing outbuildings are now gone), have suffered. Many of these lost artifacts are well-documented and could be authentically reconstructed.

Interpretation can fill many gaps, and as illustrated here, there are many period illustrations, maps and early photographs dedicated to the landscape resource. These should be better employed to tell the story and to build appreciation for these expansive, significant and beautiful historic resources—the nineteenth-century designed landscapes preserved in the Hudson River Valley of New York State. ❧

List of Illustrations

APPENDIX A: VISITING LANDSCAPE GARDENS ON THE HUDSON

Blithewood: Annandale-on-Hudson, Bard College Campus (845) 758-6822, www.bard.edu

The present large house (called Blithewood Manor) and associated formal gardens remodeled the property in the late 1890s and are not reflective of the Romantic-period Donaldson residence. The octagonal gatehouse (1841) and the approach drive lined with old white pines remain, but the modern campus setting has obliterated any sense of the historic conditions. The site is not interpreted.

Clermont: 1 Clermont Ave., Germantown, NY 12526, New York State Office of Parks, Recreation and Historic Preservation, Taconic Region (518) 587-4240, www.nysparks.state.ny.us and www.friendsofclermont.org

The original house (as rebuilt after the Revolutionary War, with many alterations) remains, but the grounds are only vaguely reflective of the historic situation. Idele, Chancellor Robert R. Livingston's separate residence, is a ruined foundation at the end of a large parking lot. Close by, open lawns, grills and picnic tables serve state park visitors. Several interpretive panels present aspects of the site's history. Occasional fee.

Highland Gardens, **Millbrook**, **Kenwood** and other properties are private property and their landscapes are changed immeasurably from their historic conditions.

Hyde Park: Vanderbilt Mansion National Historic Site, 4097 Albany Post Road (U.S. Rt. 9), Hyde Park, NY 12538, National Park Service (845) 229-9115, weekends (845) 229-7770

The grounds are open without fee. The spectacle of the river views is deservedly famed, and the isolation of the house siting (the fourth classical-style edifice to occupy the same spot) is well preserved. The old stable is the visitors' center, and the original walled gardens are now lovingly maintained in a semblance of their 1930s appearance. The site is adversely affected by vehicles and crisp asphalt roadways that, fortunately, follow historic routes. The historic landscape features and plantings are mostly gone.

Idlewild: Cornwall-on-Hudson (several private properties) The house grounds are now a residential neighborhood, and the Calvert Vaux-designed house is unrecognizable. The steeply sloping ravines of Idlewild and Funnychild brooks remain still an "idle wild" revealed in the spring before the site's rampant vegetation blankets all views.

Knoll (Lyndhurst): 635 South Broadway, Tarrytown, NY 10591, National Trust for Historic Preservation (914) 631-4481, www.lyndhurst.org

The grounds are open to the public without a fee, but it requires a lucid knowledge of the property's complex history to make sense of the remnants that remain. Landscape guide material is available at the visitors' center.

Locust Grove: Samuel Morse Historic Site, 2683 South Road (U.S. Rt. 9), Poughkeepsie NY 12601 (845) 454-4500, www.lgny.org

An idiosyncratic but well-operated museum property, the grounds are open without fee, including the extensive riverfront that is a hidden resource in the otherwise dreary sprawl along U.S. Rt. 9. The landscape is interpreted and maintained to all periods up to the most recent, non-historic owners, creating an odd mix. Garden beds from the most recent own-

ers (not Samuel F. B. Morse) remain and are maintained. The riverfront is much overgrown and spatially unrecognizable from Morse's intentions.

Montgomery Place: River Road, Annandale-on-Hudson, Historic Hudson Valley (914) 631-8200, weekends (914) 271-8981, www.hudsonvalley.org

Mothballed in recent years, Montgomery Place will likely remain the spectacular public-access property it has been since 1988, with whatever opening hours and levels of interpretation can be mustered. Check the current specifics, and go for the gracious house surroundings and the Hudson Valley views. The Sawkill, the quintessentially romantic setting, can be explored.

Olana: 5720 Rt. 9G, Hudson, NY 12534, New York State Office of Parks, Recreation and Historic Preservation, Taconic Region (518) 828-0135, The Olana Partnership (518) 828-1872

The grounds are open all year, and a fee is sometimes charged in summer. The extensive acreage is reached by over five miles of carriage drives, carefully designed by Frederic Church, that offer many opportunities for scenic pedestrian touring. Numerous interpretive panels provide background regarding the designed landscape.

The Point: Old Post Road, Staatsburg, NY 12580, New York State Office of Parks, Recreation and Historic Preservation, Taconic Region (845) 828-0135

Inquisitive visitors are left on their own when touring this abandoned site. It's a jungle out there. The house is a near-ruin, and the prominent outbuildings postdate the Romantic period development. Bring your imagination and try to recreate the original site. With understanding, you may go home with more than a case of poison ivy.

Springside: Academy Street, Poughkeepsie, NY 12602, Springside Landscape Restoration, Inc. (845) 454-2060, www.springsidelandmark.org

Open to the public for self-guided tours, the site is preserved, but remains a shadow of its former splendor, overgrown and under-maintained. Several interpretive panels help visitors re-imagine the past. Currently, site features that postdate Downing's involvement are included in the interpretation.

Sunnyside: Sunnyside Lane, Tarrytown, Historic Hudson Valley (914) 631-8200, www.hudsonvalley.org

This well-restored and sophisticated museum property includes the grounds in the ticket price. Close to the cottage, the landscape nearly replicates its historic conditions, and this area evokes an authentic feel for Irving's sensibilities. Other aspects of the site are imperfectly preserved (the old kitchen garden is a parking lot), but provide a good sense of the overall layout.

Wilderstein: Morton Road, Rhinebeck, NY 12572, Wilderstein Preservation, Inc., (845) 876-4818, www.wilderstein.org

A work in progress, Wilderstein's historic drives and pathways, laid out by Calvert Vaux's office, can be followed, but the spatial qualities of the landscape, its historic features and plantings, and many details are neither restored nor maintained.

APPENDIX B: VISITING THE BEST OF THE ENGLISH LANDSCAPE GARDENS

If you can dodge the notorious English rain, spring, summer and autumn are great times to visit the country's world-renowned eighteenth-century landscape gardens that prefigured those developed in the Hudson River Valley. The eighteen gardens noted here are regularly opened to the public. Some are premier attractions, but others, despite their importance to our interests, are lesser-known historic sites whose opening times vary with the seasons. The author will vouch for the worthiness and historic importance of these sites, but it is best to plan ahead regarding specifics before setting out.

Visiting the English countryside to experience its famous designed landscapes can be most conveniently undertaken on driving tours from several smaller cities that are of interest in themselves. For example, Oxford, easily reached by train from London, makes a good base for visiting three iconic landscape gardens located one after another towards the north. First, ten miles away at Woodstock is Blenheim, Capability Brown's most important work and famous for its lake and vast designed acreage. Only five miles farther is William Kent's most notable extant creation, well preserved at Rousham. Saving the best for last, about twenty-five miles north of Oxford and easily reached fifteen miles from Rousham is Stowe at Buckingham. This site, with its older, formal layout, dramatically illustrates the radical transformation brought on by landscape gardening, starting with William Kent and into the age of Capability Brown. Stowe is superbly restored and interpreted by the National Trust, presenting a cornucopia of landscape garden effects.

London can be a jumping-off point for visiting three very early and influential landscape gardens easily reached on the west and southwest side of the metropolis. All are well-restored today. Painhill, the fantastical landscape of noted amateur Charles Hamilton in the period 1738–1773, and Claremont, another 1730s landscape garden from William Kent, are only a few miles apart near Esher, Surrey. Even closer to the city is Lord Burlington's and William Kent's Chiswick, near Hammersmith, an excellent, if imperfectly restored, example of the earliest phase of landscape gardening.

You will need to go pleasantly afield for the next group of important landscape gardens. Stay in the lovely cathedral city of York in central England. It is only twelve miles east from there to Castle Howard (of Brideshead Revisited fame), developed in the period 1720–30s and recognized as one of England's most expansive designed landscapes, heroic in its dramatic effects. Twenty miles northeast from York is Rievaulx Terrace, a theatrical landmark in the history of landscape gardening dating to the 1750s and credited to amateur Thomas Duncombe. Nearby, outside Ripon, is Studley Royal, another amateur effort from the 1720s–40s. Both Rievaulx Terrace and Studley Royal used old abbey ruins as follies in their designed landscapes.

To the west, about 1½ hours by train from London, is the gracious Georgian city of Bath. Traveling from there up the River Severn about thirty-five miles are two splendid old gardens. First is Westbury Court, a perfectly restored National Trust property that is perhaps England's best example of Anglo-Dutch gardening common in the 1690s and early eighteenth century. Garden design in the Anglo-Dutch style continued in the Hudson River Valley up until the Revolutionary War. On the opposite bank of the Severn, a few miles south of Gloucester, is Painswick. Dated from the 1740s, it was in a transitional style antecedent of the full flowering of landscape gardening, and today considered the best Rococo garden in the country. Bath can also be a base for seeing one of the largest landscape gardens in Britain, Cirencester Park, located thirty miles to the northeast in Gloustershire. This property, the pioneering effort of amateur Allen Lord Bathhurst, influenced his close friend, Alexander Pope. Also, just outside Bath, is Prior Park, an example of the work of Capability Brown. Finally, some fifteen miles south of Bath is perhaps the finest restoration of a landscape garden in all of England—Stourhead in Wiltshire. Built by master amateur Henry Hoare in 1718–24, the site is now a premier National Trust property.

To see the work of the "picturesque improvers," who directly influenced landscape gardening on the Hudson, stay in the little cathedral city of Hereford in the Wye River Valley and travel in a loop, first north twenty-five miles to Ludlow and Downton, the home of Richard Payne Knight. Then, thirty-five miles farther north, outside Shrewsbury in Shropshire, is Hawkstone Park, a late-nineteenth-century landscape garden clearly influenced by romanticism. Circle back into central Wales and see Hafod, near Devil's Bridge, a wildly Picturesque-style landscape laid out by amateur Thomas Johnes after 1783, located about sixty-five miles west from Hereford. Finally, drive, or better yet, walk the Wye Valley, recreating one of the early tours in search of the picturesque, and below Tintern Abbey, about thirty miles south, experience the dramatic paths at Piercefield, a storied eighteenth-century landscape garden famed for its views over the River Wye and numerous whimsical features, today deteriorated.

NOTES

CHAPTER 1. HISTORICAL BACKGROUND

1. Kenneth Clark, *Civilization* (New York: Harper & Row, 1969), 271.

2. Nicolai Cikovsky, Jr., ed., *Lectures on the Affinity of Painting with the Other Fine Arts, by Samuel F. B. Morse* (Columbia, MO: University of Missouri Press, 1983).

3. A. J. Downing to Robert Donaldson, 12/26/1840, Collection of Richard Jenrette. Apparently Downing was unaware of several of William Gilpin's important works, including his *Essay on Prints* (1768) and *Three Essays on Picturesque Beauty* (1792), as well as *Observations on several parts of North Wales* (1773), *Observations on the River Wye, and several parts of South Wales* (1782), *Observations on parts of Western England ... [and] the Isle of Wight* (1798), *Observations on the coasts of Hampshire, Sussex and Kent* (1804) and *Observations on several parts of the counties of Cambridge, Norfolk, Suffolk and Essex* (1809).

4. John Fowler, *Journal of a Tour in the State of New York, in the Year 1830* (London, 1831), as quoted in Roger Haydon, ed., *Upstate Travels, British Views of Nineteenth Century New York* (Syracuse University Press, 1982), 41.

5. Anonymous author, "Thoughts of a Hermit ... ," *The Port Folio*, Vol. 6 (July 1815), as quoted in Edward J. Nygren, "From Views to Visions," *Views and Visions* (Washington, DC: Corcoran Gallery of Art, 1986), 25.

6. For a good discussion of the Hudson's distinct setting, see Raymond J. O'Brien, *American Sublime, Landscape and Scenery of the Lower Hudson Valley* (New York: Columbia University Press, 1981) and Walter L. Creese, *The Crowning of the American Landscape*, Chapter on the Hudson Valley (Princeton, NJ: Princeton University Press, 1985), 43–98.

7. Laurence Sombke, "Landscape Architecture in Hudson Valley Reflects 18th Century View on Nature's Wild and Chaotic Glory," *Albany Times Union*, September 19, 1999.

8. For background on A. J. Downing, see: David Schuyler, *Apostle of Taste: Andrew Jackson Downing, 1815–1852* (Baltimore, MD: The Johns Hopkins University Press, 1996); George B. Tatum, "Introduction: The Downing Decade (1841–1852)" and "Nature's Gardener," in George B. Tatum and Elizabeth Blair MacDougall, eds., *Prophet with Honor, The Career of Andrew Jackson Downing 1815–1852* (Washington, DC: Dumbarton Oaks, 1989), 1–42, 43–80; and Judith K. Major, *To Live in the New World, A. J. Downing and American Landscape Gardening* (Cambridge, MA: M.I.T. Press, 1997).

9. A. J. Downing to Robert Donaldson, 7/16/1845, Collection of Richard Jenrette.

10. A. J. Downing, *Landscape Gardening*, 2nd edition (1844), 33.

11. For John Claudius Loudon, the Gardenesque style and Regency-period landscape design, see Melanie Louise Simo, *Loudon and the Landscape* (New Haven, CT: Yale University Press, 1988).

12. J. C. Loudon, *Gardener's Magazine*, Vol. 8 (December 1832), 701.

13. *The Cultivator*, Vol. 2 (March 1845), 80.

CHAPTER 2. PRELUDE: THE COLONIAL PERIOD

14. "Master Plan for Philipse Manor Hall State Historical Site," Mary Dougal, Historic Site Manager, New York State Office of Parks, Recreation and Historic Preservation, Taconic Region (hereafter OPRHP), February 1984, and Kristin L. Gibbons, "A Brief History of the Garden at Philipse Manor Hall Prior to 1850," OPRHP, August 20, 1974, and Thomas C. Cornell, "Some Reminiscences of the Old Philipse Manor House in Yonkers and Its Surroundings" (1878), and Stefan Bielinski, "Philipse Manor Research Report Frederic Philipse III," Office of State History, February 1972.

15. Background on Van Cortlandt Manor is extensive and compiled in the library of Historic Hudson Valley. See: Antoinette F. Downing, "Research Report" (3 vols.), December 1953, and "Interpretive Paper," May 1959; and, more recently, Robert M. Toole, "Van Cortlandt Manor Historic Landscape Study," Historic Hudson Valley, February 15, 1993.

16. For background on Livingston Manor, see: Ruth Piwonka, *A Portrait of Livingston Manor, 1686–1850* (Friends of Clermont, 1986); Richard T. Wiles, *The Livingston Legacy* (Annandale-on-Hudson, NY: Bard College, 1987); and Clare Brandt, *An American Aristocracy: The Livingstons* (Garden City, NY: Doubleday, 1986).

17. For background on Clermont see: Bruce E. Naramore, Historic Site Manager, "Master Plan for Clermont State Historic Park," OPRHP, August 1982.

18. Ann Elizabeth Bleecker (d. 1783), published posthumously in 1793. The date of the poem is not recorded, but it is believed to be in the 1760s.

19. For background on The Pastures, see: Thomas D. Ciampa, "Schuyler Mansion Landscape Report," State of New York, Office of Parks and Recreation, The Division for Historic Preservation, Bureau of Historic Sites, September 1976, and *Schuyler Mansion: A Historic Structure Report*, State of New York, Office of Parks and Recreation, 1977.

20. L. B. Proctor, *Historic Memories of the Old Schuyler Mansion* (not dated), said to be a quotation from the *Gentleman's Magazine* (London, 1790), as quoted in *Schuyler Mansion: A Historic Structure Report*, 34.

CHAPTER 3. CLERMONT, "A COMPLETE FAIRY LAND," AND LANDOR'S COTTAGE

21. For background on this period, see 133–159; U. P. Hedrick, *A History of Horticulture in America* (New York: Oxford University Press, 1950).

22. Julian Ursyn Niemcewicz, *Under Their Vine and Fig Tree. Travel through America in 1797–1799*, 1805, Collection of the New Jersey Historical Society.

23. Horatio Gates Spafford, *Gazetteer of the State of New York* (Albany, NY: B. D. Packard, 1824, reprint, Interlakin, NY: Heart of the Lakes Publishing, 1981).

24. Niemcewicz.

25. Spafford.

26. On the French cultural links, see Roger G. Kennedy, *Orders from France, The Americans and the French in a Revolutionary World—1780–1820* (University of Pennsylvania Press, 1989).

27. Helen W. Reynolds, *Dutchess County Doorways* (Dutchess County, NY: 1931), 89–90.

28. Family history related by John Winthrop Aldrich, a descendant of the Armstrongs, in conversation with the author.

29. Research information on Montgomery Place is from Jacquetta M. Haley, "The Creation of a Country Estate: Montgomery Place, 1802–1986" (research report/training material), September 1987–February 1988, Historic Hudson Valley, Tarrytown, New York.

30. Janet Livingston Montgomery to Robert R. Livingston, May 29, 1802, as quoted in Haley, 9.

31. Ibid., August 4, 1802, as quoted in Haley, 12n.25.

32. Jacquetta M. Haley, "Montgomery Place Chronologies," Historic Hudson Valley, February 1988, 2.

33. A. J. Downing to John Jay Smith, November 15, 1841, as quoted in Judith K. Major, "The Downing Letters," *Landscape Architecture*, LXXVI (1986), 52.

34. For background on the development of the English park, see Susan Lasdun, *The English Park, Royal, Private & Public* (New York: The Vendome Press, 1992).

35. Washington Irving to Henry Brevoort, January 2, 1813. George S. Hellman, ed., *The Letters of Washington Irving to Henry Brevoort* (New York: G. P. Putnam's Sons, 1915).

36. W. A. Reichart and L. Schlissel, eds., *Washington Irving, Journals and Notebooks, Vol. II, 1807–1822* (Boston: Twayne Publishers, 1981), 14–17.

37. Wallace Bruce, *The Hudson*, 1882 (reprint, New York: Walking News, 1982), 65.

38. Henry T. Tuckerman, "Washington Irving," *Homes of American Authors* (New York: George P. Putnam, 1853), 36.

39. Edgar Allan Poe introduced Ellison in an article entitled "The Landscape Garden," published in October 1842 in the *Ladies Companion*. "The Landscape Garden" was later incorporated into a longer piece, "The Domain of Arnheim," published in March 1847 in the *Columbian Lady's and Gentleman's Magazine*. "Landor's Cottage," subtitled "A Pendant to The Domain of Arnheim," written in 1849 just before Poe's death, was later published in his *Complete Works*.

CHAPTER 4. HYDE PARK (VANDERBILT)

40. Even in the colonial period a few professional landscape designers worked in the New York City area. In 1758, Theophilos Hardenbrouck advertised his work as a "surveyor," offering "studies in Parks and Gardens." In 1768, Thomas Vallentine advertised that he "surveys land" and offered to layout "gardens and improvements." In 1802 nurseryman Joseph P. Taylor advertised "all kinds of shrubs" from his "Washington Garden" at Greenwich. The above sample is quoted from the "Subject File," Historic Hudson Valley Library, Tarrytown, NY.

41. The best source of researched information on David Hosack is Claire K. Feins, "Doctor David Hosack at Hyde Park:" A Report for the Vanderbilt Mansion National Historic Site at Hyde Park," Vanderbilt Mansion National Historic Site, 1950.

42. David Hosack to James Thacher, January 1, 1829, as quoted in Feins, 2.

43. William Wilson, "Notice of the Gardens at Albany and of Dr. Hosack's Estate, Hyde Park," *The New York Farmer and Horticultural Repository*, June 1829.

44. James Thacher, "An Excursion on the Hudson," *New England Farmer*, November 26–December 3, 1830.

45. Anonymous, "Country Seats near New York," *The New England Farmer*, September 4–October 2, 1829, as quoted in Feins, 5.

46. Thacher, "An Excursion ... ," 1830.

47. Harriet Martineau, *Retrospect of Western Travel* (3 vols.) (London: 1838). Volume I recorded her visit to Hyde Park in 1834.

48. David Hosack to William Bard, March 7, 1829.

49. Philip Hone, Diary, September 17, 1829.

50. Thacher, "An Excursion ... ," 1830.

51. Patrick Shirreff, "A Tour through North America, Together with a Comprehensive View of the Canadas and United States, As Adapted for Agricultural Emigration," *American Quarterly Review*, 18 (March–June 1835), 384.

52. Charles A. Murray, *Travels in North America During the Years 1834, 1835 and 1836* (2 vols) (New York: Harpers and Brothers, 1839), 2, 230.

53. Thomas K. Wharton, "Diaries and Scrapbook (1830–34)," (n.p.), July 12, 1832. Wharton's papers are the collection of the Manuscript and Archives Department, the New York Public Library.

54. Anonymous, "County Seats ... ," 1829.

55. Thacher, "An Excursion ... ," 1830.

56. Wharton, "Diaries," July 15, 1832.

57. Ibid., July 9, 1832.

58. Martineau, *Retrospect ... ,* 1838.

59. Thacher, "An Excursion ... ," 1830.

60. Wharton, "Diaries," July 1832.

61. David Hosack to Judge Jesse Buel, January 1831.

62. Wharton, "Diaries," November 1832, July 10, 1832, and November 1832.

CHAPTER 5. MONTGOMERY PLACE

63. Edward Livingston to Henry Carleton, October 24, 1835, as quoted in Jacquetta M. Haley, "The Creation of a Country Estate: Montgomery Place, 1802–1986," Research Report/Training Manual, Historic Hudson Valley, 1987–88.

64. Edward Livingston to Auguste Davezac, December 16, 1835.

65. These purchases are detailed in Jacquetta M. Haley, *Pleasure Grounds* (Tarrytown, NY: Sleepy Hollow Press, 1988) 29–32.

66. Cora Barton to A. J. Davis, August 14, 1863, as quoted in Haley, *Pleasure Grounds*, 79.

67. A. J. Downing to Robert Donaldson, September 21, 1846, collection of Richard Jenrette.

68. A. J. Downing to Thomas P. Barton, December 31, 1846, as quoted in Haley, *Pleasure Grounds*, 33.

CHAPTER 6. BLITHEWOOD

69. A. J. Downing to A. J. Davis, as quoted in Jean Bradley Anderson, *Carolinian on the Hudson—The Life of Robert Donaldson* (Raleigh, NC: The Historic Preservation Foundation of North Carolina, 1996), 176.

70. For background on A. J. Davis as related to Robert Donaldson, see Susanne Brendel-Pandich, "From Cottages to Castles: The Country House Designs of Alexander Jackson Davis," in *Alexander Jackson Davis, American Architect* (New York: Metropolitan Museum of Art, 1992), 58–79.

71. Jane B. Davies, "Davis and Downing: Collaborators in the Picturesque," *Prophet with Honor, The Career of Andrew Jackson Downing, 1815–1852* (Washington, DC: Dumbarton Oaks, 1989), 81–123.

72. Susan Gaston Donaldson to William Gaston, September 8, 1832, as quoted in Anderson, *Carolinian on the Hudson*, 155.

73. Hans Jacob Ehlers, "Defense Against Abuse and Slander with some strictures on Mr. Downing's Book on Landscape Gardening," 1852. The pamphlet was self-published and only a few copies are thought to exist, one in the collections of the New York Public Library.

74. A. J. Downing to Robert Donaldson, April 24, 1847, collection of Richard Jenrette.

75. Robert Donaldson to A. J. Davis, December 4, 1852, as quoted in Anderson, 230.

76. For background on Ehlers, see Robert M. Toole, "Hans Jacob Ehlers: 'The profession of a landscape gardener, principally on the banks of the Hudson,'" *The Hudson Valley Regional Review*, Annandale-on-Hudson, Bard College, 15:1, March 1998, 1–46.

CHAPTER 7. SUNNYSIDE

77. Henry T. Tuckerman, "Washington Irving," *Homes of American Authors* (New York: George P. Putnam, 1853), 51.

78. Notably, in 1798, Englishman James Malton published "An Essay on British Cottage Architecture," wherein he addressed those "noblemen and gentlemen of taste, who build retreats for themselves, with desire to have them appear as cottages," as quoted in E. A. Wade, "James Malton—Picturesque Pioneer," *The Picturesque* (Hereford, England: The Picturesque Society, 3, Summer 1993), 19. A list of early English studies of the *cottage ornée*, all published in London, would include: William Atkinson, "Views of Picturesque Cottages with Plans" (1805); Edmund Bartell, Jr., "Hints for Picturesque Improvements in Ornamental Cottages" (1804); Thomas Downes Wilmot Dearn, "Sketches in Architecture ... Cottages and Rural Dwellings" (1807); and W. F. Pocock, "Architectural Designs for Rustic Cottages, Picturesque Dwellings, Villas & c., with Appropriate Scenery, Plans and Descriptions" (1807).

79. Ebenezer Irving to William Irving, June 1, 1835. Washington Irving's letters are compiled by R. M. Aderman, H. L. Kleinfield and J. S. Banks, eds., *Washington Irving's Letters* (Boston: Twayne Publishers, 1979).

80. Ebenezer Irving to Peter Irving, July 8, 1835.

81. Washington Irving to Peter Irving, October 8, 1835.

82. Washington Irving to Catharine Paris, November 16, 1832.

83. Washington Irving to Sabrina O'Shea, September 18, 1847.

84. Washington Irving to Sarah Storrow, May 25, 1841.

85. Ibid., June 13, 1841.

86. Ibid., September 17, 1842.

87. Washington Irving to Catharine Paris, March 22, 1838.

88. Washington Irving to Pierre M. Irving, May 18, 1838.

89. N. P. Willis, "A Visit to Sunnyside," *The Home Journal* (New York: August, 1857).

90. Washington Irving to Sarah Van Wart, October 24, 1838.

91. Washington Irving to Sarah Irving, May 29, 1842.

92. Washington Irving to Peter Irving, July 8, 1835.

93. Ibid.

94. Washington Irving to Sarah Van Wart, early December 1840.

95. Washington Irving to A. J. Downing, September 28, 1850.

CHAPTER 8. KNOLL (LYNDHURST)

96. Washington Irving to Sarah Storrow, June 21, 1841.

97. "Sketches by a Rambler," *Pocantico Gazette* (September 1, 1846).

98. "The Architects and Architecture of New York," *Brother Jonathan* (New York: July 15, 1843).

99. Robert Bolton, Jr., *History of the County of Westchester*, 2 vols. (New York: Alexander S. Gould, 1848), 1:197.

100. A. J. Davis, "A Description of the Paulding Villa," no date.

101. Philip Hone, *The Diary of Philip Hone, 1828–1851*, 2 vols. (New York: Dodd, Mead & Co., 1927), 2:550.

102. Thomas J. Scharf, *History of Westchester County, New York*, 2 vols. (Philadelphia: Preston & Co., 1886), 1:242.

CHAPTER 9. MILLBROOK AND KENWOOD

103. Robert Bolton, Jr., *History of the County of Westchester*, 2 vols. (New York: Alexander S. Gould, 1848), 1:197.

104. Philip Hone, *The Diary of Philip Hone*, 2:381.

105. A. J. Downing to A. J. Davis, October 16, 1840.

106. Washington Irving to Sarah Storrow, June 21, 1841.

107. A. J. Downing to William P. Van Rensselaer, August 9, 1844.

108. H. R. Schoolcraft, *Notes on the Iroquois* (Albany, NY: E. H. Pease and Co., 1847), 75.

109. *Collections of the History of Albany*, Vol. 1 (Albany, NY: J. Munsell, 1865).

CHAPTER 10. LOCUST GROVE

110. For background on Morse's connection to early American art, see William Kloss, *Samuel F. B. Morse* (New York: Harry N. Abrams, 1988). Kloss called Morse the "finest portrait painter of his generation" and evaluated his significance in broader terms, saying he "ranked high among Americans of the revolutionary and federal era whose lives were distinguished by the breadth of their interest and knowledge and their success in varied endeavors." See also Paul J. Staiti, "Ideology and Politics in Samuel F. B. Morse's Agenda for a National Art," *Samuel F. B. Morse* (New York: National Academy of Design, 1982), 7–53.

111. Samuel F. B. Morse to Lucretia Morse, August 1823. Morse correspondence is compiled in Edward Lind Morse, ed., *Samuel F. B. Morse: His Letters and Journals*, 2 vols. (Boston: 1914).

112. Samuel F. B. Morse to Sidney Morse, October 29, 1846.

113. Ibid, July 30, 1847.

114. Ibid., September 12, 1847.

115. Ibid., October 12, 1847.

116. Samuel F. B. Morse to M. Sherell, April 4, 1849. The letter makes clear that the work described was done in the previous season.

117. Samuel F. B. Morse to Sidney Morse, July 9, 1848.

118. Ibid., September 12, 1847.

119. A. J. Davis to Samuel F. B. Morse, September 1, 1852.

120. Ibid., September 5, 1852.

121. Deed description, dated April 1, 1850 (John B Montgomery and Isabelle, his wife to Samuel F. B. Morse), Dutchess County Courthouse, Book 92, p. 306.

122. Innis Young, untitled essay (Harvard University), 1914.

123. Samuel F. B. Morse, *Lectures*, 1826.

124. Samuel F. B. Morse to Charles F. vonFleischmaan, March 6, 1852.

125. Samuel F. B. Morse to John P. Brown, April 4, 1851.

126. Samuel F. B. Morse to a cousin, August 12, 1871.

CHAPTER 11. HIGHLAND GARDENS

127. Charles Mason Hovey, "Residence of A. J. Downing, Botanical Garden and Nurseries," *The Magazine of Horticulture*, 7 (November 1841), 401–411.

128. George W. Curtis, "Memoir of the Author," (Introduction) *Rural Essays* (New York: George P. Putnam & Co., 1853), xxxii

129. A. J. Downing, *Cottage Residences* (4th edition, 1852), 222.

130. Anonymous (Clarence C. Cook), "A Visit to the House and Garden of the Late A. J. Downing," *The Horticulturist*, 3 (January 1853), 21–27.

131. A. J. Downing to John Jay Smith, March 29, 1852, as quoted in David Schuyler, *Apostle of Taste . . . .*, 170.

132. Curtis, "Memoir ..," 1853, xxxii–xxxiii.

CHAPTER 12. SPRINGSIDE

133. For background on Downing and "rural cemeteries," see David Schuyler, *The New Urban Landscape* (Baltimore: The Johns Hopkins University Press, 1989), 37–56.

134. Downing had written an article on rural cemetery development in *The Horticulturist* (July 1849).

135. *Poughkeepsie Eagle*, January 5, 1850.

136. Matthew Vassar, Jr., diary entry, November 25, 1850.

137. *Poughkeepsie Eagle*, December 7, 1850.

138. A. J. Downing, *The Horticulturist*, February 1851, 98.

139. *Poughkeepsie Eagle*, April 9, 1851.

140. Ibid., July 6, 1850.

141. Ibid., July 10, 1852.

142. Calvert Vaux, *Villas and Cottages* (New York: Harpers & Brothers, 1857), 299.

143. *Poughkeepsie Eagle*, May 8, 1852.

144. Anonymous, "Ode to Springside," *Poughkeepsie Eagle*, June 12, 1852.

145. *Poughkeepsie Eagle*, July 10, 1852.

146. Ibid., June 12, 1852. The evaluation came from a Professor Russell Comstock, said by the newspaper to be "a man of good taste and superior judgment in rural matters."

CHAPTER 13. IDLEWILD, THE POINT AND WILDERSTEIN

147. Henry James, *A Small Boy and Others*, 1913. The scenes remembered took place in the mid-1850s when Henry James was about eleven years old. See William Wilson, "Henry James as a Small Boy in Rhinebeck," *The Hudson Valley Regional Review*, Annandale-on-Hudson: Bard College, 8:2 (September 1991), 93.

148. N. P. Willis, *Outdoors at Idlewild, or The Shaping of a Home on the Banks of the Hudson* (New York: Charles Scribner, 1855). Also, several essays concerning Idlewild were included in *The Convalescent* (New York: Charles Scribner, 1859). These books are compilations of Willis's "Letters" to the *Home Journal*, with these letters appearing periodically from the spring of 1853 through 1855.

149. Lorenzo Sears, *American Literature in the Colonial and National Period* (Boston: Little, Brown, and Co., 1909), 226.

150. Henry Beers, *Nathaniel Parker Willis* (American Men of Letters Series) (Boston: Houghton, Mifflin & Co., 1885), 225.

151. T. Addison Richards, "Idlewild, The Home of N. P. Willis," *Harper's New Monthly Magazine*, XVI:XCII (January 1858), 150.

152. Ibid., 159–60.

153. Washington Irving to John P. Kennedy, August 31, 1854.

154. Franklin Delano Roosevelt to Margaret Suckley, October 1935.

CHAPTER 14. OLANA

155. Frederic E. Church to Thomas Cole, May 20, 1844.

156. Henry Q. Mack, diary entry dated November 4, 1872.

157. Theodore Cole, diary entry dated April 25, 1861.

158. Ramon Paez to Frederic E. Church. September 15, 1862.

159. Frederic E. Church to Joseph Church, May 13, 1864.

160. Ibid., April 15, 1864.

161. Ibid., May 13, 1864.

162. Frederic E. Church to Theodore Cole, July 28, 1865.

163. Frederic E. Church to William H. Osborn, respectively, June 13, 1867 and March 26, 1867.

164. Frederic E. Church to Erastus Dow Palmer, October 22, 1867.

165. Frederic E. Church to William H. Osborn, October 25, 1867.

166. Frederic E. Church to Erastus Dow Palmer, July 7, 1869.

167. Ibid., September 22, 1869.

168. Frederic E. Church to Mr. Austin, September 16, 1869.

169. Frederic E. Church to A. C. Goodman, July 21, 1871.

170. Frederic E. Church to Erastus Dow Palmer, May 3, 1871.

171. Theodore Cole to Frederic E. Church, May 24, 1868.

172. Frederic E. Church to Edward A. Weeks, October 13, 1869.

173. Susan Hale to Edward Hale, November 15, 1903.

174. F. N. Zabriskie, "'Old Colony Papers,' An Artist's Castle and Our Ride Thereto," *The Christian Intelligencer*, September 10, 1884.

175. Ibid.

176. "Homes of America, V," *The Art Journal*, New York, August 1876, 248.

177. Frederic E. Church to A. C. Goodman, July 21, 1871.

178. Frederic E. Church to William H. Osborn, July 22, 1871.

179. Zabriskie, "Old Colony Papers ... ," 1884.

180. Frederic E. Church to Charles D. Warner, August 15, 1887.

181. "Homes of America, V," August 1876, 248.

182. Frederic E. Church to Amelia Edwards, September 2, 1877.

183. "Homes of America, V," August, 1876, 248.

184. H. W. French, *Art and Artists in Connecticut* (Boston: Lee and Shepard, 1879), 131.

185. Frederic E. Church to Erastus Dow Palmer, respectively, May 19, 1879 and June 22, 1875.

186. Ibid., October 18, 1884.

187. Emma Carnes, diary entry dated, respectively, August 23, 1884 and September 4, 1884.

188. Frederic E. Church to Erastus Dow Palmer, October 18, 1884.

189. Emma Carnes, diary entry dated September 7, 1885.

190. Frederic E. Church to Erastus Dow Palmer, June 20, 1886.

191. Frank J. Bonnelle, *The Boston Sunday Herald*, September 7, 1890.

192 Thomas Cole, "Lecture on Arts," in Marshall Tymn, ed., *The Collected Essays and Prose Sketches of Thomas Col,* (St Paul, MN: John Colet Press, 1980), 108.

193. Charles Eliot, "Some Old American Country-Seats," *Garden Forest*, Vol. III, No. 115 (May 7, 1890), 223.

194. Landscape gardening has been disparaged since the advent of America's infatuation with Italianate gardens in the 1890s (promoted by the work of Charles A. Platt—1861–1933). See, for example, Henry V. Hubbard and Theodora Kimball, *Landscape Design*, (Boston, 1959), which spent a few pages out of over 400 hurling invectives at English landscape gardening, such as the following: "Tired of geometrical shapes, the landscape gardeners introduced shapes which were not organized in any other way, . . [and so] were not worthy to be called design at all." Softening only a bit, Norman Newton, in his comprehensive history, *Design on the Land* (Boston, 1971), spent 13 pages out of 700 on landscape gardening and concluded that the whole movement was an unfortunate digression in the ancient, firmly geometric traditions of garden design.

BIBLIOGRAPHICAL ESSAY

The endnotes to each chapter cite historical documentation and source material that supports my discussion of landscape gardening in the Hudson River Valley. The references presented below, offered with no pretense to completeness, cite broader contributions to the study of historic landscape gardening and site-specific research, grouped in seven areas of focus. The first category suggests general readings in garden history that place the study of eighteenth- and nineteenth-century landscape gardening within the broadest context. The second group narrows the study to English (and Dutch) garden history, a subject that has seen significant contributions in the past thirty years, and one with special resonance to the early American scene. Next are works specifically addressing English landscape gardening, a facet of garden history that has been given much attention in recent years. This is followed by a focus on the picturesque aesthetic and picturesque landscape gardening as formulated in England, themes that have special resonance along the Hudson River. These sections include period works that are considered literary landmarks in the evolution of the theory of landscape gardening. Several can be sampled online, from reprints, or as excerpted in scholarly publications. The fifth category compiles works related to American landscape gardening. Sixth are works related to the Hudson River Valley and its native son, Andrew Jackson Downing, and his contemporaries. Finally, sources of background study for each of the gardens highlighted in this study, and their creators, are presented.

GENERAL GARDEN HISTORY

There are several excellent titles from the past thirty years that survey the broad history of garden design, including landscape gardening. The most recent is Elizabeth Barlow Rogers, *Landscape Design, A Cultural and Architectural History* (New York: Harry N. Abrams, 2001). See also: Christopher Thacker, *The History of Gardens* (Berkeley and Los Angeles: University of California Press, 1979); F. R Cowell, *The Garden as a Fine Art* (Boston: Houghton Mifflin, 1978); Geoffrey and Susan Jellicoe, *The Landscape of Man* (London: Thames & Hudson, 1975); William Howard Adams, *Nature Perfected: Gardens Through History* (New York: Abbeville Press, 1991); George Plumptre, *The Garden Makers, The Great Tradition of Garden Design from 1600 to the Present Day* (London: Pavilion Books, 1993); Monique Mosser and Georges Teyssot, *The History of Garden Design, The Western Tradition from the Renaissance to the Present Day* (New York: Thames & Hudson, 2000). For a comprehensive coverage with subject and person entries arranged in alphabetical order, see: Patrick Goode and Michael Lancaster, eds., *The Oxford Companion to Gardens* (Oxford and New York: Oxford University Press, 1986).

GARDEN HISTORY IN THE BRITISH ISLES

British garden history has prompted a plethora of investigations over the past thirty years, including Christopher Thacker, *The Genius of Gardening: The History of Gardens in Britain and Ireland* (London: Weidenfeld and Nicolson, 1994), and Laurence Fleming and Alan Gore, *The English Garden* (London: Michael Joseph, 1979). There are several compilations, such as Gervase Jackson-Stops, *An English Arcadia 1600–1990* (Washington: The American Institute of Architects Press, 1991). Unique is Roy C. Strong, *The Artist in the Garden* (New Haven, CT and London: Yale University Press, 2000), which uses artistic imagery to trace English garden history from the sixteenth to the nineteenth centuries. The late-seventeenth-century Anglo-Dutch garden style that so influenced colonial-period America before the landscape garden is revealed in David

Jacques and Arend Jan van der Horst, *The Gardens of William and Mary* (London: Christopher Helm, 1988), and in John Dixon Hunt, ed., special issue on Anglo-Dutch gardens, *Journal of Garden History*, 8:2 and 3, 1988. There are several important English garden history journals, notably *Garden History* (London: The Garden History Society), since 1973, and the *Journal of Garden History* (London: Taylor & Francis), initiated in 1981. Both include numerous scholarly articles that cover the broad scope of British garden history, although other areas of interest are also covered (see below).

LANDSCAPE GARDENING IN THE BRITISH ISLES

In the past thirty years the history of English landscape gardening has been the subject of several excellent publications, most notably, perhaps, John Dixon Hunt and Peter Willis, eds., *The Genius of the Place: English Landscape Gardens, 1620–1820* (Cambridge, MA: M.I.T. Press, 1990), which is an anthology of critical historical writings, with an informative analysis. The early history of landscape gardening, specifically the role of Alexander Pope and the Augustan Age, is insightfully presented in Peter Martin, *Pursuing Innocent Pleasures: The Gardening World of Alexander Pope* (Hamden, CT: Archon Books, 1984). For a more comprehensive treatment of the history of landscape gardening, see David Jacques, *Georgian Gardens, The Reign of Nature* (Portland, OR: Timber Press, 1984). Also, David C. Stuart, *Georgian Gardens* (London: Robert Hale, 1979), and Miles Hadfield, *The English Landscape Garden* (Aylesbury, England: Shire Publications, 1977). All the major English practitioners of landscape gardening have been given separate study, including John Dixon Hunt's *William Kent, Landscape Garden Designer* (London: A. Zwemmer, 1987), Thomas Hinde's *Capability Brown, The Story of a Master Gardener* (London and New York: W. W. Norton & Co., 1986) and Stephen Daniels's *Humphry Repton, Landscape Gardening and the Geography of Georgian England* (New Haven and London: Yale University Press, 1999). For the contributions of John Claudius Loudon, who so influenced the career of A. J. Downing, see Melanie Louise Simo, *Loudon and the Landscape* (New Haven, CT and London: The Yale University Press, 1988). Some older scholarship used the word "picturesque" as synonymous with landscape gardening in the natural style, as distinct from the picturesque variant that evolved in the 1790s. This unfortunate confusion can be experienced in otherwise groundbreaking volumes such as Nikolous Pevsner, *The Picturesque Garden and Its Influence Outside the British Isles* (Washington, DC: Dumbarton Oaks, 1974) and John Dixon Hunt, *The Picturesque Garden in Europe* (London: Thames & Hudson, 2002). Landscape gardening is related to broader concerns of the rural economy and aesthetics in Ann Bermingham, *Landscape and Ideology, The English Rustic Tradition, 1740–1860* (Berkeley and Los Angeles: University of California Press, 1986). The scholarly journals *Garden History* and the *Journal of Garden History* have numerous contributions related to landscape gardening. A sample would include Fiona Cowell's study of a contemporary of Lancelot "Capability" Brown, "Richard Woods—1716–93", *Garden History* 14:2, Autumn 1986, and John Dixon Hunt, "Humphry Repton and Garden History," *Journal of Garden History* 16:3, July–September 1996.

THE PICTURESQUE

The picturesque aesthetic and Picturesque landscape gardening as defined by A. J. Downing have been covered in selected studies, many published in scholarly journals over recent decades. The oldest book-length treatment is Christopher Hussey's classic, *The Picturesque; Studies in a Point of View* (London: 1927). On picturesque scenery, see Malcolm Andrews, *The Search for the Picturesque* (Stanford, CA: Stanford University Press, 1989). The critical role of William Gilpin is usually discussed within broader studies, but independent research has added to current understandings as, for example, Joan Percy, *In Pursuit of the Picturesque* (Surrey Gardens Trust, 2001). The picturesque improvers are the subject of Stephen Daniels and Charles Watkins, eds., *The Picturesque Landscape, Visions of Georgian Herefordshire* (Nottingham, England: University of Nottingham, 1994). Regency-period gardening in the years when the practice of landscape gardening was in flux, from the 1790s to the 1830s, is incisively discussed in Mavis Batey, *Regency Gardens* (Aylesbury, England: Shire Publications, 1995). Also, a sample of individual articles in the scholarly publications *Garden History* and the *Journal of Garden History* would include Marvis Batey, "The Picturesque: An Overview," and Sophieke Piebenga, "William Sawrey Gilpin (1762–1843): Picturesque Improver" (*Garden History*, 22:2, Winter, 1994), and Jay Appleton, "Some Thoughts on the Geology of the Picturesque" (*Journal of Garden History*, 6:3, July–September 1986). A notable contribution to the scholarly study of the picturesque aesthetic has been the publication of the journal *The Picturesque* (Hereford, England: The Picturesque Society), since 1992. There have been sixty-nine issues through spring 2010. Many of the essays have addressed the genesis of what A. J. Downing later codified as the Picturesque design mode and its impact on landscape gardening. See, for example, David Whitehead, "[Humphry] Repton and the Picturesque Debate" from the inaugural issue (1, Winter 1992–3), Jack Calow, "In Search of the Origins of the Picturesque" (30, Spring 2000), and Jay Appleton, "Some Thoughts on the Geology of the Picturesque" (35, Summer 2001). One article was a report from the colonies, Robert M. Toole, "Picturesque Landscape Gardening in the Hudson River Valley, New York State" (10, Spring 1995). *The Picturesque* has also reprinted important historical publications, most notably Uvedale Price's *Essay on the Picturesque*, excerpts from Humphry Repton's writings on landscape gardening, and several of William Gilpin's works. Historical works published in the era when landscape gardening was evolving in England and influential in America provide a strong literary foundation for the study of landscape gardening in the Hudson Valley, beginning with William Shenstone (1714–63) *Unconnected Thoughts on Gardening* (1764), which included the memorable line, "I think the landscape painter is the garder's [sic] best designer." Thomas Whately's (d. 1772) *Observations on Modern Gardening* (1770), an early "treatise" on landscape gardening, largely followed the ideas of Lancelot "Capability" Brown and so influenced Samuel F. B. Morse and his Hudson Valley contemporaries. Even more widely influential was Horace Walpole (1717–97), whose *History of the Modern Taste in Gardening* (1780) traced the origins of landscape gardening as an art form. William Gilpin (1724–1804) provided writings that visited distinct regions of Britain and described the landscape as related to picturesque scenery. The broader popularity of the picturesque aesthetic was directly linked to landscape gardening by Richard Payne Knight (1750–1824), notably in *The Landscape, A Didactic Poem* (1794), and his close-by neighbor, Uvedale Price (1747–1829), whose multivolume work, *An Essay on the Picturesque* (1794), showed how simple vernacular scenes and unfettered nature could be made part of a landscape garden. Humphry Repton's prolific writings included *Fragments on the Theory and Practice of Landscape Gardening* (1816) and numerous "Red Books" (sheathed in red leather) wherein he proposed alterations to the landscape using "before" and "after" drawings.

AMERICAN LANDSCAPE DESIGN HISTORY

An early collection of essays that treated not only American, but also related English garden design, is Robert P. Maccubbin and Peter Martin, eds., *British and American Gardens in the Eighteenth Century* (Williamsburg, VA: The Colonial Williamsburg Foundation, 1984). There have been other anthologies: Walter T. Punch, *Keeping Eden, A History of Gardening in America* (Boston: The Massachusetts Horticultural Society, 1992); Therese O'Malley and Marc Treib, eds., *Regional Garden Design in the United States* (Washington, DC: Dumbarton Oaks, 1995); and Bonnie Marranca, ed., *American Garden Writing: Gleanings from Garden Lives Then and Now* (New York: PAJ Publications, 1988). Other works are organized around a particular time period. A good coverage of garden design in the pre-romantic era is Therese O'Malley, "Landscape Gardening in the early National Period," in Edward J. Nygren, ed., *Views and Visions, American Landscapes Before 1830* (Washington, DC: The Corcoran Gallery of Art, 1986), 133–159. Concise entries highlight "designers" and "places" in William H. Tishler, ed., *American Landscape Architecture* (Washington, DC: National Trust for Historic Preservation, 1989). A broadly comprehensive treatment, mostly unsourced, is Ann Leighton's *American Gardens of the Nineteenth Century, For Comfort and Affluence* (Amherst, MA: The University of Massachusetts Press, 1987). This volume and others show that American writers have not always understood the role of landscape gardening, a situation that can be traced from the earliest contributions such as Rudy J. Favretti's and Joy Putman Favretti's otherwise pioneering *Landscapes and Gardens for Historic Buildings* (Nashville, TN: American Association of State and Local History, 1978). In this volume, landscape gardens are described as "pleasure grounds" that "should probably not be called gardens." More useful are titles covering separate regions of the United States. One of the best of this group is Peter Martin, *The Pleasure Gardens of Virginia, from Jamestown to Jefferson* (Princeton, NJ: Princeton University Press, 1991). Others include Alan Emmet, *So Fine a Prospect, Historic New England Gardens* (Hanover, NH: University Press of New England, 1996). There have been several compilations on American garden history published in the periodical *Journal of Garden History*. See, for example, Barbara Wells Sarudy, "Eighteenth-Century Gardens of the Chesapeake," 9:3, July–September 1989, and C. Allan Brown, ed., "New Perspectives on Southern Gardens," 16:2, April–June 1996. More generalized discussions of landscape with its connotations for design include Walter L. Creese, *The Crowning of the American Landscape* (Princeton, NJ: Princeton University Press, 1985), Raymond J. O'Brien, *American Sublime, Landscape and Scenery of the Lower Hudson Valley* (New York: Columbia University Press, 1981), and U. P. Hedrick's classic, *A History of Horticulture in America to 1860* (Oxford: Oxford University Press, 1950).

HUDSON VALLEY AND ANDREW JACKSON DOWNING

Except for the work before you, there has not been a comprehensive study of landscape gardening in the Hudson Valley. A few authors have discussed the topic, usually as related to A. J. Downing. Architectural historians have sometimes been confused by the terminology and correct attributions of the art form represented by landscape gardening, which has had little scholarly attention in America. An early and unique contribution was Joel Elias Spingarn, "Henry Winthrop Sargent and the Early History of Landscape Gardening and Ornamental Horticulture in Dutchess County, New York," *Year Book*, 22 (Dutchess County Historical Society, 1937). The works of Andrew Jackson Downing are available in many regional libraries as well as in reprints. Downing published three editions of *Treatise on the Theory and Practice of Landscape Gardening, Adapted to North America* (1841). The second edition (1844) was extensively revised and expanded from the original, as to a lesser extent was the third edition (1849, actually titled the 4th edition). Downing also wrote *Cottage Residences* (1842), with subsequent editions during his lifetime in 1844, 1847 and 1852. Downing's *The Architecture of County Houses* was issued in 1850, and again in 1852. Finally, Downing edited the influential journal *The Horticulturist* from July 1846 until his death in July 1852. Many of his best essays from that publication were compiled in *Rural Essays*, edited by his friend George William Curtis (New York: 1853). Downing also wrote numerous articles for other publications, and his technical work, *The Fruit Trees of America* (1845), while not directly germane to our discussion of landscape gardening, was reissued every year until Downing's death in 1852. Contemporary scholarship regarding A. J. Downing has blossomed in recent years. For a biography of Downing, see David Schuyler, *Apostle of Taste: Andrew Jackson Downing, 1815–1852* (Baltimore: The John Hopkins University Press, 1996). See also, George B. Tatum and Elizabeth Blair MacDougall, eds., *Prophet with Honor, The Career of Andrew Jackson Downing, 1815–1852* (Washington, DC: Dumbarton Oaks, 1989). The literary context of Downing's career can be gainfully sampled in Adam Sweeting, *Reading Houses and Building Books, Andrew Jackson Downing and the Architecture of Popular Antebellum Literature, 1835–1855* (Hanover, NH: University Press of New England, 1996), and Judith K. Major, *To Live in the New World, A. J. Downing and American Landscape Gardening* (Cambridge, MA: M.I.T. Press, 1997). The best treatments for the role of Alexander Jackson Davis is Jane B. Davies's essay "Davis and Downing: Collaborators in the Picturesque," from *Prophet with Honor* (1989), 81–123, and Amelia Peck, ed., *Alexander Jackson Davis: American Architect, 1803–1892* (New York: Rizzoli International Publications, 1992), especially the contribution of Susanne Brendel-Pandich, "From Cottages to Castles: The Country House Designs of Alexander Jackson Davis," 59–80. The best coverage of Calvert Vaux are William Alex and George B. Tatum, *Calvert Vaux: Architect and Planner* (New York: 1994), and Francis R. Kowsky, *Country, Park & City, The Architecture and Life of Calvert Vaux* (Oxford and New York: Oxford University Press, 1998).

THE GARDENS (AND THEIR CREATORS)

Hyde Park (SAMUEL BARD, DAVID HOSACK AND ANDRÉ PARMENTIER)
Incorporated into the national park system as an historic site in 1940, the landscape has been generally ignored in the interpretation of the property. Hyde Park's history and background related to its important residents can be gleaned from two biographies, John Brett Langstaff, *Doctor Bard at Hyde Park* (New York: E. P. Dutton and Co., 1942), and Christine Chapman Robbins, *David Hosack, Citizen of New York* (Philadelphia: The American Philosophical Society, 1964). For André Parmentier, the professional landscape gardener who worked with Hosack, see Pleasance Crawford and Stephen A. Otto, "André Parmentier's Two or Three Places in Upper Canada," *Journal of the New England Garden History Society* (Boston, MA: Massachusetts Horticultural Society, 5, 1997), and Ann Leighton, *American Gardens of the Nineteenth Century*, 1987, 123–132. The Hyde Park landscape was systematically studied in Patricia M. O'Donnell, Charles A. Birnbaum, Landscapes, Inc., and Cynthia Zaitzevsky, *Cultural Landscape Report for Vanderbilt Mansion National Historic Site, Site History, Existing Conditions and Analysis* (Boston, MA: National Park Service, 1992). For the author's contribution, see Robert

M. Toole, "Wilderness to Landscape Garden: The Early Development of Hyde Park," *The Hudson Valley Regional Review* (Annandale-on-Hudson: Bard College, 8:2, September 1991).

Montgomery Place (EDWARD LIVINGSTON FAMILY, THOMAS BARTONS, A. J. DAVIS AND A. J. DOWNING)
Incorporated as a historic site under the auspices of Historic Hudson Valley in 1986, Montgomery Place was given considerable research in its earliest years of operation. The landscape was not ignored; see Jacquetta M. Haley, ed. and introduction, *Pleasure Grounds, Andrew Jackson Downing and Montgomery Place* (Tarrytown, NY: Sleepy Hollow Press, 1988). For the role of A. J. Davis as a designer of classical structures, as exemplified at Montgomery Place, see Jane B. Davies, "Alexander J. Davis, Creative American Architect," from Amelia Peck, ed., *Alexander Jackson Davis: American Architect, 1803–1892* (1992), 9–22, and Jane B. Davies, ed., *A. J. Davis and American Classicism* (Tarrytown, NY: Historic Hudson Valley, 1989).

Blithewood (ROBERT DONALDSON, A. J. DAVIS)
This historic property, much altered from its condition in the 1840s, is now an undistinguished part of the Bard College campus. It is not presented or interpreted to its ownership under Robert Donaldson in the period 1839–52. For background on Robert Donaldson, see: Jean Bradley Anderson, *Carolinian on the Hudson—The Life of Robert Donaldson* (Raleigh, NC: The Historic Preservation Foundation of North Carolina, 1996). There have been tangential efforts to discuss the landscape; see Jane B. Davies, "Davis and Downing: Collaborators in the Picturesque," from *Prophet with Honor*, 81–123, and Helen Wilkinson, "The Story of Blithwood [sic]," *Year Book* (Poughkeepsie, NY: Dutchess County Historical Society, 15, 1930, 19–23.

Sunnyside (WASHINGTON IRVING)
For background on Washington Irving as related to Sunnyside, see Stanley Brodwin, ed., *The Old and New World Romanticism of Washington Irving* (New York: Greenwood Press, 1986). Therein, note especially Ralph M. Aderman, "Washington Irving as a Purveyor of Old and New World Romanticism," 13–25, and Jeffrey Rubin-Dorsky, "Washington Irving as an American Romantic," 35–48. The landscape was comprehensively discussed in Robert M. Toole, with Jacquetta M. Haley, "Sunnyside Historic Landscape Report" (Historic Hudson Valley, December 1995). This study was condensed and disseminated in Robert M. Toole, "An American Cottage Ornée: Washington Irving's Sunnyside, 1835–1859," *Journal of Garden History*, 12:1, January–March 1992, 52–72. For a good and early analysis linking Sunnyside to romanticism, see Deborah Clyde, "Sunnyside and Romanticism," unpublished report for Sleepy Hollow Restorations, 1983.

Knoll (Lyndhurst) (PAULDINGS AND A. J. DAVIS)
The early landscape at Knoll was not given due consideration after the site was acquired by the National Trust for Historic Preservation in 1964. In a special edition of *Historic Preservation* (Washington, DC: National Trust for Historic Preservation, 17:2, March–April 1965), a half-dozen articles were included on aspects of the property. Most focused on Davis's Gothic Revival house, and there was little mention of the landscape. This discrepancy was righted in the report by the landscape architectural firm, Landscapes, and David Schuyler, "Lyndhurst Landscape History, Existing Conditions and Interpretive Brochure," 1993, and Landscapes, "Lyndhurst Historic Landscape Report: Significance, Analysis & Treatment,"

1996, both commissioned by Lyndhurst (National Trust), Tarrytown, NY. The author's contribution is Robert M. Toole, "Lyndhurst's Picturesque Design," *Nineteenth Century* (Philadelphia, PA: Victorian Society in America, 19:2, Fall 1999), 4–10.

Millbrook AND *Kenwood* (HENRY SHELDON AND JOEL RATHBONE)
These sites are not designated historic properties and have been little studied. At Millbrook, even the site is today unrecognizable, so that excerpted visitors' commentaries are the only source of information on Sheldon's creation. Kenwood has been mentioned in several histories of the Albany area, but none have focused attention on the estate's designed landscape.

Locust Grove (SAMUEL F. B. MORSE)
Samuel F. B. Morse's theories on the art of landscape gardening are reprinted in Nicolai Cikovsky, Jr., ed. and introduction, *Lectures on the Affinity of Painting with the Other Fine Arts, by Samuel F. B. Morse* (Columbia, MO and London: University of Missouri Press, 1983). Morse's life is reviewed in Kenneth Silverman, *Lighting Man, The Accursed Life of Samuel F. B. Morse* (New York: Alfred A. Knopf, 2003). The landscape was studied in Robert M. Toole, "Locust Grove Historic Landscape Report" (Poughkeepsie, NY: Young-Morse Historic Site, 1992). This report was disseminated in Robert M. Toole, "The 'Prophetic Eye of Taste': Samuel F. B. Morse at Locust Grove," *The Hudson Valley Regional Review* (Bard College, 12:1, March 1995) and reprinted in *America's First River: The History and Culture of the Hudson River Valley* (Poughkeepsie, NY: Hudson River Valley Institute, 2009), 181–208.

Highland Gardens (A. J. DOWNING)
Because of its disappearance as an identifiable site, Downing's home has not been widely studied. For a lone pioneering researcher, see Arthur Channing Downs, Jr., "Downing's Newburgh Villa" (Toronto, Canada: *Bulletin of the Association for Preservation Technology*, 4, 1972), 1–113. See also, George B. Tatum, "Introduction: The Downing Decade (1841–1852)," and "Nature's Gardener," *Prophet with Honor*, 1989, 1–80, and David Schuyler, *Apostle of Taste*, 1996, 24–26, 212–18.

Springside (MATTHEW VASSAR AND A. J. DOWNING)
See Robert M. Toole, "Historic Landscape Report, 1852, Springside Landscape Garden," Hudson River Sloop Clearwater and Scenic Hudson, Inc. 1987, and Robert M. Toole, "Springside—A. J. Downing's Only Extant Garden," *Journal of Garden History*, 9:1, 1989, 20–39. Also, summarizing the historic landscape report, see Harvey K. Flad, "Matthew Vassar's Springside: "... the hand of Art when guided by Taste," from *Prophet with Honor*, 219–257.

The Point/Idlewild/Wilderstein (HOYTS, CALVERT VAUX/
N. P. WILLIS/SUCKLEYS)
William Emmet's Wittmount, William Kelly's Ellerslie and John B. James's Linwood are but three of about three dozen estates that form a notable array of contiguous country seats aligned along the eastern shoreline of the Hudson River from Hyde Park in Dutchess County to north of Clermont State Historic Site in Columbia County. For background on these properties and their landscapes, see Robert M. Toole, "Inventory and Evaluation: Landscape Architecture in the Sixteen Mile and Clermont Estates Historic District" (Hudson River Shorelands Task Force, 1980). This research document was included in the material submitted for the designation of the area as the Hudson River National Historic Landmark District. For

The Point, see Doyle & Doyle, "A Landscape Management Plan for 'The Point'," New York State Office of Parks, Recreation and Historic Preservation, Taconic Region, and The Friends of Mills Mansion, June 1998. For an early discussion, see Robert M. Toole, "The Point," *NAHO Magazine*, New York State Education Department/New York State Museum, 17:2 (Summer 1984), 3–5. For background on Nathaniel Parker Willis, see Cortland Auser, *Nathaniel P. Willis* (New York: Twayne Publications, 1969), and Robert M. Toole, "'Illustrated and Set to Music': The Picturesque Crescendo at Idlewild," *Journal of the New England Garden History Society*, 4, Spring 1996, 1–12. For background on Wilderstein and the Suckley family, see Cynthia Owen Philip, *Wilderstein and the Suckleys: A Hudson River Legacy* (Rhinebeck, NY: Wilderstein Preservation, 2001). For background research on the Wilderstein landscape, see Maloney Associates/Landscape, "Cultural Landscape Report for Wilderstein," Wilderstein Preservation, 1996, and Noel Dorsey Vernon, "Wilderstein: A Brief Landscape History," Ball State University (student project), 1982, revised by the author, March 1989. For background on Top Cottage and Margaret Suckley, see Geoffrey C. Ward, *Closest Companion* (Boston & New York: Houghton Mifflin Co., 1995). For background on the landscape at Top Cottage, see Robert M. Toole, "Landscape Study," research report for John G. Waite, Associates, Architects, 1997.

Olana (FREDERIC E. CHURCH)
For background on Frederic E. Church, see Franklin Kelly, et al., *Frederic Edwin Church* (Washington, DC: National Gallery of Art, 1989), James A. Ryan, *Frederic Church's Olana* (Hensonville, NY: Black Dome Press, 2001), Robert M. Toole, "Olana Historic Landscape Report," 1996, and "Olana Landscape Restoration Plan," 2002, New York State Office of Parks, Recreation and Historic Preservation, and Friends of Olana/The Olana Partnership, and Robert M. Toole, "The Art of the Landscape Gardener: Frederic Church at Olana," *The Hudson River Valley Review*, (Poughkeepsie, NY: Marist College, 21:1, Autumn 2004), 38–63

About the Author

Robert M. Toole is a landscape architect whose private practice in Saratoga Springs, New York, initiated in 1975, has specialized in historic landscape study and restoration while also providing design services on a variety of landscape design projects, including campus planning, environmental assessments and many private residences.

INDEX